Y0-EMJ-185

DEFENSE POLICY IN THE
REAGAN ADMINISTRATION

DEFENSE POLICY
In the **REAGAN**
ADMINISTRATION

☆☆

EDITED BY

William P. Snyder
James Brown

1988
NATIONAL DEFENSE UNIVERSITY PRESS
WASHINGTON, DC

NDU Press publications are sold by the US Government Printing Office. For ordering information, call (202) 783-3238, or write to: Superintendent of Documents, US Government Printing Office, Washington, DC 20402.

Library of Congress Cataloging-in-Publication Data

Defense policy in the Reagan administration.

Papers in this volume were commissioned for and presented at a conference organized by the Southwestern Regional Program in National Security Affairs, held in Dallas, Tex., Apr. 1986.
    Includes bibliographies.
    1. United States—Military policy—Congresses. 2. United States—Politics and government—1981—Congresses. I. Snyder, William P. (William Paul), 1928–   II. Brown, James, 1934 May 1–
UA23.D423   1988   355'.0335'73   88–9967

Edited by William Mizelle, Editmasters/Mizelle, Washington, DC, under contract DAHC32–87–A–0014.

Proofread by Editorial Experts, Inc., Alexandria, Virginia, under contract DAHC32–87–A–0012.

First printing September 1988

CONTENTS

FOREWORD

*I*N THE MINDS OF MANY observers, the Reagan administration was associated with policies redirecting the nation's energies to provide for a stronger defense. By substantially increasing defense budgets, the administration did more than merely underwrite improvements in military forces; it undertook initiatives that changed both the image and reality of America's national defense and its central role in the common defense of the free world.

This book assesses those initiatives. It examines the policies and programs that were the center of controversy during the Reagan years. It concentrates upon the most important issues, like the Strategic Defense Initiative, the 600-ship Navy, and the hefty increase in the Defense budget.

Critics and supporters of the Reagan initiatives do agree on one point: The Reagan administration came into office with the intent of strengthening defense policy. How well the administration succeeded in that effort and the cost of that success are vigorously debated in these pages.

BRADLEY C. HOSMER
Lieutenant General, US Air Force
President, National Defense University

ACKNOWLEDGMENTS

*T*HE ESSAYS IN THIS VOLUME were presented at an April 1986 conference held in Dallas, Texas, organized by the Southwestern Regional Program in National Security Affairs, a grouping of faculty at institutions in Texas, Louisiana, and Oklahoma with interests in national security issues. We are indebted to the participants in that conference for their thoughtful papers and their stimulating discussion of the many controversial aspects of the Reagan administration's defense policies. Our desire to publish this collection was understandable, given the quality of the papers and the discussion.

Financial support for the Southwestern Regional Program and the conference came from several sources: the National Strategy Information Center, the Inter-University Seminar on Armed Forces and Society, and the Ora Nixon Arnold Foundation. We are grateful for their support and the help of their representatives: Mr. William Bodie, Dr. Jay Williams, and Professor Cecil Johnson. We also acknowledge the assistance of Professor Dennis S. Ippolito and Bryan Jones, chairmen, respectively, of the political science departments of Southern Methodist University and Texas A&M University. Finally special thanks are due Mrs. Maria Thurman for her typing and preparation of the manuscript.

The merits of the work belong to the authors; the editors are responsible for errors of fact or interpretation.

WILLIAM P. SNYDER
JAMES BROWN

INTRODUCTION

A safer world will not be realized simply through honorable intentions and good will.... No, the pursuit of the fundamental goals our nation seeks in world affairs—peace, human rights, economic progress, national independence, and international stability— requires a dedicated effort to support our friends and defend our interests. Our commitment as peacemaker is focused on these goals.

—Ronald Reagan

When the Reagan administration entered office in 1981 the détente of the 1970s had already ended. The military buildup initiated earlier by President Carter and soon to be expanded by President Reagan decisively reflected the gulf that had grown between the United States and the Soviet Union.

In the 1980 presidential campaign, Mr. Reagan had sounded the call to arms against what he viewed as a dire and immediate danger—an accelerating Soviet threat to America's national security. Détente was disastrous, he contended, because it ignored the realities of Soviet expansionism and failed to stop the shift in the balance of strategic nuclear power in favor of Moscow. To address these problems, Mr. Reagan promised a rapid buildup of US military forces and large increases in defense spending.

It was assumed at the time that President Reagan would break radically with past policies and programs of the Nixon, Ford, and Carter administrations. This proved only partially correct. The President eschewed calls for quick fixes to redress the so-called "window of vulnerability," and crash programs to increase conventional weapons production and combat strength. Rather, the President's new initiatives involved across-the-board increases in ongoing defense programs. The one exception was the Navy. In essence, the initial Reagan initiatives did not change overall American strategy; rather, they focused on the resources needed to implement existing strategic goals successfully.

These initiatives required, and received, a sharp and sustained increase in defense spending. Congress was reluctant to finance these increases by cuts in the "Great Society" social programs that had been enacted during the Johnson administration. In addition, a generally stagnant economy seemed to demand fiscal stimulus; the administration responded with, and Congress approached, reductions in Federal tax revenues. In combination these measures resulted in a massive Federal deficit whose size increased substantially with each passing year. By 1984 the deficit exceeded $150 billion, and public concern over Federal fiscal policies could not easily be ignored.

The congressional response was Gramm-Rudman-Hollings, which mandated spending reductions and projected a balanced budget by the early 1990s. A throttling-back of Government spending has now set in and outlays are now growing at a rate roughly equal to overall economic growth. And, after its sharp increase during President Reagan's first term, inflation-adjusted defense spending settled into a no-growth (actually slightly negative growth) pattern early in the second term.

In the strategic area, President Reagan combined strategic force modernization with new arms control initiatives. In addition to continuing the Carter initiatives regarding air-launched cruise missiles, force modernization involved procurement of the B–1B bomber, limited deployment of the MX missile, research and development on the single warhead missile, Midgetman, and a revamping of the strategic command, control, communications, and intelligence (C^3I) systems. Arms control proposals—developed reluctantly and belatedly according to the President's critics—involved sharp reductions in the levels of both intercontinental and intermediate-range systems. These proposals were initially unacceptable to the Soviets and attracted mixed support among arms control devotees. But the President's most controversial initiative came in March 1983. Mr. Reagan directed establishment of a comprehensive and intensive research program to develop a defense against ballistic missiles. The Strategic Defense Initiative, SDI or "Star Wars," added a note of uncertainty regarding the future of strategic nuclear deterrence. Equally, SDI threatened basic Soviet assumptions regarding its strategic relationship with the United States.

The Reagan initiatives, however, involved more than strategic force modernization, arms control, and SDI. Former Secretary of State Alexander M. Haig, Jr., warned that the changing conventional military balance cast "a shadow over every significant geopolitical decision.... It influences the management of international crises and the terms on which they are resolved." In short, deterring future Soviet threats or outright aggression was possible only if the United States possessed capable conventional land, air, and sea forces. As a consequence, the Reagan administration adopted four initiatives related to conventional forces—an increase in the Navy's fleet from about 450 warships to more than 600; an imprecise plan to pressure peripheral Soviet interests around the world in order to gain military leverage in other areas of critical interest to the United States; a move to accelerate development and procurement of "smart" battlefield weapons and to increase the stockpile of war materials needed in a protracted conflict in Europe; and finally, steps to increase the level of training and combat readiness of existing conventional forces.

Of the four initiatives, a larger Navy was by far the most ambitious and costly. President Reagan succeeded in persuading Congress to approve construction of two additional nuclear-powered aircraft carriers, at an estimated cost of $6.8 billion. The carrier request was symbolic of the President's acceptance of the consensus among US military planners that conventional forces were becoming more crucial than at any time since Moscow achieved nuclear parity.

Without trivializing the military threat to the United States and its allies, congressional observers feared that the President's approach would be self-defeating. Less confident than Mr. Reagan about funds for defense and concerned that his initiatives would sharply alter relations with both Moscow and America's NATO allies, Congress was only cautiously supportive. Other observers advanced proposals regarding a range of issues not dealt with by the administration: reform of defense organizational arrangements, restructuring of weapons procurement policies, and changes in force structure and operational procedures, particularly as they apply to NATO Europe. Each of these proposals rested on the perception that the armed forces were infatuated with expensive and technologically complex weaponry, that military organizations, especially headquarters and agencies, were overstaffed at the officer level, and that military educational programs were deficient in important respects.

*   *   *

For an April 1986 conference in Dallas, a diverse group of civilian and military scholars from several universities and governmental agencies took the opportunity to discuss the Reagan administration's defense policies. The essays prepared for that conference and included here, detailed and insightful observations on the several topics touched upon in this introduction, have since been revised, updated, and edited for this volume. The editors believe that this collection provides, under one cover, one of the first comprehensive studies of the Reagan administration's national security policies. That the authors reflected on these issues for some months also makes possible, perhaps, more reasoned and perceptive judgments of the long-term implications of the policies of this administration.

Part I of this collection includes five papers on regional and global issues. The first is by Schuyler Foerster, who analyzes the efforts of President Reagan to alter the agenda of arms control from the legacy of SALT (Strategic Arms Limitation Talks). Foerster notes that President Reagan has pursued simultaneously a major strategic modernization program and sharp reductions in both strategic and intermediate nuclear weapons. Both initiatives were designed to overcome the perception of strategic vulnerability that developed in the 1970s. The paper examines the legacy of SALT, the dilemma of extended deterrence in NATO, and evolving US positions in both strategic and intermediate arms control negotiations. It is Foerster's contention that while the two initiatives are compatible in the near term, success in arms control will ultimately require the United States and its allies to reassess their nuclear strategies and force modernization programs.

The second paper, by Paul Godwin, considers US policies in Asia. Godwin argues that the United States has viewed Northeast Asia as strategically more critical than Southeast Asia. The geographic proximity of China, Japan, the two Koreas, and the Soviet Union in Northeast Asia has greater potential for conflict than exists among the smaller, less developed nations in Southeast Asia. The Reagan administration, Godwin observes, has accepted this view, with some adjustments, set in motion by previous administrations. The author contends that security relations in Asia, for both Washington and Moscow, are far more complex, fluid, and politically sensitive than in Europe. In fact, the United States under Mr. Reagan has been able to firm up loose coalitions of allies and friends in the Asia-Pacific region. But it must now strengthen its cooperative ties to friendly, if nonaligned, states, thereby strengthening the political context required for a successful defense policy.

Peter Zwick is the author of the third paper. He examines the reasons for Mr. Reagan's shift from the harsh criticism of the Soviet Union that characterized his first term to what the author terms a "realistic" approach. He suggests that it is the ascendancy of Mikhail Gorbachev that led to this change. In addition, Gorbachev's leadership style and the politics he adopted in his first year point to a new era in Soviet foreign policy: a differentiated approach to the West and to the Third World. In effect, Gorbachev hopes to raise the cost of confrontational rhetoric to the United States and to increase the payoff for "realism" in American foreign policy. Zwick questions whether President Reagan will understand and be willing to play by rules that necessitate a commitment to diplomacy and negotiated settlements based on mutual benefits.

John F. Guilmartin tackles what is the most topical element of the conflict spectrum with his wide-ranging historical analysis of terrorism. Guilmartin believes that the use of military force to counter terrorism has been "reasonably effective." But he goes on to say that any long-term approach requires fundamental reform of the "military instrument." More is involved than new equipment: the defense establishment must understand, appreciate, and learn to utilize more effectively the leadership and training of its personnel.

The final chapter in this part is Roy Werner's essay on security assistance policies. He traces their evolution as a support tool of containment and as a political lever with nonaligned nations. Security assistance programs, Werner notes, have not been used as economic programs linked to the balance of payments and trade deficits. He also points out that the burdensome trade deficits faced by the United States may require such a consideration. In addition, this paper examines two fundamental questions regarding security assistance: the supplier's responsibility to evaluate a recipient's use of the weapons it receives, and criteria appropriate to this evaluation. Regardless of the how or why provided, security assistance should be viewed as only a secondary contribution; in the end peaceful resolutions of conflict will ultimately require solutions that do not entail coercive mechanisms.

The second part includes three papers on defense resource requirements. The first, by Dennis S. Ippolito, focuses on defense spending and budgeting. The paper reviews historical patterns of defense spending and the relationship of defense outlays to the rest of the Federal budget. Ippolito contends that the Reagan defense buildup has not, despite the popular perception, solely or even primarily been responsible for the worsening of the Federal budget deficit. Ippolito believes that President Reagan is in a unique position to achieve what was considered impossible when he came to office in 1981, namely, long-term growth in defense and a reduction in the relative size of the Federal budget. From any perspective, according to Ippolito, this would represent one of the most important budget policy accomplishments of the modern era.

David Segal and Nathan Hibler discuss manpower and personnel policies and conclude that the United States is in a far better posture in the late 1980s than a decade earlier. Recruitment goals have been met and the quality of personnel has improved markedly. Segal and Hibler attribute these improvements to increases in military compensation, to establishment of educational incentives, and to the relatively high civilian youth unemployment of recent years. The authors are concerned that under budgetary constraints both manpower and personnel accounts may become vulnerable. In addition, existing benefits, if cut or eliminated, will affect the military's ability to compete in the marketplace for the quality personnel essential in an all-volunteer force. Weakening of recruitment incentives will necessitate additional recruitment from the secondary labor market: women and minority group members. Such a strategy raises concerns apparent during the 1970s: Will disadvantaged elements of society be greatly overrepresented in the armed forces and, in case of war, suffer disproportionate casualties?

Dov Zakheim contends that the defense programs in the Gramm-Rudman-Hollings era must of necessity remain roughly similar to those proposed prior to the introduction of this deficit reduction legislation. He reasons that US forces must continue to support commitments that have existed for several decades. Altering these commitments is unlikely since they are constructed on the basis of political relationships developed since World War II. Zakheim believes that Gramm-Rudman-Hollings will not appreciably affect the defense budget, but will engender changes in other areas of governmental spending.

Part III considers forces and weapons systems. It opens with a chapter on land warfare by William Staudenmaier. Staudenmaier contends that fiscal austerity will prevent the Army from achieving the force structure its leaders believe required by the threat facing the United States. As a consequence, the Army, which requires 860,000 soldiers to man an 18-division force, must choose between a "hollow Army" or cuts in its force structure. Staudenmaier is also concerned that the equipment necessary to fight effectively will not be forthcoming during this period of austerity. Ultimately, the United States will be forced to rely primarily on air and naval forces in situations short of war, with the Army's rapid deployment capability available for appropriate circumstances. To improve overall flexibility, Staudenmaier therefore suggests a reallocation of defense spending, reducing general purpose NATO force expenditures by 6 percent, with this savings applied to contingency forces, thereby increasing them by 25 percent.

The Navy has been the prime beneficiary of the Reagan administration's largess. John Williams amplifies and details the strategic concept known as the "Maritime Strategy," which formed the basis for that Service's expansion. The Maritime Strategy evolved within the Navy, and dictates how increased naval capabilities would be used to deter, and possibly to fight, a conventional conflict with the Soviet Union. Critics of the strategy, Williams points out, view the Maritime Strategy primarily as a rationale for the expanded forces the Navy has long desired. Williams suggests that the current Maritime Strategy will be difficult to sustain in the light of budgetary retrenchment. The dilemma this poses for the Navy is that the threat to our national commitments is unlikely to decline.

A discussion of the Air Force follows. Thomas Fabyanic examines this Service and notes that the Air Force in 1986 was a far superior military instrument, quantitatively and qualitatively, to the one inherited by President Reagan in 1981. Some of the changes that have brought this about were motivated by civilians, for example, Midgetman and Special Operations Forces; others were promoted by the Air Force, an institution that Fabyanic contends is too hardware-oriented. This latter quality hamstrings the institution in its ability to develop effective strategic concepts, leaving the Service vulnerable to pleas for new systems whose warfighting values are suspect.

The last article in part III is a discussion of the Strategic Defense Initiative (SDI). Slater and Goldfischer are skeptical, contending that confusion and inconsistency on the part of the Reagan administration characterize that program. As presently conceived, SDI will likely lead both to an arms race and to crisis instability. There *are* good arguments for a ballistic missile defense, according to Slater and Goldfischer, but the bad arguments put forth by the Reagan administration have all but buried the good ones. The authors discuss reasons why SDI is worth pursuing: for safeguarding against clandestinely retained nuclear weapons and against third-party or terrorist attacks.

In part IV, Jacques Gansler examines readiness issues and acquisition policies. Gansler argues that both Congress and the executive branch have historically focused on problems of "fraud and abuse." Both institutions, he believes, should shift their attention to a needed restructuring of the planning, budgeting, and acquisition process, along the lines proposed by the Packard Commission. In addition, Gansler suggests reforms that would change the "culture" of procurement and, by providing incentives for efficiency, contribute to improvements in the acquisition process.

Lawrence Korb suggests that the Department of Defense achieved commensurate improvements in readiness and hardware capabilities during the Reagan era. These improvements were a result of a 52 percent real growth in the defense budget (discounting for inflation) between fiscal year 1980 and fiscal year 1985. However, Korb is not optimistic that readiness and sustainability will continue to be adequately funded. The fiscal year 1986 budget declined by 6 percent in real terms, the largest drop in 15 years, and the short-term outlook does not appear hopeful for budget increases. The challenge will be to maintain the balance between modernization and readiness in a period of budget retrenchment. If this is not done, Korb argues, the gains in readiness of the early 1980s will be lost quickly.

*   *   *

The authors and editors hope this volume opens new vistas and suggests directions that heretofore have not been pursued by this or previous administrations. Furthermore, for scholars, we hope these articles will stimulate further analysis and debate of the issues examined in this volume. Clarification of the strengths and weaknesses of past policies will ultimately assist in understanding the multidimensional security needs of the United States and its alliance partners in the decades ahead.

DEFENSE POLICY IN THE
REAGAN ADMINISTRATION

☆☆

Part I

REGIONAL AND GLOBAL ISSUES

THE REAGAN ADMINISTRATION AND ARMS CONTROL: REDEFINING THE AGENDA

Schuyler Foerster

NO PRESIDENT ENTERS THE OVAL OFFICE with a blank agenda, nor does he enjoy the unconstrained freedom to shape an agenda. Observers may debate the extent to which a President can shape the destiny of his administration, or whether his accomplishments are significantly determined by the various political systems—international and domestic—in which he is but one, albeit important, actor. In the arenas of defense policy, nuclear strategy, and arms control, a President's latitude is more constrained by systemic factors than it is in other policy arenas. For the United States, no less than for other states, arms control in particular is interwoven with both high and low politics, at the domestic level, within an alliance framework, and in an East-West international context.

Much of the arms control agenda was already in place when Ronald Reagan entered the Oval Office. Equally, the President inherited a situation in which there was a strong impetus to pursue arms control initiations. Because arms control is a contractual process between two independent (sovereign) actors, each party must approach the process with a sense of *strength* with which to negotiate, even as each party is brought to the process out of a sense of *vulnerability*. Although these

5

two elements—strength and vulnerability—are arguably part of any contractual process, they are especially salient in the nuclear business where both the measures of power and the magnitude of risk involve such high stakes.

It is commonplace to note that, political and ideological conflicts notwithstanding, the United States and the Soviet Union share a common interest in war avoidance and nuclear confrontation. This mutual vulnerability of the nuclear age provides an incentive for each to seek a regulated strategic relationship as one means to enhance national security. Conceivably, arms control can provide mutual benefits in a nonzero sum game context. Yet the United States and the Soviet Union approach this security dilemma of the nuclear age with different geostrategic outlooks, different perspectives on the utility of nuclear weapons and of military force in general, and, accordingly, different force structures. For either to feel confident about its ability to secure its interest in such negotiations, therefore, each side requires sufficient manifestations of military strength to sustain leverage in the negotiations.

The Reagan administration entered office at a time when US military strength was viewed as inadequate to sustain an efficacious bargaining position. Perhaps more to the point, the sense of American vulnerability was especially high. In his first Annual Report to Congress, Defense Secretary Weinberger stressed "the long overdue modernization of our strategic forces."[1] Noting that arms control was "a melancholy chapter in the troubled history of the last decade or two," Weinberger was specific about the source of US "disappointment": "Our land-based deterrent forces have become highly vulnerable even though one of our main purposes in SALT was to prevent such vulnerability."[2]

In many ways, the Reagan administration has attempted to redefine the agenda of arms control, and in many respects it has succeeded in doing so. It is not so clear, however, that the redefinition will be as complete and as straightforward as hoped by the administration. There seemed, from the outset, to be a sense that a rebuilding of strength would be the antidote to vulnerability, with strategic modernization and a return to new forms of arms control proceeding in sequence. As events evolved, however, the same vulnerability that drove the pursuit of strength also compelled deliberate moves in arms control. Indeed, the pursuit of arms control was necessary as a concomitant condition for the pursuit of military strength.

Even as the Reagan administration seemed bent on redefining the agenda, it could not escape the fact that it had inherited a policy framework from its predecessors. To understand the context of arms control in the Reagan administration, therefore, it is necessary to explore the legacy which it inherited. The next section discusses the relationship between strategy and arms control, since the latter cannot be—or ought not to be—disconnected from the former. Subsequent sections summarize the legacy of the SALT process in the 1970s, lamented by Weinberger in his first annual report, and the alliance dimension of US strategy and arms control.

The unsuccessful negotiations on both intermediate nuclear forces in Europe and strategic weapons between 1981 and 1983 provide the context in which the Reagan administration sought to define its own approach to arms control. That period laid the foundation for the latest efforts, ongoing in Geneva since March 1985. That process has revealed a security dilemma, inherent to the nuclear age, with profound implications for US policy.

Nuclear weapons are a significant element of national military power for superpowers, but possession of a strategic nuclear arsenal does not automatically provide a deterrent, nor does it necessarily translate into an efficacious political instrument. Regardless of one's offensive prowess, societal vulnerability is a reality which can be only partly mitigated by military strength. Weapons programs are necessary instruments for one's strategy, but they also provide the necessary leverage for arms control processes which that same vulnerability compels. The Reagan administration has pursued both substantial improvement in the US strategic arsenal and a dramatic reorientation of the arms control agenda. Success in the former is a hedge against failure in the latter, but improved capabilities also serve as levers for success in the latter. There remains, however, the possibility that success in both arenas may create fundamental incompatibilities between the two policy directions.

Strategy and Arms Control in the Nuclear Age

Well over a decade ago, amid a debate on whether or how detente would alter the postwar international system, Michael Howard wrote:

The objective of strategy has remained unchanged since before the advent of the nuclear age—coercing one's opponent into abandoning his preferred course of action by posing the alternative of unacceptable punishment; but that object was not to be achieved less by manipulation of actual forces than by manipulation of risks.[3]

In many respects arms control has evolved into a component of defense policy, serving to complement a state's ability to manipulate others' perception of risk. Arms control has left its maternal source, idealistic notions of disarmament, and has become integral to the strategic frameworks in which weapons find their utility.

The distinction between arms control and disarmament is an important one. As Thomas Schelling and Morton Halperin pointed out 25 years ago, arms control is "concerned less with reducing national *capabilities* for destruction in the event of war than in reducing the *incentives* that may lead to war or that may cause war to be the more destructive in the event it occurs."[4] Similarly, Hedley Bull noted at the same time that disarmament—the reduction or abolition of arms—need not be controlled, although arms control involves the necessary element of restraint in arms policies.[5] Such restraint may apply to the character of weapons, to their deployment, or to their employment; it need not involve a reduction in the level of armaments and, indeed, may not necessarily be incompatible with the increase in certain types of armaments as long as that increase is within a framework of restraint on future policies.

Ideally, arms control can facilitate the creation of a strategic relationship in which antagonists can subsequently reduce levels of armaments. The essential element of arms control, however, remains the stability of the relationship between strategic adversaries rather than levels of armaments. There may be other side benefits—reducing the effects of war, building mutual confidence between adversaries, or lowering the costs of defense—but the central utility of arms control is its ability to reduce the chances of war by minimizing miscalculation, misperception, and anxiety in a crisis and by reducing the incentives for starting a war.[6]

The development of arms control thinking along these lines paralleled the evolution of deterrence theory itself as the latter adapted to the realities of the missile age. In particular, Mutual Assured Destruction (MAD) derived as much from arms control theory as from deterrence theory. Proceeding from the premise that nuclear warfare was not—and should not be—a usable instrument of state policy, MAD made possible certain distinctions in weaponry that, in turn, provided a foundation on which arms control could develop. Invulnerable retaliatory capabilities and vulnerable societies were essential to mutual deterrence. It followed, then, that weapons which were vulnerable, capable of disarming an adversary's retaliatory force, or capable of defending one's own society were "destabilizing"; weapons which were invulnerable, capable of destroying an adversary's society, but not threatening to an adversary's capability to retaliate were "stabilizing." In short, the traditional preference of defense over offense, at least for arms control purposes, was in a fashion reversed: deterrence rested on an offensive retaliatory capability, while the avoidance of defense—at least for one's society—helped to ensure that any incentive for initiating war would be absent.

The Legacy of SALT

In practice, the Strategic Arms Limitations Talks (SALT) embodied a process which had no element of disarmament associated with it. Limits on intercontinental ballistic missile (ICBM) and submarine-launched ballistic missile (SLBM) launchers in the 1972 SALT I Interim Agreement on Offensive Weapons reflected the US and USSR force structures, either deployed or under construction, for the five-year duration of the treaty. When combined with the Anti-Ballistic Missile (ABM) Treaty, however, SALT I appeared to institutionalize parity; both the United States and the USSR would preserve their invulnerable retaliatory capabilities and endure a "mutual hostage relationship."

Yet institutionalizing MAD as a strategic framework for superpower relationships has been elusive. In the wake of SALT I, it became evident that the Soviet Union did not share the US theoretical view that societal vulnerability and assured retaliatory capability were desirable elements of a strategic framework. The reasons are political, ideological, historical, and cultural, as well as strategic. Some subsequently argued that it was irrelevant whether the Soviets accepted societal vulnerability as a desirable state of affairs: the mutual hostage relationship remained, for the foreseeable future, an inherent and unavoidable feature of the nuclear age.[7] Others, however, viewed Soviet persistence in pursuing ABM technology, increased investment in civil defense, and fascination with large, heavy ICBMs as indicative of a continuing effort to find an escape from that hostage relationship.

Likewise, SALT I did not effectively block those Soviet efforts. With respect to the ABM Treaty, even a generous interpretation of Soviet activity suggests they have pushed the limits of the treaty's provisions in probing the possibilities of ABM territorial defense.[8] Of more immediate concern, the Soviets began to exploit the advantages which larger ICBM throw-weight capability gave them by deploying multiple independently targetable reentry vehicles (MIRVs) in the wake of SALT I. The United States had only indirectly succeeded in restraining Soviet "heavy" ICBM deployment in SALT I. Subsequently, MIRVed Soviet SS–18 replaced the 308 SS–9 "heavy" ICBMs but multiplied the allowable number of independently targetable countersilo-capable warheads by a factor of 10. Similarly, despite attempts to block the substitution of "heavy" ICBMs for "light" ICBMs, the Soviets began to replace their SS–11 ICBMs with the SS–19, with three times the throw-weight and MIRVed with six warheads.[9]

The growth of a Soviet countersilo capability led many to speak of a possible "window of vulnerability" for the United States. The dominant issue in arms control became not the institutionalization of MAD but removal of a threat to the US land-based ICBM force. According to the logic of MAD, each side could maintain a capability to destroy the other's society, but to use that capability would only invite the other side to retaliate in like fashion. Only a first strike which effectively disarmed the adversary would avoid that suicidal outcome. Countersilo-capable MIRVed ICBMs, however, created the ominous possibility that sufficient warheads could be targeted against an adversary's ICBM force, effectively disarming the only leg of the triad capable of striking hard targets. While over 55 percent of US strategic warheads were in SLBMs and almost 25 percent of its warheads on intercontinental bombers, it would have the capability to retaliate against such a Soviet strike *only* by assuring the destruction of Soviet society.[10] In short, after losing its ICBMs, the United States would still have the assured destruction capability called for by MAD. The Soviet Union, however, would still retain *its* assured destruction capability as well. Thus, under the logic of MAD it would be irrational for the United States to retaliate against a Soviet first strike against the US ICBM force.

Such a theoretical possibility propelled a defense debate that has gone to the very roots of the nuclear dilemma. MAD has been criticized as a dubious "theory of prewar deterrence" that has seduced the United States into ignoring the essential requirements of a strategy in the event deterrence failed; what was needed was a clear notion of how military power could achieve

political ends *in war*.[11] This debate is often cast in
Glenn Snyder's classic categorization of deterrence
versus defense or, more precisely, deterrence by punishment versus deterrence by denial. Deterrence by the
threat of devastating punishment is the essence of
MAD, recalling Bernard Brodie's characterization of
the atomic bomb as the "Absolute Weapon": the very
destructiveness of nuclear weapons has made them the
"weapon to end war," because such destructive power
is presumed to have no political utility. MAD merely
extends this feature to its logical conclusion and offers a
framework of stability in which the "balance of terror"
is not quite so precarious. Deterrence by denial requires
the ability to deny an adversary military—and hence
political—success by keeping nuclear weapons usable in
the event deterrent threats fail. Such "warfighting"
notions are anathema to MAD, precisely because the
weapons favored under one theory are incompatible
with those favored by the other.

In reality, the United States has never had a totally
"MAD"-oriented force posture. The technology necessary for MIRVing, for increased accuracy in ICBM and
SLBM warheads, and for associated command, control,
communications, and intelligence (C^3I) had advanced
considerably, paralleling the development of Soviet
strategic warfighting capabilities. The "Schlesinger
Doctrine," embodied in the 1974 National Security
Decision Memorandum (NSDM) 242, called for greater
flexibility in targeting options to allow limited nuclear
strikes as an alternative to indiscriminate response. The
MK–12a RV and warhead, more accurate than its predecessors, was deployed on 300 Minuteman IIIs, and
comparable technology will provide each of the 10 MX
warheads with a hard-target kill capability. Similarly,
the countersilo-accurate Trident D5, still to be

deployed, will transform the SLBM force from its traditional role as a force capable only of assuring the destruction of Soviet socioeconomic assets.

These technological developments led to a new targeting strategy in the Carter administration, Presidential Directive 59 (PD 59), which was carried over in the Reagan administration as National Security Decision Directive 13 (NSDD 13). Fundamentally similar, both strategies primarily target Soviet political structures and command and control networks, as well as military targets, in the attempt to provide the President with options besides the destruction of Soviet society.[12] The force structure required by this strategy involves increased numbers of warheads, greater hard-target kill capability, and a substantial investment in both ground-based and space-based C^3I capabilities. The search for strategic defense options represents merely an extension of this logic, not based on a desire to achieve a first-strike capability against the Soviet Union, but based on a reluctance to stay locked into a mutual hostage relationship whereby an American President has only the options of surrender or suicide in response to Soviet attack.

The Carter administration's "countervailing strategy" was announced in August 1980, in the wake of his withdrawal of the ill-fated SALT II Treaty from ratification proceedings in the Senate. While the failure of SALT II certainly did not cause this shift in strategic thinking, it represented a general disillusionment with an arms control process that did not appear to be improving the US strategic predicament.[13] Like its saline predecessor, SALT II largely ratified existing force structures. While it succeeded in imposing limits on MIRV-capable weapons systems, and indirectly capped the number of warheads available to each side, it did not fundamentally alter a marked Soviet advantage in hard-target kill-capable ICBMs. Opponents of the treaty, among them Carter's successor, rejected it as "fatally flawed" because it seemed to legitimize this theoretical instability. Proponents of the treaty noted, in rebuttal, that the USSR was at least restrained in future weapons developments, while the United States did not have to alter its existing plans for strategic modernization.[14]

The Alliance Dimension

The utility of nuclear weapons—and, hence, the desirability of alternative schemes for controlling them—is only partly understood in the context of the US-Soviet competition. Were the United States to be concerned only with the security of its own territory, the dilemmas of the nuclear age would be less complicated, although still not simply resolved. The requirements for "extended deterrence"—the deterrence of attacks against allies—are different from those of "basic deterrence"—the deterrence of attacks against oneself. The logic of MAD is at least theoretically applicable in a relationship between two nuclear-armed adversaries, since it offers little or no incentive for either side to initiate a nuclear strike. The logic of MAD does not, however, provide much solace for the Western European allies of the North Atlantic Treaty Organization (NATO). The doctrine of flexible response obliges NATO to defend against, for example, a Soviet invasion with conventional forces, but contemplates the possibility that NATO might have to escalate to the nuclear level in that defense. In short, NATO might find itself the first to use nuclear weapons, and the United States—the provider of that extended deterrent guarantee—would have to authorize that first use.

Such use of nuclear weapons can now take three forms: tactical or battlefield weapons, intermediate nuclear forces based in Europe, and the US strategic nuclear arsenal. So-called tactical nuclear weapons could be used against targets confined to the European theater of operations. Designed as a link in a chain of graduated response ranging from conventional defense to strategic nuclear retaliation against the USSR, these weapons are being unilaterally reduced to 4,600 in Europe, down from a peak of some 7,000 weapons in the 1970s. Although they pose a threat to attacking forces, they are not capable of striking the territory of the USSR.

Until 1983, the only effective way to keep the Soviet Union from being a "sanctuary" in a war which they might initiate in Europe was to use the US strategic arsenal. Clearly such use of weapons would require that US strategic nuclear weapons be in fact "usable"— capable of achieving desired political ends. A purely MAD force posture would not provide that option, but as noted above, counterforce weapons and targeting run counter to the logic of MAD. Moreover, to the extent that the Soviet Union remains in a position to employ nuclear weapons against US strategic assets—and thereby deter US strategic use—the credibility of US extended deterrence may be even more questionable than that of the US basic deterrent threat.

Helmut Schmidt, then Chancellor of the Federal Republic of Germany (FRG), stressed this conflict between the requirements of extended deterrence and the realities of superpower nuclear parity to the NATO allies in 1977:

[Strategic parity] will make it necessary during the coming years ... to reduce the political and military role of strategic nuclear weapons as a normal component of defense and deterrence; the strategic nuclear component will become increasingly regarded as an instrument of last resort, to save the *national* interest and *protect the survival of those who possess these strategic weapons of last resort.*[15]

A paradox existed: to the extent SALT I succeeded in institutionalizing superpower parity and MAD, it tended to undermine the extended deterrent foundations of NATO. To the extent that the SALT process failed to deal successfully with the strategic predicament posed by Soviet ICBM developments, it further exacerbated this paradox. Only by creating a balance between NATO and Warsaw Pact conventional forces could NATO reduce its reliance on the United States extended-deterrent guarantee. Since that was not forthcoming, NATO turned to a third form of nuclear weapons—Long-Range Intermediate Nuclear Force (LRINF)—to bolster the "coupling" of the defense of Western Europe and the US extended deterrent.

NATO's 1979 dual-track decision envisioned the deployment of 572 US Pershing II and ground-launched cruise missiles (GLCMs) in Western Europe, beginning in 1983, unless the Soviet Union agreed to negotiate appropriate reductions in their nuclear missiles—specifically their new SS–20s—aimed at Western Europe. No agreement was forthcoming, and deployments continue although NATO councils persistently stress their willingness "to modify, halt, reverse, or dispense altogether with LRINF missile deployment as part of a balanced, equitable and effectively veritable arms control agreement."[16] The missiles' significance lies in their capability to target the Soviet Union from Europe, so that the USSR could not expect to remain a sanctuary in a European conflict. Two somewhat paradoxical arguments existed for the deployments. First, the missiles were a threat to the Soviet heartland even if the

United States decided to defer use of its strategic arsenal
in a European conflict. Second, they manifested a continuing US commitment and, some argued, made the
escalation to strategic nuclear exchange between the
superpowers more nearly inevitable, thereby deterring
the Soviet Union.

What has evolved over the past decade, however,
is an increasingly blurred distinction between what had
previously been two separate "balances of power"—the
theater balance in Europe and the superpower nuclear
balance. The SALT process had been possible in part
because it had confined itself to the bilateral superpower
relationship. In the currency of SALT I, "strategic"
was equated to "intercontinental": neither the limited
Soviet nuclear capability against NATO—inaccurate
SS–4 and SS–5 missiles—nor the limited US "forward-
based systems" (FBS), such as tactical aircraft capable
of striking targets in the Soviet Union, were included in
SALT I. SALT II likewise deferred the knotty issues of
Soviet INF (Intermediate-Range Nuclear Force)—
including the newly deployed SS–20—and NATO's
FBS, and skirted new "gray area" systems such as the
Soviet Backfire bomber and US cruise missiles.[17] Negotiations were difficult enough when the United States
and Soviet Union had to contend with asymmetrical
forces and doctrinal perspectives. They seemed nigh
impossible if the negotiators' differing geostrategic
positions in Europe were included. Even had the negotiations remained ostensibly bilateral, the accompanying
intra-alliance negotiations would have been onerous.
Given that politics remains the "art of the possible,"
arms control remains the "act of the negotiable": gray-
area systems seemed destined to be deferred to "SALT
$N + 1$." In this case, however, SALT III required SALT
II, but the Soviet invasion of Afghanistan and the subsequent "suspension" of SALT II ratification in the

United States—all within a month of NATO's "dual-track decision"—boded ill for SALT III.

Changing the Parameters of Arms Control: 1981–1983

In his first press conference after his inauguration, Reagan set a harsh rhetorical tone to US-Soviet relations:

[The Soviets] have openly and publicly declared that the only morality they recognize is what will further their cause [of promoting world revolution and a one-world socialist or communist state], meaning they reserve unto themselves the right to commit any crime, to lie, to cheat, in order to attain that, and that is moral, not immoral, and we operate on a different set of standards. I think when you do business with them ... you keep that in mind....[18]

This and similar statements by other officials signaled the administration's intention to change the framework which had characterized previous arms control efforts.

LRINF. The immediate arms control agenda for the Reagan administration was not strategic nuclear weapons but LRINF. Having affirmed in February 1981 US support for the 1979 NATO dual-track decision on LRINF, Reagan announced the US negotiating position in November. Dubbed the "Zero Option," the proposal envisioned cancelling Pershing II and GLCM deployments—still two years away—in exchange for Soviet dismantling of SS–4, SS–5, and SS–20 intermediate-range missiles, including those SS–20s deployed in the Ural Mountains and the Soviet Far East.[19]

The political merit of the Zero Option lay in its simplicity. The President could claim the "moral high ground" and restore "disarmament" to arms control by stressing that Soviet agreement could permit "the removal of an entire class of weapons." Not included within the framework of the proposed LRINF negotiations were US theater systems in Europe, British and

French nuclear forces, either side's aircraft or sea-based systems, or shorter-ranged Soviet systems like the SS–21, –22, or –23. Subsequent debates revolved around the "real" balance in Europe, with public and private organizations and individuals on all sides weighing in with various calculations and measurement schemes.[20]

What made much of the debate over "the balance" meaningless, of course, was that NATO's proposed LRINF deployments had little to do with a Soviet theater nuclear threat that somehow needed to be "matched" militarily. The Soviets enjoyed a nuclear capability against NATO even before the first SS–4 was deployed in 1959. Indeed, one can even argue that SS–20s are preferable to obsolete SS–4s and SS–5s by virtue of their mobility: the invulnerability of the SS–20s—notwithstanding the increased military threat they pose—renders them less likely to be used preemptively in a crisis. NATO's fundamental strategic problem, which provided the impetus for the 1979 dual-track decision, was that the central strategic relationship—even under an anticipated SALT II agreement—would at best be one of parity and mutual deterrence. Given the failure to achieve a conventional force balance, as Schmidt noted in 1977 and Henry Kissinger reiterated in 1979,[21] the extended deterrent foundations of NATO were less than solid. This "deterrence gap"—not the SS–20s themselves—provided the basis for viewing Soviet military power as potentially capable of nuclear blackmail. The parallel debate on "no first use" of nuclear weapons in Europe was not, moreover, unrelated to the LRINF dilemma.[22]

Not surprisingly, there was considerable debate within the Reagan administration about the LRINF negotiating framework. Secretary of State Alexander Haig was certainly not alone in suggesting that "we wouldn't want it even if we could have it.''[23] Because LRINF deployments were designed to reinforce the US extended deterrent guarantee, elimination of Soviet LRINF did not solve the problem. For others, the Zero Option was a guarantee that no agreement would be forthcoming, that the Pershings and GLCMs would be deployed on schedule, and that the Soviet Union would find itself defeated politically, both because the United States would have captured the moral high ground in the propaganda battle and because the alliance would have demonstrated the unity and resolve necessary for exacting Soviet concessions on other issues.

Alliance cohesion was not a foregone conclusion, however, as the LRINF negotiations in Geneva dragged on. Allied pressure—itself a source of vulnerability for the United States—mounted as governments in whose countries the missiles were to be deployed urged flexibility in the US negotiating position. Even if the Zero Option solution was for everyone not the most desirable outcome from a strategic point of view, an arms control agreement became valued for its political merit. It would pressure—indeed restore—a political process between the superpowers which would mitigate European anxiety; it would enable European governments to undercut opposition movements whose members had taken to the streets in the thousands, and it might at least restrain continuing Soviet military developments.

In an address to the American Legion in February 1983, Reagan offered some flexibility for the Zero Option. He continued to insist that French and British systems could not be included and that SS–20s deployed in the Far East could not be excluded from an agreement (reflecting pressure from allies in Asia too). He left open, however, the possibility of a limited agreement, provided that ''equality of rights and limits''

and "effective measures of verification" were maintained.[24] Although helpful politically, this show of flexibility produced no progress. Willingness in principle to
consider alternatives to the Zero Option, or what had
become known as the "Zero-Zero Option," did not
remove the fact that there was no agreement on what
kinds of "equal limits" could be established. Clearly
the United States could not accept a freeze that left the
Soviets with more than they had in 1979, but neither
could the Soviets be expected to dismantle existing systems while NATO deployed theirs. Moreover, the
increasing complexity of the "balance" calculations
coincided with the beginning of a leadership succession
crisis in Moscow, during which no substantive policy
demarches could be expected.

On 23 November 1983, in the wake of the Soviet
shootdown of a Korean airliner, one day after the West
German Parliament approved the deployment of Pershing IIs, and the day the first GLCMs arrived in the
FRG, the Soviet delegation suspended indefinitely its
participation in LRINF negotiations. Two weeks later,
on 8 December, the Soviet delegation to the START
negotiations followed suit.[25]

START. In the November 1981 televised address in
which he laid out his Zero Option for LRINF, Reagan
also declared that his new agenda for strategic arms
control was not SALT but START—Strategic Arms
Reduction Talks. These negotiations began in June 1982
in Geneva.

As with the LRINF negotiations, the United States
began with a hard-line "linkage" position of no negotiations unless Soviet concessions were evident in other
areas and evolved to a position of apparent simplicity,
with the potential for disarming critics even if it did not

successfully disarm the Soviets. A year before, during his Senate confirmation hearings, Eugene Rostow, the new Director of the Arms Control and Disarmament Agency (ACDA), had urged a return to "effective containment" as a necessary precursor to the fruitful pursuit of "detente and arms control."[26] Rostow subsequently highlighted the need for preliminary discussions on ways to verify compliance before beginning any formal negotiations on arms reductions.[27]

Linkage is a double-edged sword, as the United States discovered during the Nixon administration and the complex nexus of agreements that characterized the heyday of detente during the early 1970s. Linkage suggests a contingent willingness to seek agreement on one issue, provided that other issues are made part of the process or that prior concessions are made.

To hold agreement in one arena hostage to concessions on other issues suggests that one is willing to defer the benefits of agreement if those concessions are not forthcoming.

At the outset of the Reagan administration, the rhetoric of linkage was strong. As Secretary of State Haig told the Foreign Policy Association in July 1981,

we will seek arms control, bearing in mind the whole context of Soviet conduct world-wide.... Linkage is not a creation of US policy, it is a fact of life.[28]

Given concurrent crises in Poland, Central America, and the Middle East, then, one should not have expected much progress in arms control. For the Reagan administration, there were reasons enough not to hasten back to a strategic arms control forum. It was, after all, the first year of his term; the administration's own position and bureaucratic process were still in flux; the political dynamics of LRINF demanded more immediate attention; and there remained the nagging problem of whether to reject or adhere to the SALT II treaty.

During the first year of office, moreover, the Reagan defense program incorporated some striking defense reductions on both budgetary and strategic grounds: Titan II ICBMs were earmarked for retirement, as were the last remaining eight submarines carrying Polaris SLBMs. Reagan's strategic modernization program, on the other hand, remained largely in the development stage, and several of its elements were not yet firm. The Carter administration's program for 200 MX missiles rotating among 4,600 Multiple Protective Shelters (MPS), for example, was soon cut to 100 missiles, with 40 to be deployed in existing silos.[29] By May of 1982, the proposed basing mode had been changed to Closely Spaced Basing (CSB) which relied on "fratricide"— and perhaps on ABM cover—to preserve their invulnerability, but this concept met with little enthusiasm on Capitol Hill.[30]

Any application of linkage to strategic arms control, therefore, seemed doomed, and indeed, there were no preliminary negotiations on verification. The Reagan administration was not in a position to undercut an existing—albeit dormant—arms control regime if, as the Joint Chiefs of Staff (JCS) pointed out in 1981, there was nothing the United States would do differently in the absence of SALT II restraints. Accordingly, the State Department had already announced on 4 March 1981, "We will take no action that would undercut existing agreements so long as the Soviet Union exercises the same restraint."[31] Despite imposition of martial law in Poland in December 1981, LRINF negotiations continued because, as Haig noted, there was "a fundamental advantage to the West as well as to the East" in continuing that dialogue.[32] Two weeks later, however, "deterioration" of the Polish situation caused a delay in the expected announcement of a date for negotiations on strategic arms.

In his commencement speech in Eureka, Illinois, on 9 May 1982, Reagan outlined his START proposal, calling for substantial reductions—approximately one-third—in US and Soviet strategic arsenals.[33] The notion of a one-third reduction was not a new one. Senator Henry Jackson had proposed a one-third reduction as a framework for SALT II as early as 1973, and Carter opened his administration with an abortive one-third "Deep Cuts" proposal in March 1977.[34] Reagan's proposal was directed specifically against the Soviet ICBM threat to US ICBMs. Strategic warheads were to be reduced to 5,000, with a subceiling of 2,500 ICBM warheads, and ICBM and SLBM launchers were to be reduced to 850. Although the United States would have had to reduce its deployed warheads approximately 30 percent, compared to 26 percent for the Soviets, Soviet ICBM warheads would have had to be reduced 53 percent while the United States still had room for 500 warheads (or 50 MX) after Titan II retirement. The Soviets were hardly receptive to this approach, arguing that it discriminated against the mainstay of their defense. They offered instead a reduction in both sides' delivery vehicles. Although this would have forced the USSR to reduce theirs six times the number required of the United States, the fundamental strategic relationship would have remained essentially unchanged: The Soviets, with a substantial advantage in hard-target kill warheads, would still pose a threat to the US ICBM force.[35]

By early 1983, there had been no progress in Geneva, and the US ICBM modernization program was in disarray as the administration searched for a politically acceptable basing mode for MX. In January,

Reagan commissioned retired USAF Lieutenant General Brent Scowcroft, who had advised his three predecessors, to form a "Blue Ribbon" committee to examine the administration's strategic force modernization program and arms control posture. The Report of the President's Commission on Strategic Forces, released on 6 April 1983, had a major effect on the direction of US policy. In the main, the commission endorsed the broad contours of administration policy—including basing 100 MXs in existing and presumably vulnerable Minuteman silos—but redirected US policy in several key areas. First, MX was to be only a transitional weapons system, pending development of a small, single-warhead ICBM (dubbed "Midgetman"). The near-term vulnerability of existing ICBM silos was deemed acceptable because of the prospects of "superhardening" and by virtue of the "operational uncertainties" the Soviets would face in disarming the US with a first strike. Fundamentally, however, the MX offered a potential "bargaining chip" for arms control, although those words were not used: of the six reasons cited in support of the MX, the first two addressed the need to influence Soviet willingness to negotiate by keeping the MX program going and the need to demonstrate US "national will and cohesion." Other reasons reflected principally a desire to retain the MX as a means of preserving the targeting flexibility outlined in PD 59 and NSDD 13, not just to sustain the US basic deterrent but to enhance the extended deterrence guarantee to NATO.[36]

Of more potential long-term significance, the Scowcroft Commission urged development of Midgetman and a shift in arms control toward reductions in warheads rather than launchers. Instability in the US-Soviet strategic relationship, the commission contended, derived from the proliferation of MIRVed warheads on

ICBMs, providing a warhead-to-target ratio conducive to a Soviet first strike. Ideally, if both sides returned to single-warhead ICBMs, there would be no such incentive to preempt, especially if their deployment modes were mobile or otherwise less vulnerable. This required, however, a change in arms control policy: from a strategic point of view, limitations on launchers served to limit the number of targets the other side needed to hit; from a practical standpoint, the 850-launcher ceiling envisioned by the opening START proposal precluded any program like Midgetman. Indeed, the JCS had favored the 850-launcher ceiling precisely because it would provide a target set which could be covered by US systems.[37] On 8 June 1982, Reagan dropped the launcher ceiling from the US START proposal to bring it in line with the Scowcroft Commission's recommendations.

The Scowcroft Commission laid the foundation for a crucial compromise on MX in the Congress and bipartisan support for the administration's START proposals. Led by Congressman Les Aspin, this support produced congressional authorization for the initial procurement increments of MX, coupled with the development of a "build-down" proposal offered to the Soviets in late 1983. Build-down proposals varied in their complexity but involved a net reduction in warheads as each side modernized its forces: conceptually, if any side persisted in deploying heavy MIRVed systems, the price would be disproportionately higher in terms of the simultaneous reductions that such an agreement would require.[38] Of more immediate significance, however, "linkage" had been applied in US domestic politics: the price for MX was an arms control proposal that Congress had participated in developing, just as NATO's dual-track decision of 1979 had coupled modernization with an arms control initiative.

The timing of the build-down proposal was hardly conducive to success. Soviet-American relations had been soured by the Korean airliner shootdown, and NATO's LRINF deployments were pending. Andropov had disappeared from public view and another Soviet succession struggle had begun even before revelation that the incumbent had died. The Soviets suspended both LRINF and START negotiations to regroup at home. The 13 months of the Chernenko period, beginning in February 1984, provided a respite for both sides to contemplate new directions in nuclear policy and, for the United States especially, to reflect on basic premises.

The Scowcroft Commission had articulated a way to integrate force modernization, nuclear strategy, and arms control policy. The first three years of the Reagan administration represented a classical example of building a position of strength which could provide leverage in arms control. Considerable leverage was needed: what was desired was nothing less than a major restructuring of the Soviet strategic force posture. The United States was likewise at a strategic crossroads. On 23 March 1983, Reagan announced his Strategic Defense Initiative (SDI) which portended a major transformation of both US strategy and, potentially, force posture. The US arms control policy no longer accepted, except by default with SALT II, a nominal freeze on force levels which could be verified with relative ease. Disarmament, in a fashion, had returned to arms control in the form of major reductions, while the currency of arms control had changed from launchers to warheads. When negotiations resumed, with Gorbachev as the new Soviet leader and Reagan reelected in a landslide, the agenda of arms control had changed, perhaps irreversibly.

The Geneva Arms Control Agenda

On 12 March 1985, the United States and the Soviet Union reopened arms control negotiations in Geneva, having agreed in January "that the subject of the negotiations will be a complex of questions concerning space and nuclear arms both strategic and intermediate range with all the questions considered and resolved in their interrelationship."[39] Three separate negotiating fora were subsumed under one umbrella. Two were resurrections of the START and LRINF negotiations which the Soviets had abandoned in late 1983. The third was a new issue, space-based defenses, reflecting a Soviet desire to thwart SDI. The Soviets stressed from the outset that any agreement required progress in all three negotiations while the United States stressed that agreement in one forum should not be hostage to any other.

What is at stake in Geneva is what the Reagan administration has termed its "strategic concept":

During the next ten years, the US objective is a radical reduction in the power of existing and planned offensive nuclear arms, as well as the stabilization of the relationship between offensive and defensive nuclear arms, whether on earth or in space. We are even now looking forward to a period of transition to a more stable world, with greatly reduced levels of nuclear arms and an enhanced ability to deter war based upon an increasing contribution of non-nuclear defenses against offensive nuclear arms.[40]

The centerpiece of this "strategic concept" is strategic defense: the ability, as Reagan outlined in March 1983, to "intercept and destroy strategic ballistic missiles before they reached our own soil or that of our allies."[41] The Strategic Defense Initiative, in Reagan's vision, means nothing less than providing "the means of rendering these nuclear weapons impotent and obsolete." As such, it strikes at the very core of postwar deterrence thinking which has been based on the premise that deterrence derives from the threat of offensive retaliation. The power of the concept stems as well from rising concern about the prospects of "nuclear winter" in the event of even limited nuclear exchanges.[42]

In essence, the Reagan administration had decided to pursue strategic stability based not on the nuclear weapon as the "Absolute Weapon" but on a new "Absolute Weapon" which could defend nonlethally and nondestructively against nuclear weapons. The controversy over SDI revolves principally around assessments of its feasibility and the form it might take. Although that can hardly be resolved before specific technologies can be assessed, the theoretical issue is not premature. The Strategic Defense Initiative is not only the centerpiece of Reagan's "strategic concept," which can only be described as "long-term," it is also the central issue in ongoing Geneva negotiations. How one views the prospects of strategic defense—however premature that assessment may be—colors one's assessment of what is desirable and negotiable in Geneva.

Critics of SDI have rightly noted Soviet concern about US breakthroughs in defensive technology and at the same time warned of the difficulties in fulfilling this strategic vision.[43] A defense which meets this Administration's criteria—survivability of the defensive systems themselves and marginal cost-effectiveness[44]—may not be readily achievable. Yet both these criteria are necessary for stability. If defense is not cheaper than offensive countermeasures, then one has only succeeded in creating an open-ended spiral of anxiety and instability. If defensive systems are not survivable, then offensive systems are not rendered "obsolete" and, worse, the side which possesses the defense may succumb to a "Maginot Line mentality." In that case, there remains an incentive to strike first to disarm vulnerable defenses on which the defender has relied excessively; this instability could persist even after both sides have weathered the presumably unstable "transition" and deployed their respective defenses.

Such criticism of what remains only a hypothetical defensive strategy has led many to suggest that SDI be exploited as the quintessential bargaining chip to exact substantial Soviet concessions on offensive arsenals and thereby close firmly the "window of vulnerability." In short, SDI should be traded for the existing threat to US land-based ICBMs, thereby restoring MAD. Yet, SDI remains, as the administration has reiterated, "A research program ... conducted in accordance with a restrictive interpretation of the [ABM] treaty's obligations."[45] Barring verification of a ban on "purposeful" research programs—as opposed to testing or deployment of established systems—SDI is not readily negotiable in any arms control agreement, especially since the USSR and allies not party to the agreement conduct similar research.

Before the 19–20 November 1985 Reagan-Gorbachev summit meeting, the administration attempted to assure the Soviets by offering "five to seven years notice" in advance of deployment to allow negotiations on defensive systems. As Ambassador Paul Nitze told a House Foreign Affairs subcommittee, "the research program was not on the table" but that "other aspects of the program" were negotiable.[46] One month after the summit, Reagan announced that the United States would continue to abide by the SALT II Treaty after its expiration, despite "a continuing pattern of Soviet noncompliance."[47] The US position had evolved to one of apparent flexibility to preserve an arms control process which had picked up momentum since the summit.

More significant, the President had become personally involved in the process, indicating a significant departure from earlier administration arguments that ''arms control without agreements'' might be preferable to the political drama of negotiations and presidential summitry.[48]

It seems clear that, in many respects, the Reagan administration has developed a more intense commitment to the arms control process. On the one hand, the US negotiating position appears stronger than it did five years before. Regardless of whether SDI is or even could be a bargaining chip, the possibility that it might be negotiable in the long term has enticed the Soviets into an apparently greater commitment to the process as well, for economic and political if not strategic reasons. By the same token, the administration is commensurately more vulnerable to the demise of arms control. The President's personal involvement, both his strategic vision of dramatic reductions and his involvement in summitry, makes it harder to resist the process. Meanwhile, the costs of US commitment are tangible: adherence to SALT II required that the United States dismantle a Poseidon submarine when the seventh Trident submarine was deployed in the fall of 1985 and that two more Poseidons be dismantled when the next Trident was to be deployed in 1986. In that decision, Reagan rejected recommendations which called for only ''selective'' or ''qualified'' adherence to SALT by only drydocking the submarines.[49]

Since the United States claimed it could go no further in meeting Soviet concerns about SDI, thus precluding a straight SDI versus heavy-ICBM deal, a new arms control framework evolved that enabled both sides to approach their goals in a different way. The very structure of the Geneva negotiations provided the logic of the framework: because individual issues seemed immune to agreement, but multiple negotiation contexts existed simultaneously, the answer seemed to lie in ending the distinction between strategic and theater (LRINF) forces and allowing trade-offs to occur between them.

Thus, both the United States and the USSR proposed in advance of the summit apparently similar positions which limited all nuclear "charges" (warheads) to 6,000. Significant differences remained, particularly in the various subceilings and in the definitions of what was and was not to be included. Nonetheless, certain common elements existed on which future negotiations could build, most notably a drastically reduced warhead ceiling and, within that, substantial reductions in ICBM warheads.[50]

On 15 January 1986, Gorbachev offered a sweeping proposal which called for the phased removal of all nuclear weapons by the end of the century, incorporating his own version of Reagan's Zero Option on LRINF, but excluding both British and French systems and Soviet systems in Asia.[51] Although not directly negotiable as an integrated package, it provided Reagan an opportunity to respond both to the general thrust of the proposal and to the Soviet inclination to seek an interim agreement on LRINF. Specifically, Reagan endorsed the goal of removing nuclear weapons by the year 2000 and proposed that both sides begin by dismantling all US and Soviet LRINF missiles within three years.[52]

At the same time that significant differences remain in the US and Soviet proposals, the political climate seems more conducive to some kind of agreement than in previous years. First, the Soviets have indicated a willingness to move on LRINF in the near term without prior agreement on SDI, and they appear to have accepted that, for the moment, research programs are beyond the scope of negotiations. Second, the overall framework for arms control has evolved to one inextricably linked with notions of disarmament, and both sides have made numerous statements indicating continued interest in such an objective. The consequences of such an agreed framework are dramatic, however, and involve difficult choices which, historically, arms control has not required.

Arms and Arms Control—Whither Strategy?

The prospect of an agreement on LRINF has raised important questions about its strategic impact that had remained largely muted when there was little prospect of agreement. The basic issue had been raised earlier, in August 1969, after Kurt-Georg Kiesinger, then FRG Chancellor, discussed with newly elected President Nixon the US plans for SALT:

[SALT] raises serious questions ... about whether the outcome of such talks could not produce a situation that would be worse for the European NATO partners than the present situation ... [producing] a less credible deterrent.... [I]t would reflect a change for Europe, [since] the *Soviet medium range rockets, which are targeted only on Europe, will not be covered as well.*[53]

Then the issue was how SALT might increase the significance of imbalances in LRINF and conventional forces. Now the issue is how an LRINF agreement might increase the significance of imbalances in shorter range systems and conventional forces. As FRG Chancellor Helmut Kohl noted in response to the Reagan-Gorbachev LRINF proposals, ''We cannot agree to an accord on medium range weapons if something is not done to limit conventional weapons and shorter range nuclear systems.''[54] West German, French, and British officials have reacted warily to the LRINF proposal, stressing, as one British official noted, that ''a denuclear world, or even a world with substantial nuclear reductions, that is not accompanied by changes in Soviet conventional strength is not acceptable.''[55] The heart of the issue is the current framework of deterrence, particularly in Europe. As one West German official explained, ''The whole idea of bringing the [LRINF] missiles over here was to reinforce the nuclear link between Europe and the United States.... We will probably go through a new debate now over how credible is the American nuclear umbrella.''[56]

Nuclear weapons, and the prospect of global holocaust, have provided the vehicle by which East and West have, as Michael Howard noted, manipulated risks rather than actual forces in their mutual strategic competition. It has been a precarious relationship, riddled with complex theories, contradictory premises, and paradoxical prescriptions for strategy. By and large, it has been, until recently, an accepted reality. Even unlikely advocates of nuclear power, such as Egon Bahr in the FRG, have embraced it:

For once, nuclear weapons must be praised. I do not know whether, without the extreme effectiveness of their deterrence, the world would have been wise enough to steer past the rocks of deep-seeded conflict and differences of interest between East and West without a general conflagration in Europe.[57]

Bahr's words were spoken in a different age, when the nuclear dilemmas seemed almost academic to those who viewed the detente of the early 1970s with optimism. Now, over a decade later, that optimism is unjustified: notwithstanding a mutual interest in conflict avoidance, the superpowers remain fundamental political, ideological, and strategic antagonists.

Mutual vulnerability to nuclear destruction has, however, created an impetus to seek an alternative framework. Both superpowers talk rhetorically about rendering nuclear weapons obsolete. For the United States, the concern is with ballistic missiles, which provide the greatest threat to the United States, the vehicle is a combination of arms control and strategic defense. For the Soviet Union, the focus is on nuclear weapons in general, with a conscious recognition that a totally de-nuclear world would enhance the political significance of Soviet conventional power, even if the United States returned to its historical position of territorial invulnerability. That, after all, was one of the Soviet objectives behind their proposed treaty on the Prevention of Nuclear War, signed with significant modification in 1973.[58]

The corollary to altering the foundation of postwar nuclear deterrence—assuming this is both desirable and feasible—is how one transitions between frameworks. The United States, for its part, has reacted to its perceived vulnerability of the 1970s with a deliberate program of strategic modernization, coupled with SDI. As noted at the outset, the pursuit of strength is arguably a necessary precondition to the pursuit of arms control, which vulnerability likewise compels. Given the skepticism—even disillusionment—about the ability of arms control to remove that vulnerability, however, strategic modernization efforts are justifiable as a hedge against the failure of arms control. A dilemma arises, however, when arms control appears to have promise, but the costs of arms control involve elements of that strategic modernization effort. That dilemma was easily avoided when arms control took the form of capping existing arsenals while letting programs under development be continued. When arms control begins to mesh with disarmament, then hard choices emerge.

Such choices certainly involve SDI, but arguably that choice is premature insofar as both sides, at least for the time being, defer negotiations on what constitutes a "research program." The hard choices are in offensive weapons programs under development which, even now, necessitate dismantling of existing systems to stay within the residual SALT framework. The United States has, at present, approximately 10,000 warheads deployed on SALT-counted systems.[59] In various stages of development are the MX and Midgetman ICBMs, Trident D5 SLBMs, the B–1 and "Stealth" bombers, and cruise missiles launched from a variety of platforms. To stay within a proposed framework of 6,000 warheads, even assuming an agreement eliminating LRINF, the US strategic force of the 1990s could— depending upon the weapons mix—easily find itself with fewer launch platforms and more adverse warhead-to-target ratios than is the case now.[60]

On the positive side, however, a smaller Soviet ICBM force—coupled with a more dispersed US ICBM force—could result in greater stability, especially if the Trident D5 force can remain invulnerable and still provide flexible targeting despite the fewer submarines involved.

The implications of drastic reductions in superpower nuclear arsenals—and of changes in the specific weapons mixes allowed in such an arms control regime—are immense. To the extent that such reductions reduce incentives for one superpower to preempt in a crisis, then the stability of the basic deterrent relationship is improved, and the world is safer. The development of strategic defenses could force a major shift in force structures if ballistic missiles are indeed rendered "impotent and obsolete." Cruise missiles and air-breathing platforms would become more important, with associated pressures to improve their accuracy and survivability. To the extent that such developments render nuclear weapons unusable, however, Europe could become safer for conventional war, and the extended deterrent relationship encompassing NATO could be undermined. The pressures to find new and more usable weapons systems in such a strategic relationship would be great. Conventional force ratios would become even more important in the NATO theater, accelerating developments in non-nuclear weapons technologies to enable NATO to keep the Soviet Union "at risk" as part of its deterrent strategy.

There is clearly no inexpensive exit from the post-war security dilemma. Economic pressures have already called into question the logic surrounding the Scowcroft Commission's recommendations on long-term development of the single-warhead Midgetman. Undersecretary of Defense Donald Hicks has suggested, for example, doubling the size of Midgetman to enable it to carry three MIRVed warheads instead of one, arguing that 170 MIRVed Midgetman (510 warheads) would be only 60 percent of the cost of 500 single-warhead Midgetman ICBMs.[61] Nuclear weapons have always been the cheaper form of deterrence, and multiple-warhead systems likewise tend to provide more target coverage at less cost. Ultimately, one must match strategy and weapons within realistic resource constraints.

Strategy is commonly defined as the "calculated relationship between ends and means," and ends and means inevitably exist in a dynamic and uncertain relationship. It is certainly premature to assume that the process of arms control will move in the years ahead along the lines sketched out by current proposals, much less remove the dilemmas which the nuclear "Sword of Damocles" has posed. History provides little basis for optimism on this count. The current agenda for arms control is more comprehensive and interrelated than it has been in the past, but comprehensiveness increases the complexity of negotiations. As the current proposals of LRINF suggest, there will always be pressure to segment the agenda so that difficult issues can be handled in isolation and in a more incremental fashion. On the other hand, the relationships among each forum and others—including conventional force negotiations in Vienna—are unavoidable, as the allied response to the LRINF proposal indicates. It may be that, as Paul Nitze argued in NSC 68—26 years ago—one should "insist on concurrent agreement" on the control of both nuclear and nonnuclear forces.[62]

These dilemmas are chronic symptoms of a nuclear reality that has been both a blessing and a curse. There are no simple resolutions for this nuclear dialectic. Rather, they provide the boundaries of political latitude in which President Reagan and other Presidents have had and will have to operate, no matter what their strategic vision. The current nuclear debate—whether manifested in controversies over SDI, strategic modernization, NATO force posture, or approaches to arms control—is ultimately a healthy one, as it compels reflection on the foundations of strategy in the nuclear age. It raises the central questions of what role the "Absolute Weapon" of 1945 will play in the security relationships of the year 2000, of what strategy we need to ensure that security, and what means we choose to achieve that end.

Notes

1. Caspar W. Weinberger, Secretary of Defense, *Annual Report to Congress: Fiscal Year 1983* (Washington, DC: GPO, 8 February 1982), p. I–17.

2. Ibid., p. I–19.

3. Michael E. Howard, "The Relevance of Traditional Strategy," *Foreign Affairs* 51, no. 2 (January 1973): 264.

4. Thomas C. Schelling and Morton H. Halperin, *Strategy and Arms Control* (New York: Pergamon Press, Reprinted Edition, 1985), p. 3.

5. Hedley Bull, *The Control of the Arms Race: Disarmament and Arms Control in the Missile Age* (New York: Frederick A. Praeger, Publishers, Second Edition, 1965), pp. vii–viii.

6. Jerome H. Kahan, *Security in the Nuclear Age: Developing US Strategic Arms Policy* (Washington, DC: The Brookings Institution, 1975), pp. 277–85.

7. See Spurgeon M. Keeny, Jr., and Wolfgang K.H. Panofsky, "MAD Versus NUTS: Can Doctrine or Weaponry Remedy the Mutual Hostage Relationship of the Superpower?" *Foreign Affairs* 60, no. 2 (Winter 1981/82): 287–304.

8. See President Reagan's unclassified report, "Soviet Noncompliance with Arms Control Agreements," United States Department of State, Bureau of Public Affairs, Special Report #136, December 1985.

9. For further discussion on the "SS–19 loophole," see Strobe Talbott, *Deadly Gambits* (New York: Vintage Books, 1984), pp. 212–16. Regarding estimates as to whether the SS–19 has a countersilo capability, see Michael R. Gordon, "CIA Downgrades Estimate of SS–19 ... Saying Missile Too Inaccurate for First Strike," *National Journal* 29 (20 July 1985): 1692.

10. Data on US and Soviet strategic force postures in this paper are drawn from the International Institute for Strategic Studies, *Military Balance 1985–1986* (London: IISS, 1985).

11. See, for example, Colin Gray, "Nuclear Strategy: The Case for a Theory of Victory," *International Security* 4, no. 1 (Summer 1979): 54–87.

12. For a detailed description, see Jeffrey Richelson, "PD–59, NSDD–13, and the Reagan Strategic Modernization Program," *Journal of Strategic Studies* 6, no. 2 (June 1983): 125–46.

13. See Richard Burt, "The New Strategy for Nuclear War: How it Evolved." *New York Times*, 13 August 1980, p. 3, and

Michael Getler, "Changes in U.S. Nuclear Strategy," *Washington Post,* 14 August 1980, p. 3.

14. Strobe Talbott, *Endgame: The Inside Story of SALT II* (New York: Harper and Row, 1980), pp. 279–94, and Talbott, *Deadly Gambits,* pp. 219–21.

15. Helmut Schmidt's speech at the 10 May 1977 NATO summit meeting, in *Survival* 19, no. 4 (July/August 1977): 177–78 (emphasis added).

16. NATO Special Consultative Group (SCG), Chairman's Press Statement, 14 January 1986, NATO Press Release (86) 02.

17. See Gregory Treverton, "Nuclear Weapons in Europe," Adelphi Paper No. 168 (London: IISS, Summer 1981), and Talbott, "Endgame," pp. 185–90.

18. Presidential Press Conference, 29 January 1981, in *Survival* 23, no. 3 (May/June 1981): 129–30.

19. For excerpts from the President's speech of 18 November 1981, see *Survival 24,* no. 2 (March/April 1982): 87–89.

20. For a particularly useful summary, see H.J. Neuman, *Nuclear Forces in Europe: A Handbook for the Debate* (London: IISS, 1982).

21. See Kissinger's speech, "NATO: The Next Thirty Years," September 1979, in Kenneth A. Meyers (ed), *NATO: The Next Thirty Years* (Boulder, CO: Westview Press, 1981), pp. 3–14.

22. McGeorge Bundy *et al.,* "Nuclear Weapons and the Atlantic Alliance," *Foreign Affairs* 60, no. 4 (Spring 1982): 753–68, and Karl Kaiser *et al.,* "Nuclear Weapons and the Preservation of Peace: A German Response to No First Use," *Foreign Affairs* 60, no. 5 (Summer 1982): 1157–70.

23. Quoted in Talbott, *Deadly Gambits,* p. 71. For a related strategic argument, see Steven Canby and Ingemar Doerfer, "More Troops, Fewer Missiles," *Foreign Policy,* no. 53 (Winter 1983–84): 3–17.

24. For excerpts from Reagan's speech to the American Legion Annual Conference, 22 February 1983, see *Survival* 25, no. 3 (May/June 1983): 128–29.

25. Talbott, *Deadly Gambits,* pp. 205, 342.

26. Henry Trewhitt, "Rostow Expects SALT Delay, Pushes Containment Policy," *Baltimore Sun,* 23 June 1981, p. 1, and Michael Getler, "Rostow's Testimony Illustrates Reagan's Shifts on Arms Control," *Washington Post,* 24 June 1981, p. 12.

27. "Arms Control Chief Makes Compliance a Condition," *Baltimore Sun,* 25 July 1981, p. 2.

28. Seymour Weiss, "Secretary Haig's New Framework for Arms Control," *Wall Street Journal*, 27 July 1981, p. 17.

29. Walter Pincus, "Behind Reagan's Tough Talk, A Unilateral Arms Reduction," *Washington Post*, 10 January 1982, p. D–1.

30. "Is This MX Mode Final?" *New York Times*, 23 May 1982, p. E–4.

31. Talbott, *Deadly Gambits*, pp. 224–26.

32. Don Oberdorfer, "US Defense Launching Arms Talks," *Washington Post*, 22 January 1982, p. 1. Haig's comment on LRINF negotiations was at a news conference on 6 January during the visit of FRG Chancellor Helmut Schmidt.

33. Herbert Scoville, "Deterring Deterrence," *New York Times*, 23 May 1982, p. E–23. For the text of the Eureka College Commencement Address, see *Weekly Compilation of Presidential Documents*, 9 May 1982, pp. 599–604.

34. For Jackson's proposal, see *Washington Star-News*, 9 December 1973. On Carter's proposal, see Talbott, *Endgame*, pp. 58–63.

35. Stockholm International Peace Research Institute, *1983 SIPRI Yearbook* (London: Taylor and Frances, Ltd., 1983), table 3.3, p. 61. See Talbott, *Deadly Gambits*, pp. 233–99, for a description of the pre-Eureka negotiations within the United States and the Soviet response.

36. Report of the President's Commission on Strategic Forces, 6 April 1983, pp. 16–18.

37. Talbott, *Deadly Gambits*, pp. 261–62.

38. See Alton Frye, "Strategic Build-Down: A Context for Restraint," *Foreign Affairs* 62, no. 2 (Winter 1983/84): 293–317. Also Glenn A. Kent with Randall J. DeValk and Edward L. Warner III, *A New Approach to Arms Control*, Rand Report R–3140–FF/RC (Santa Monica, CA: The Rand Corporation, June 1984).

39. From the text of the Joint US-USSR Statement of 8 January 1985, in *Survival* 27, no. 2 (March/April 1985): 90.

40. Ambassador Paul H. Nitze, "The Alastair Buchan Memorial Lecture," *Survival* 27, no. 3 (May/June 1985): 98–108, here p. 104. See also Talbott, *Deadly Gambits*, pp. 358–59.

41. Reagan's speech to the nation, 23 March 1983, in *New York Times*, 24 March 1983, p. 20.

42. See Carl Sagan, "Nuclear Winter and Climatic Catastrophe," *Foreign Affairs* 62, no. 2 (Winter 1983/84): 257–92. For excerpts from the Defense Department's Report to the Congress on

"The Potential Effects of Nuclear War on the Climate," see *Survival* 27, no. 3 (May/June 1985): 130–34.

43. For example, McGeorge Bundy *et al.*, "The President's Choice: Star Wars or Arms Control," *Foreign Affairs* 63, no. 2 (Winter 1984/85): 264–78, and Harold Brown, "The Strategic Defense Initiative: Defense Systems and the Strategic Debate," The Foreign Policy Institute, School of Advanced International Studies, Johns Hopkins University, 14 December 1984.

44. Nitze, "The Alastair Buchan Memorial Lecture," p. 105.

45. See Nitze's speech to the North Atlantic Assembly in San Francisco, 15 October 1985.

46. Walter Pincus, "U.S. Drafts Response on SDI," *Washington Post*, 23 October 1985, p. 1.

47. John J. Fialko, "U.S. to Honor Expiring Arms Pact Despite Violations by the Soviets," *Wall Street Journal*, 24 December 1985, p. 13. For the President's annual report on Soviet compliance with arms control agreements, see note 8, *supra*.

48. See, for example, ACDA Director Kenneth L. Adelman's "Arms Control With and Without Agreements," *Foreign Affairs* 63, no. 2 (Winter 1984/85): 240–63.

49. See Leslie H. Gelb, "Arms Treaty: Issue Put Off," *New York Times*, 11 June 1985, p. 10, and Walter Pincus, "Navy Picks Two Missile Subs for Possible '86 Dismantling," *Washington Post*, 27 November 1985, p. 2.

50. For a summary of the proposals, see "Reagan Makes a New Offer," *Time*, 11 November 1985, pp. 18–21.

51. See "A Farewell to Arms?" *Time*, 27 January 1986, pp. 18–20.

52. Michael Gordon, "U.S. is Weighing 3 Responses to Gorbachev Plan on Arms," *New York Times*, 4 February 1986, p. 12; Bernard Weintraub, "Reagan Offers a Plan to Cut Missiles," *New York Times*, 23 February 1986, p. 1; and Don Oberdorfer, "U.S. Plan Would Abolish Intermediate-Range Arms," *Washington Post*, 24 February 1986, p. 1.

53. In an interview with Suedwestfunk, in Boris Meissner (ed), *Die deutsche Ostpolitik, 1961–1970: Kontinuitaet und Wandel (Dokumentation)* (Cologne: Wissenschaft und Politik, 1970), 374–76 (emphasis added).

54. Quoted in James M. Markham, West Europe Cool to Removal of U.S. Medium-Range Missiles," *New York Times*, 25 February 1986, p. 3.

55. Quoted in William Drozdiak, "W. Europeans Uneasy About Losing Missiles," *Washington Post,* 17 February 1986, p. 1.

56. Ibid.

57. Egon Bahr, "German *Ostpolitik* and Superpower Relations," 11 July 1973 speech at Tutzing, FRG, in *Survival* 15, no. 6 (November/December 1973): 296-300.

58. See Henry A. Kissinger, *Years of Upheaval* (London: Weidenfeld and Nicolson, Michael Joseph, Ltd., 1982), pp. 274–86.

59. Based on data from the IISS *Military Balance, 1985–1986, passim.*

60. For a discussion of alternative force mixes under such an arms control regime, see Barry Schneider and Michael Ennis, "Strategy, Policy, and the US Arms Reduction Proposal," *Armed Forces Journal International,* January 1986, p. 63.

61. George C. Wilson, "Bigger Midgetman ICBM Draws Fire From Panel," *Washington Post,* 19 February 1986, p. 5.

62. From National Security Council Document 68 (NSC 68), "United States Objectives and Programs for National Security," 1950, in *Foreign Relations of the United States, 1950,* Volume I: *National Security Affairs; Foreign Economic Policy* (Washington, DC: GPO, 1977), p. 275.

THE UNITED STATES AND ASIA: THE SUCCESS OF CONTINUITY?

Paul H. B. Godwin

A SIA HAS BEEN A REGION of major strategic importance to the United States throughout the 20th century, but Europe has usually ranked higher than Asia in the strategic perceptions of American leaders. This remained true in the post-World War II period despite the fact that Korea and Indochina were the locale of two of America's most frustrating wars. Since World War II, US strategic perceptions of Asia have been driven by the United States' global competition with the USSR, and the central area of concern for both Moscow and Washington has been their confrontation in Europe. Even the Sino-American rapprochement that so dramatically changed the strategic map of Asia was seen by its architects as falling within the scope of the United States' worldwide conflict with the USSR, and not primarily as an Asian initiative.[1] As the Carter administration worked toward diplomatic recognition of China, this same global focus was the primary policy context.[2]

Within Asia, the United States has viewed Northeast Asia as more critically important than Southeast Asia. China, the USSR, Japan, and Korea are in close proximity in the northeast, but Southeast Asia is far from the center of major potential military confrontation. Korea became host to the largest continuing American military presence in Asia, and the defense of Korea and Japan became the center of US security concerns in Asia. Even in its Indochina war, the United States was more concerned with containing Sino-Soviet influence than it was with protecting any carefully defined American interest in Southeast Asia.

None of these observations is meant to imply that the United States has no intrinsic interests in Asia or that US Asian interests are perceived as unimportant by American political leaders. Rather, they are meant to state that in terms of American defense and security policy, Asia is ranked below Europe, and that within Asia itself the northeast sector has been seen as the most important in American security concerns. In Secretary of Defense Weinberger's *Annual Report to the Congress,* for fiscal year 1987, the Secretary demonstrated both the continuing preeminence of Europe in America's strategic planning, and that American defense and security policies remain driven by US global competition and conflict with the USSR.[3] Within East Asia, Secretary Weinberger continued the now traditional emphasis of Northeast over Southeast Asia. As in the past, even with the radical change in Sino-American relations, Soviet and North Korean military capabilities in and adjacent to Northeast Asia required the Secretary to place primary emphasis on American security relations with Korea and Japan. The Vietnamese occupation of Cambodia and Soviet use of the former American military facilities at Cam Ranh Bay receive attention, but in his analyses of the military balance in the region, Secretary Weinberger's concern highlighted primarily Northeast Asia.[4]

The Reagan administration's approach to defense and security issues in East Asia followed the pattern that emerged after WW II. Although the United States has direct and growing interests in the region as a whole,

US defense policy is designed around America's world-wide military commitments and the administration's perception of the global balance of power between the West and the Soviet Union. In defining its defense policies and military force structure, the United States is faced with the complex task of reconciling global, regional, and subregional interests. Within Asia this is a difficult task because the region is extremely diverse, and American interests and those of its friends and allies in the region form less than a clear and compelling set of choices. If anything, the choices faced by Washington are marked more by ambiguity than clarity.

In distinct contrast to the relatively stable patterns of political alignment in Europe, the breakdown of Sino-Soviet relations in the 1960s brought radical change to the patterns of strategic alignment in Asia. Once allied with the USSR in direct opposition to the United States and its Asian allies, by the late 1970s Beijing had not only broken with Moscow, but was seeking to participate in a grand coalition led by the United States in opposition to the USSR's "global hegemonism"—a phrase used by China to specify the Soviet Union's worldwide strategy of expansionism. But, even as the Reagan administration assumed office, Beijing was reassessing its alignment with the United States and moving toward a strategy in which China was to have greater freedom of movement between Moscow and Washington. Indeed, the first three years of Sino-American relations in the Reagan administration were riddled with a series of bilateral conflicts. American arms sales to Taiwan, disagreements over the pace of US technology transfers, and a number of other issues related to trade put Beijing and Washington into a downward spiral as Sino-Soviet relations entered the first stage of a rapprochement. Moscow, responding to the obvious deterioration in Sino-American relations, began to show great interest in reopening the "normalization" talks broken off by China in the aftermath of the Soviet invasion of Afghanistan. Following personal and public appeals by Brezhnev, the first post-Afghanistan talks were held in Beijing between 5 and 21 October 1982.

As the Reagan administration began reviewing its Asian defense policies, one of the central features of previous administrations' strategy to oppose the USSR was undergoing change. Beijing had decided that defiance of Moscow expressed through open alignment with the United States no longer served China's interests. In Beijing's revised security logic, such an alignment not only served to provoke the USSR unnecessarily, but also reduced China's influence in the Third World because Beijing was being perceived as dependent on the United States for its security.[5] Moving from a position of alignment with the United States to one of "independence," China entered into a pattern of negotiations with Moscow, or "consultations," as the Chinese prefer to call them, designed to reduce tension in Sino-Soviet relations. In doing so, Beijing presented Washington with a Chinese foreign policy different from that faced by the Carter administration.

US Defense Policies in Asia

The defense guidance produced by the Office of the Secretary of Defense in 1982 for the years 1984–1988 represents the first set of policies that can be viewed as entirely the work of the Reagan administration. Even so, the basic problems defined by the Reagan administration were identical to those of the Carter administration. American concerns continued to focus on the Soviet military buildup of its forces adjacent to

Northeast Asia; Soviet military use of the bases at Cam Ranh Bay; Vietnamese occupation of Cambodia; and the threat to the Persian Gulf and Southwest Asia created by the Soviet occupation of Afghanistan. In short, the Reagan administration faced the dilemma of how to determine defense policies and strategies for a military force structure overextended by a widening set of military commitments. The policies that emerged focused on creating a sustained American military buildup and developing an effective coalition strategy, for American forces alone could not cope with what the administration saw as an increasing set of potential military conflicts created by growing Soviet military capabilities and access to overseas bases.

Washington's response did not differ in any major dimension from the approach taken in the later years of the Carter administration: the states of East Asia had to be prepared to do more in their own defense, including the defense of Persian Gulf oil. Although not explicitly stated by Secretary of Defense Brown, he clearly implied that forces could be swung from Europe and Asia to participate in defending access to Gulf oil. He argued that American commitment to the Persian Gulf served the interests of both American European and Asian allies, and that by increasing their own defense efforts Asian and European allies would permit US forces to be moved from their theaters of operation without endangering local security.[6]

The *Fiscal Year 1984–1988 Defense Guidance*, as reported in the press and "background use only" discussions with Government officials, indicates that the Reagan administration directly faced the possible need to "swing" US forces from Asia to the Persian Gulf area in the event of a crisis involving the USSR.[7] Furthermore, some military units based in the continental

United States, Hawaii, and the Far East were to be viewed as potential reinforcements for Southwest Asia rather than necessarily as reserves for Northeast Asia. Within such a strategy, Japan and South Korea were to assume greater responsibility for their own defense. Japan, in particular, was to be strongly urged by the Reagan administration to become a more active military ally. The countries of Southeast Asia were to be responsible for countering Vietnamese expansion and for facilitating the movement of US forces from the West Pacific to the Indian Ocean and the Persian Gulf region.

Although reported to be a "new" military strategy, Secretary of Defense Harold Brown's report presented to the Congress in January 1981 clearly contained the same strategic concepts as those used by the Reagan administration. With the creation of the Rapid Deployment Joint Task Force (RDJTF) in response to the Iranian revolution (which removed a valuable ally from US planning) and the Soviet invasion of Afghanistan, military units already assigned other responsibilities were made available to the RDJTF commander for potential projection into Southwest Asia. Some of these units would already be assigned to the Pacific Command (PACOM) and would, if necessary, be assigned to the RDJTF in a crisis. The swing concept was clearly implied by the RDJTF's creation. In his closing argument for greater defense efforts by US allies to assist in the deployment of RDJTF forces to Southwest Asia, Secretary Brown stated:

We cannot do it all. If our European and Asian allies will not increase their defense efforts appropriately, the American people are likely to demand some scaling down of our own plans and programs.[8]

The Reagan administration continued this approach to American Asian defense policy, but put greater emphasis on the modernization and expansion of PACOM forces and increasing the military stockpiles necessary to sustain US forces in prolonged combat. The objective was to increase US military capabilities while at the same time developing a more viable coalition strategy to offset Soviet military strength. Increasing Soviet military capabilities were seen as stemming not only from the continuing buildup and modernization of Soviet forces, but also from growing Soviet use of the military facilities at Cam Ranh Bay in Vietnam. These issues were joined by the growth of North Korean military capabilities and the continuing guerrilla war in Vietnam, which threatened to spill over into Thailand. Indeed, military issues were the only major problems perceived by the Reagan administration, for with the exception of the Philippines, Asia was seen as a region where American friends and allies were prime examples of political stability and economic growth.

The changing role of China and Japan. By early 1983, however, it was evident that Washington was making a change in American political-military strategy for Asia. Whereas since 1972 prior administrations had tended to look to China as providing a major counterweight to Soviet military power in Asia, the Reagan administration saw Japan as playing a major role in future US military planning for the region. However, the shift was made despite the fact that Beijing continued to view Moscow as the only major military threat to its security. A number of factors contributed to the Reagan administration's decision to shift its focus from Beijing to Tokyo.

First, it was recognized that it would be many years before China's defense modernization program would give the Chinese armed forces, especially air and naval forces, the capability to counter Soviet forces effectively in the region. Beijing had assigned defense modernization the lowest priority in its overall modernization goals, and anticipated only very slow and incremental improvement in its weapons systems and equipment. China believed that its growing nuclear capabilities were creating a more credible deterrent against a nuclear war with the Soviet Union, and that a slow and deliberate modernization of its conventional forces would continue to provide sufficient capability to defend China in the unlikely event of a major conflict with the USSR. There was some disagreement between Chinese civil and military leaders on this issue. The dominant view inside the Chinese ruling hierarchy, however, was that the USSR did not present a military threat that required a major reallocation of resources from the civil sector of the economy to support a rapid modernization of the armed forces.[9] The Reagan administration, although agreeing that the United States should play a limited role in modernizing Beijing's defense capabilities, believed that China would not become an active partner in US defense strategies—a position also held by Beijing. Rather, China would play a passive role, its defense policies a function of parallel concerns rather than active participation.

Chinese foreign-policy strategy announced at the Party Congress in October 1982 also contributed to the Reagan administration's revised view of China. By declaring its policy to be one of "independence" and refusing to join any "big power or group of powers," Beijing explicitly denied any intention of forming a "strategic relationship" with the United States.[10] The reopening of Sino-Soviet negotiations in October 1982 served notice to Washington that China was able to manage its conflict with the USSR without American assistance. Thus Washington had to reevaluate the "strategic triangle" concept that had dominated strategic planning for Asia during most of the past decade.

Japan, in sharp contrast to China, was viewed as having the potential to play a much more active role in American defense planning. This position was first articulated in the 1982 defense guidance document. Japan's potential value as a more active partner in American coalition strategy was to be found in a variety of factors which, although it faced some difficult political problems, provided the underpinnings for a considerably expanded defense relationship.

Japan had an existing security treaty with the United States and an emerging pattern of close military ties between the Japan Self Defense Forces (JSDF) and US forces deployed in Northeast Asia. Japan's geographical location, astride the principal sea passages taken by the Soviet Pacific Fleet when it steamed from its headquarters in Vladivostok, complemented the treaty. Similarly, Japanese airspace was on the route of Soviet air forces heading for the Pacific. The security treaty and strategic location of Japan were complemented by Japan's strong economy. As the world's second largest market economy, Japan could make a major contribution to the West's effort to maintain superiority over Soviet defense capabilities. Finally, the election of Yasuhiro Nakasone in November 1982 presented the United States with a Japanese prime minister who was determined to place greater emphasis on the US-Japan defense relationship.

The US dilemma with Japan. In its search for a more active Japanese partnership within US defense policy, the United States had to face a number of difficult problems. Japan lacked the strong public consensus required to support an expanded defense relationship with Washington. In 1976, the Japanese government had placed a restriction on defense spending that limited defense expenditures to no more than 1 percent of the gross national product (GNP). This meant that rapid modernization and growth of the JSDF's weapons and equipment were impossible. The 1-percent limit was made even more problematic by the slowdown in Japan's economic growth in the 1980s and the concomitant retrenchment in Tokyo's fiscal policies.

Within Japan, however, the ongoing debate over an appropriate Japanese defense policy entered a new phase in the 1980s.[11] In 1976, Japan had for the first time presented an explicit strategic concept to provide a rationale for its defense expenditures and to gain public support for JSDF modernization. Known as the National Defense Program Outline (NDPO), this required Japan to develop the military capability necessary to deter a limited attack. Beyond this threshold, the United States would come to Japan's assistance because the United States could not ignore a large-scale attack upon Japan. When the Japanese cabinet approved the NDPO, it also announced the policy of restricting defense expenditures to within 1 percent of the GNP. This was designed to gain public support for the NDPO by applying restrictions that would not permit a quick or massive expansion of Japanese military capabilities.

By the early 1980s, the Soviet invasion and continued occupation of Afghanistan, the buildup of Soviet military forces in the Far East, and the USSR's apparent nuclear parity with the United States raised questions about the adequacy of the NDPO as the basis for Japan's future defense planning. The growth of the Soviet Pacific Fleet, deployment of Backfires and SS–20s in the Far East, and the reinforcement of Soviet forces deployed in the "northern territories" claimed by Japan all combined to create a distinctly different security environment from that which provided the NDPO's rationale.

Alongside these developments came an increased Japanese sensitivity to American criticism that Japan was getting a "free ride" in defense, and that Japan could now easily afford to spend more in the defense of its own country. This issue, in conjunction with the rise of Soviet military power, even produced doubts in Japan about US capability and willingness to defend Japan in the future.[12] Within this political environment, Prime Minister Nakasone was able to raise the issue of Japan's contribution to Northeast Asia's defense in a more receptive milieu. Nonetheless, even within this new Japanese political and security environment, the United States had to recognize that an abrasive and obvious criticism of Tokyo's defense commitments would unravel the national consensus sought by Nakasone.

In essence, Japan and the United States were required to work together to achieve a revision of the NDPO strategy, a process made increasingly difficult by the rising criticism within the United States of the chronic and growing trade imbalance between the two countries. For the United States, the May 1981 agreement by Prime Minister Suzuki, confirmed by Prime Minister Nakasone in 1983, to develop the capability to defend the sea and airspace around Japan out to 1,000 nautical miles was a major step forward, but only the first of many steps yet to be taken.

Asia and the US-Japan defense relationship. In other parts of Asia, however, US pressure on Japan to assume greater defense responsibilities touched a raw nerve. With Japan already the major Asian economic power, there is a deep-rooted fear that in the future Japan will become a major independent military power. Nonetheless, there is also growing recognition that an expanded Japanese military role in Asia is inevitable. When such a role is directly tied to a strong American military presence in the West Pacific, a more active Japanese contribution is acceptable to most Asian states. But if the United States should shift its military resources away from Asia, Japan's future military role becomes problematic.[13] US insistence that it intends to remain a Pacific power and will continue to support its friends actively is designed to offset these fears. Prime Minister Nakasone's tour of the Association of Southeast Asian States (ASEAN, now composed of Thailand, Malaysia, Singapore, Indonesia, the Philippines, plus Brunei since 1985) in May 1983, included efforts, largely successful, to assure these countries that the future expansion of Japanese military capabilities was for defensive purposes only. Nakasone explained that the agreement to defend its sealanes and airspace out to 1,000 nautical miles was undertaken within the US-Japan treaty and was not the precursor of an independent Japanese military policy.[14]

Building a Coalition Strategy

When President Reagan scheduled his first visit to Asia in November 1983, one of his major purposes was to stress the new Pacific partnership emerging from his administration's policies. Beijing's absence from the itinerary was intended to symbolize the United States' commitment to its traditional friends and allies in the region. A China trip was in the offing, but only after Premier Zhao Ziyang's scheduled visit to the United States in January 1984. The August 1983 assassination of Benigno Aquino at Manila airport as he returned from political asylum in the United States tended to blur the trip's symbolism. Rather than a grand tour, President Reagan's itinerary was restricted to Japan and South Korea, with the visits to Thailand, Malaysia, and Indonesia canceled to avoid a Presidential visit to Manila—an event that would have suggested United States support for President Marcos. The ASEAN states, and especially Indonesia, were displeased with the decision because they believed they had to pay the price for the crumbling Philippine political situation.[15] In fact, the Indonesian leg had been added to the trip so that President Reagan could address a meeting of the ASEAN foreign ministers scheduled for November. As a consequence, even though Japan and South Korea are clearly major allies of the United States, dropping the ASEAN visits reduced the trip's symbolism as a demonstration of the new Pacific partnership and tended to reemphasize the principle of Northeast Asian preeminence in America's Asian priorities.

Building a coalition strategy based upon common security concerns continued to be difficult, and the Reagan administration sought to adjust its relations with China within its revised concept of an American-Asian strategy. Tensions with China were high, but in August 1982, Beijing and Washington signed a joint communiqué in which China pledged itself to seek only a peaceful reunification with Taiwan and the United States pledged itself to a gradual reduction of its arms sales to Taiwan. Other bilateral issues continued to strain Sino-American relations, and in February 1983, Secretary of State George Shultz was sent to Beijing in an effort to resolve these problem areas. In September Secretary of Defense Caspar Weinberger went to Beijing, after stopping off in Tokyo, to restore high-level strategic discussions and discuss possible US participation in

China's defense modernization programs. In particular, the Secretary discussed the possible sale of defensive weapons and military technology. When Premier Zhao Ziyang visited the United States in January of 1984, weapons and technology sales were among the major topics discussed. These discussions continued in March 1984, when a four-man team of defense specialists led by Zhang Pin, the son of China's defense minister, arrived in Washington. From Washington the team went on to visit several American defense industries.

The President's six-day visit to China in April of 1984, the first by an incumbent US President since 1975, symbolized the restoration of more cordial Sino-American relations. Tensions over Taiwan, technology transfers, and trade continued, but the conflict marking the first years of the Reagan administration's relations with China had clearly been reduced. Defense Minister Zhang Aiping's arrival in Washington the following June further strengthened the military relationship between the two countries. Discussions of US arms sales were followed by the defense minister's tour of American military bases and visits to defense industries. Sino-American military relations were now restored to a more normal level. The restoration of these defense ties was seen as important because, even though the administration's search for a more active Asian defense partner had focused on Japan, the Chinese relationship needed to be brought into balance with the overall objective of building an effective coalition strategy. This balance required, in Washington's view, a reduction in overall tensions and a revival of high-level meetings, dormant since 1981, between American and Chinese defense officials.

The complexity of the Reagan administration's task could be seen shortly after Zhang Aiping left the United

States. On his way home, the Chinese defense minister met with his Japanese counterpart in Tokyo.[16] This was the first time in 35 years that the senior defense officials of China and Japan had met. The Japanese insisted that the meeting was a "courtesy call" arranged at China's request. At the same time, however, Japanese defense officials described the meeting as significant and a possible precursor to future Sino-Japanese military exchanges. On the other hand, Malaysia's prime minister told Secretary of State Shultz in Kuala Lumpur that US assistance to China's economic modernization endangered Southeast Asia's security. Although the prime minister did not directly address the issue of potential US arms sales to China, he did observe that an economically strong China would also be strong militarily, and this would permit Beijing to revert to a more aggressive foreign policy in the future.[17] Thus, whereas Sino-Japanese military exchanges and agreements on Sino-American arms sales would be seen by the United States as contributing to the development of a coalition strategy in Asia, other friends of the United States in the region were not supportive of Washington's goals.

The trend of closer Sino-American military ties continued throughout 1984, as additional US military delegations went to China. Similarly, in December the Japanese Defense Agency (JDA) completed its guidelines for future Sino-Japanese military exchanges.[18] China and Japan had exchanged military attachés in 1974, but Zhang Aiping's visit granted greater momentum to the opportunity for higher-level contacts between the two defense establishments. It is also quite possible that the rapidly improving status of Sino-American defense relations encouraged Japan to review its minimal military relations with China and respond positively to China's interest in expanding Sino-Japanese military contacts.

As the Reagan administration entered its second term, the grand design for its Asian defense policy was well underway. There were problems and major issues yet to be resolved, but a basic pattern had been established that built on prior American defense policy and had the strength of consistency with the past.

US Asian Defense Policy: The Political Context

Since the 1960s, there has been a constant iteration within the United States that Washington's friends and allies are not "doing enough" in their own defense. Japan and NATO are the common targets of this criticism. More recently, the New Zealand government's decision to deny port visits by US naval vessels unless the United States declared they do not carry nuclear weapons (a declaration the United States government will not make) has led to the unraveling of the ANZUS Treaty (Australia, New Zealand, and the United States).

In his fiscal year 1987 *Report to the Congress,* Secretary Weinberger explicitly looked to compare the capabilities of the United States and its friends and allies in confronting the USSR and its allies.[19] Thus the "East Asian Balance" assesses the Sino-Soviet confrontation, including strategic missile forces; North and South Korea; Vietnam in Southeast Asia; and Japan's contribution to the collective security of the region. When economic and political factors are included in the assessment, the Secretary concludes that "from the Soviet perspective, the long-term trends in East Asia are negative, especially in the context of the worldwide competition with the West."[20] This optimism, although widely supported by specialists in Asian affairs, represents one of the most difficult problems in preparing defense policy.

Defense policy is designed to deter war and to fight potential wars in the future. Coalition strategies thus become critically dependent on political relations because agreement must be achieved on future defense commitments, commitments that require the allocation of resources. In the absence of war it is readily assumed that deterrence has been effective, but it is the absence of war that makes defense planning for the future so difficult. Present realities tend to dominate planning for future requirements. If what is being done now appears to be effective, agreeing on future scenarios requiring increased defense commitments is extremely difficult. For the United States, even though it analyzes long-term trends as going against the USSR's interest, the continued growth of Soviet military power in Asia is sufficient to require increased defense commitments from its friends and allies to supplement and complement increased American commitments. This is especially important from the Reagan administration's perspective when increased Soviet capabilities are joined by the continuing buildup of North Korean forces, the continuing Vietnamese military occupation of Cambodia, the growth in the number and capabilities of Soviet forces deploying out of Cam Ranh Bay, and the Soviet reinforcement of its forces on the southern Kurile Islands claimed by Japan. Within the region, even though a strong military presence is seen as Washington's commitment to the defense of non-Communist Asia (and Communist Asia when the People's Republic of China is included), gaining greater defense commitments from American friends and allies has been difficult.

The United States and Japan. Under the leadership of Prime Minister Nakasone, Japan has taken significant steps toward an expanded security relationship with the

United States. In large part this is due to the obvious increase in Soviet military capabilities, but is also due to a built-in Japanese desire to do enough to keep the United States marginally contented. Within Japan there remain significant obstructions to any rapid increase in Japanese military capabilities. Of major importance is Japanese public opinion, which even now is only supportive of the present level of defense efforts and a gradual increase in defense capabilities. Even so, while there is great reluctance to define the USSR as an adversary, there is increasing support for the notion that the Soviet Union is a "latent" threat.

To such caution it is also important to add the view of many Japanese that it is time to demonstrate political independence from the United States and cease accepting the status of an American military protectorate. There are also those who view Japanese-American military ties as serving US interests more than they do Japan's; specifically, that these ties serve primarily US global strategy against the USSR. Those holding this view demand that the Japanese government define its own security and defense policies rather than simply acquiesce to American demands.[21]

These factors make it very difficult for Mr. Nakasone to change overnight a set of attitudes deeply ingrained in Japanese citizens. Currently, even as Japanese attitudes toward a more active defense relationship with the United States are beginning to change, the Soviet Union under the leadership of General Secretary Mikhail Gorbachev has begun to modify Moscow's approach to Tokyo. Nakasone has aligned Japan with the West more directly than any other prime minister. The USSR, perhaps in response to Japan's closer defense relationship with the United States, in early 1986 sent Foreign Minister Shevardnadze to Tokyo in an effort to ease relations with Japan. Given Soviet determination not to discuss the "northern territories" issues or to reverse its military buildup in East Asia, it is unlikely that any major issues dividing Japan and the Soviet Union can be resolved either by Shevardnadze or the visit by Gorbachev. But gestures by the Soviet Union, such as Gorbachev's speech of 28 July 1986, in Vladivostok, will reinforce those attitudes within Japan opposing a closer and more active defense relationship between Washington and Tokyo. If the USSR should develop a more refined and subtle diplomatic approach to Japan and treat Tokyo more as a neighbor than an ally of the United States, it would be difficult for Prime Minister Nakasone or his successors to sustain the growth of a public consensus supportive of a more active role for Japan in its security relations with the United States.[22]

The United States and China. China, the only other Asian state directly confronting Soviet military power, has established its own strategy toward the USSR, albeit implicitly accepting the umbrella of American defense policies in the region. As Beijing seeks its own rapprochement with Moscow, the United States is seeking an "enduring military relationship" with China.[23] The restoration of high-level military dialogue between the United States and China prepared the groundwork for a new series of functional exchanges between the armed forces of the United States and the PRC (People's Republic of China).[24] From these exchanges and high-level negotiations, an agreement emerged in which the United States will sell weapons, military technology and equipment (antitank weapons, artillery, air defense, and surface ship antisubmarine warfare) to China.[25] The expressed purpose for these sales by the United States is to assist the PRC in defending itself against the Soviet Union.[26]

This growing Sino-American defense link supports China's effort to demonstrate to the USSR Beijing's ties with the United States, while at the same time China claims to eschew a strategic relationship with any major power. China continues to insist that its relations with the USSR cannot be normalized until the Soviet Union removes its forces from Afghanistan, stands down forces and weapons systems deployed along the Sino-Soviet border and in Mongolia, including the SS–20s, and withdraws its support for Vietnam's occupation of Cambodia. These demands are sustained even as trade, cultural, and political exchanges between Moscow and Beijing grow at what appears to be an accelerating rate. Both the United States and the USSR are involved in assisting China's economic modernization, with the United States making a direct, albeit small and restrained, contribution to the modernization of China's armed forces. American defense policy toward China is thus intimately bound not only by the political context created by Beijing's insistence on autonomy, but also by the USSR's search for a less hostile relationship with China.

The United States and the Korean Peninsula. South Korea remains the most closely aligned of all American allies in Asia. Here the United States does not question Seoul's contribution to its own defense, which is high. The political context of US policy is nonetheless very complex. Three issues are involved: the potential for extreme levels of political instability due to civil and human rights problems within Chun Doo Hwan's authoritarian political system; the future of negotiations for some form of political compromise between North and South Korea on the prospects for the peninsula's reunification; and what may be an effort by the Soviet Union to establish closer military and political ties with Pyongyang. In fact, none of these issues threatens the close ties between the United States and South Korea, but they do complicate the formulation of future US policy.

The success of Corazon Aquino's "people's power" movement in the Philippines gave new life to Chun Doo Hwan's political opposition. Events in Manila were closely followed and widely reported in the South Korean press. There are, however, distinct differences between South Korea and the Philippines that appear to negate any chance of a similar process emerging that would result in Chun Doo Hwan's downfall. Whereas the Philippine economy was in deep recession and had been for some years, the Korean economy is one of the strongest in Asia. South Korea's economic conditions are a source of support for the government rather than a seedbed for political discontent. Similarly, the Korean military support President Chun. It is almost inconceivable that there could be a defection from his government similar to the manner in which defense minister Juan Ponce Enrile and Assistant Chief of Staff Fidel Ramos refused any further support for President Marcos. Finally, the threat presented by the insurgent New People's Army's (NPA) growth in the Philippines was a function of Marcos's misrule. The threat presented to South Korea by North Korea's armed forces is far more lethal and direct than the long-term protracted conflict presented by the NPA in the Philippines. President Chun can use the North Korean threat far more effectively than Marcos could the NPA.

South Korea's politics may be volatile and President Chun's regime extremely authoritarian, but the crisis that emerged in the last few years of Marcos's rule is not present in South Korea. Even so, the United States has pressed President Chun to permit greater political freedom for his opposition. Chun had done so, perhaps noting the role of the United States in easing the way for both Duvalier and Marcos to leave their countries during periods of extreme political unrest. The United States does not want to see a repetition of the events that led to the assassination of President Park Chung Hee in 1979, and is pressing the current government to create a tradition of participatory democracy to avoid the kind of civic unrest that has undermined South Korea's political stability for the past 25 years.

The shootdown of KAL 007 in September 1983 and the Rangoon bombing in October brought tension on the peninsula to a new high. Yet these same events seem to have influenced North Korea to propose talks with the United States in which South Korea could participate, and then, early in 1984, to reopen direct talks with South Korea. Although meetings have been held in several fora, both South Korea and the United States treat them with some considerable caution. The backdrop to such caution, above and beyond a deep suspicion of Pyongyang's goals, is the continuing buildup of North Korean armed forces and redeployment of these forces closer to the demilitarized zone (DMZ) dividing the peninsula. Included in these forces are more modern weapon systems recently supplied by the USSR: SCUD surface-to-surface missiles, SA–3 surface-to-air missiles, and MiG–23 fighter bombers.[27]

Renewed Soviet interest in North Korea reflects a change in the dynamics of the international politics of the Korean peninsula. This change led to a sense of isolation in Pyongyang and contributed to a restoration of closer relations between North Korea and the USSR. President Chun's visit to Japan in 1985, the first ever by a ROK president, and his meeting with the emperor symbolized the new warmth between Seoul and Tokyo. China, perhaps seeking a relaxation of tension on the peninsula, had earlier developed unofficial relations with South Korea through trade and athletic exchanges. At the very least, China was demonstrating tacit support for the status quo on the peninsula in spite of its official support for the peaceful reunification of North and South. North Korea, seeking a more responsive ally, looked toward the USSR. Kim Il Sung visited Moscow in 1984 for the first time in 20 years, and in 1985 these ties with the USSR grew closer with the delivery of MiG–23s. With this delivery, the USSR broke any arms embargo put into effect in 1973 to prevent advanced Soviet military technology from falling into Chinese hands and to reduce the probability that Kim Il Sung would drag the USSR into an unwanted war with the United States. In August 1985, a massive Soviet delegation including First Deputy Minister of Defense Marshal Vasiliy Petrov arrived in Pyongyang to celebrate the 40th anniversary of Korea's liberation from Japan. As part of the celebration, the First Deputy Commander of the Pacific Fleet, vice-Admiral Nikolai Yasakov led a Soviet port visit of three ships to Wonsan.[28]

Moscow's revived support for Pyongyang reflects the new Soviet leadership's desire to become more politically active in the Pacific area. The USSR has few allies in the region, and North Korea was looking for a way to demonstrate its unhappiness with China's increased willingness to seek its own objectives without taking into account Pyongyang's concerns. China, on the other hand, can look to Pyongyang's willingness to negotiate with Seoul as promoting the stability Beijing needs to conduct its policy of sustaining a wide range of contact with the Communist and non-Communist world.

China may well be seeking to end North Korea's isolation from the West and Japan, and encouraging Pyongyang to expand its contacts with the outside world. Under these conditions, Beijing may not see Moscow's renewed interests in Pyongyang as unduly threatening to China's relations with North Korea.[29]

For the United States, Moscow's willingness to renew the transfer of more modern armaments to Pyongyang counteracts whatever optimism may exist from the potential restraining influence provided by the evident desire of China and the USSR to avoid war on the peninsula. Washington, Seoul, and Tokyo are all concerned that Soviet military and economic assistance to North Korea will become substantial, and that Moscow's ultimate objective is to use such aid to gain access to North Korean ports for its navy and overflight rights for its air forces. The political context of Pyongyang's relations with its neighbors is now undergoing what could well become a major transformation. It is also evident that the USSR intends to be politically more active in the region than it has been in the past. Foreign Minister Shevardnadze's visit to Japan, the first high-level visit by a Soviet leader in a decade, followed by a call on Pyongyang to reassure Kim Il Sung, and Moscow's increasingly close relationship with Beijing all serve to demonstrate the USSR's diplomatic activism in the region. Whether this reflects Mikhail Gorbachev's recognition that Soviet saber-rattling has led to Moscow's increasing isolation in Asia, or a decision to combine military strength with a new pattern of diplomacy cannot yet be determined.

The United States and Southeast Asia. The US defense policy for Southeast Asia is faced by an equally complex political environment. At one level of analysis the long-term prognosis for the American objective of building a coalition of states opposing the USSR is quite good. Continued Soviet assistance for the Vietnamese occupation of Cambodia may influence the ASEAN states in the direction of supporting the United States. However, US policy tends to focus on decrying the USSR's expansion and increased use of the military facilities at Cam Ranh Bay. The ASEAN states, on the other hand, although suspicious of long-term Soviet intentions in the region, are focused on devising a solution to what has become the Cambodia dilemma.

Today, the Cambodian situation has devolved into a stalemate. The ASEAN insists that Vietnam must withdraw its forces from Cambodia and permit a new government to be created under international supervision. Vietnamese willingness, with Soviet assistance, to pay the economic and political costs of staying in Cambodia and fighting a counterinsurgency war for some eight years has begun to divide ASEAN.[30] Malaysia and Indonesia now accept the concept that a solution to Cambodia must take into account Vietnam's security interests. China refuses to recognize a Vietnamese security interest in Cambodia and has no intention of granting Hanoi unchallenged dominance over Indochina. Thailand, seeking a buffer between itself and Vietnam, does not want to see Hanoi the dominant influence over any government in Phnom Penh and views the PRC as an ally against Vietnam. The USSR, although it sees its political objectives in non-Communist Southeast Asia frustrated by its support for Vietnam, does not want to lose its access to the Cam Ranh Bay military bases. Cam Ranh Bay grants Moscow increased capability to project military force into the Indian Ocean, South China Sea, and West Pacific, thereby increasing its ability to conduct military operations against both the United States and China.

There is now a growing belief that a solution to Cambodia must reconcile the security concerns of both Thailand and Vietnam.[31] This will be difficult to achieve. Hanoi's recent willingness to be more cooperative in assisting the United States in locating its MIAs in Indochina may well reflect Vietnam's understanding of the importance of the United States in breaking the stalemate. It may even represent Hanoi's hope that the United States could pressure China into becoming more flexible in its views. The ASEAN, on the other hand, has been pressing the United States to provide military assistance for the non-Communist guerrilla forces fighting in Cambodia.

The issues facing the United States are difficult to resolve. Washington does not want the Thai-Cambodian border to become yet another East-West flashpoint. Extensive military assistance to the non-Communist forces, who are the weakest of the three guerrilla armies opposing Vietnam in Cambodia, could create just that. Nor does Washington want simply to acquiesce to Vietnamese domination of Cambodia. Yet, as long as the Cambodian stalemate continues, broader US regional and strategic concerns with the Soviet Union's presence will not be addressed by the major regional actors who form the basis for a potential anti-Soviet coalition.

The Cambodian dilemma is that no matter how effectively ASEAN diplomacy has been preventing Vietnam from turning its control of Cambodia into a *fait accompli,* there is no "ASEAN solution." The current stalemate reflects the reality that without great-power agreement there will be no solution to the Cambodian impasse. Without a solution to the Cambodian dilemma, broader US defense interests will not become a topic of major interest in ASEAN. Even if the Cambodian problem was resolved, Kuala Lumpur and Djakarta are more concerned over China's future policies in the region than they are about the USSR. Djakarta especially may tend toward the view that the USSR presents a counter-weight against renewed hostile intentions in the region from the PRC.

In the Philippines, the political context of the strategic US military bases at Clark Field and Subic Bay reached the point where, just a few months ago, continued US access to these facilities was in considerable doubt. The Marcos oligarchy had brought the Philippine political system to the verge of a major civil war. Without a change in the political leadership it was feared that the Philippines would collapse into civil war and the United States would be required to develop new bases within a more stable political environment, preferably in American territory.[32] Even as this issue was being discussed within the Congress and the White House, Marcos fled the Philippines and political power passed to Corazon Aquino and her supporters.

The new Philippine government has assumed all of the problems plaguing the islands, but there is now a sense of hope that over time they can be resolved. With Marcos in power, there was only a sense of deepening crisis. American support for Aquino and the US role in easing Marcos's departure has, at least for the moment, restored a sense of mutual confidence between Washington and Manila. The issue of continued American access to Clark Field and Subic Bay naval base has receded into the background and there is confidence that American use of the bases will be reconfirmed in future negotiations. The Philippine crisis, however, serves to highlight the extent to which US defense strategy is critically dependent on its overseas bases, and these bases are dependent upon the political environment within which they exist.

The United States and ANZUS. In the same manner that the Philippine crisis of the past four years threw a shadow over US access to strategically critical military facilities, so a change in New Zealand's government brought the future of the ANZUS treaty into question. With the election of the Labour Party and Prime Minister David Lange in the summer of 1984, the Labour Party's longstanding antinuclear stance became a major issue for the alliance.

It is US policy not to confirm or deny the presence of nuclear weapons aboard its naval vessels. When the United States requested a port call in New Zealand for the destroyer *Buchanan* following the "Sea Eagle" ANZUS exercise scheduled for March 1985, Wellington refused on the grounds that its intelligence could not determine whether the vessel was carrying nuclear weapons. This ban on ships carrying nuclear weapons was extended to the United Kingdom's naval vessels, which also refuses to confirm or deny the presence of nuclear weapons on its vessels. A second American port visit was denied in February 1985.

Later in the year, the Australian government bowed to antinuclear sentiment among its citizens and denied logistical support for MX missile testing in the Tasman Sea. This was a change in Australian policy, which had provided support for American nuclear weapons tests. These events raised the question: Is ANZUS unraveling? The United States canceled scheduled joint military exercises, stopped exchanges of military personnel with New Zealand, and indicated that future defense cooperation with Wellington would not be assumed. The Australian government, embarrassed by the MX decision, soon assured the United States that its alliance commitments, including port calls, remained strong. By summer 1985, ANZUS had functionally become a bilateral alliance between the United States and Australia.

The American dispute with New Zealand brought renewed focus on the 34-year-old defense pact anchoring the southern end of the United States's Pacific alliances. What the United States saw was the potential for New Zealand's explicit antinuclear policy's spreading to Japan and the nearby South Pacific. New Zealand had become an important test case because US relations with New Zealand were based upon bonds that precede the 1951 treaty. Furthermore, US relations with Wellington also involved indirect American links with Southeast Asia and the South Pacific.

ANZUS is part of a pattern of regional cooperation in Southeast Asia whereby Australia keeps a squadron of fighters in Malaysia, and Malaysian and Singaporean forces train with Australian, New Zealand, and British troops on a regular basis. Australia, New Zealand, Malaysia, Singapore, and the United Kingdom signed the Five-Power Defense Arrangement in 1971, and have sustained exchange and joint training programs, and other defense links since that time. This British Commonwealth link is further expanded by other defense ties, such as those between Malaysia and Indonesia, although the Kuala Lumpur-Djakarta link is based more on a mutual suspicion if not fear of long-term Chinese intentions in the region.

The crisis with New Zealand, when viewed within the broader context of US relations with Southeast Asia and the South Pacific, illuminates the number of links, direct and indirect, that Washington has within the region. The United States has no defense links with four of the six ASEAN members but looks with favor upon the strengthening of bilateral defense ties among the ASEAN members and between Australia and New Zealand and the other members of the Five-Power Defense

Arrangement. The United States has no alliance with the PRC but includes China's conventional and strategic nuclear forces in its assessment of the East Asian military balance with the USSR, and values the emerging links between the Chinese and American armed forces.[33]

Such linkages have their own problems. Indonesia and Malaysia warn the United States against assisting China in its economic and defense modernization programs.[34] Southeast Asia as a whole is ambivalent, at best, about US pressures on Japan to contribute more to the defense of the region. At worst, some countries in Southeast Asia fear that Washington may see Japan as a potential surrogate for the United States in the West Pacific.[35] Closer cooperation between Hanoi and Washington in recovering the remains of US MIAs raises concern in Thailand that if this divisive issue were resolved, Washington would retreat from its hard-line support for Bangkok's goal of forcing Vietnamese troops out of Cambodia and the creation of a neutral government in Phnom Penh.[36] Thus, with defense policy focused on future conditions, the political environment of the present becomes critically important in securing accord for the future.

The Reagan Defense Policy in Asia: An Assessment

With all its problems, the Asia-Pacific region cannot be viewed as anything less than a success for US policy. A little more than a decade ago Asia was the setting for the greatest defeat in the history of US security policy. The charge leveled by President Thieu of the defeated Republic of Vietnam that the United States had failed to fulfill its commitment to his government was echoed by President Marcos in Manila, Singapore's Lee Kuan Yew, Japan's Foreign Minister Miyazawa, Indonesia's

Foreign Minister Malik, and President Park in South Korea.[37] It has been a long road back, and the Reagan administration's policies have been part of a continuing American effort to restore and sustain the confidence of American friends and allies in the region. There is also continuity in the Reagan administration's tendency to analyze Asia in language reminiscent of the containment policies of the 1950s and 1960s. To a great extent, this is a function of interpreting the Soviet Union's objectives as the greatest external threat to peace and stability in Asia. That is an accurate assessment, but the political crisis in the Philippines and Chun Doo Hwan's domestic political problems should warn current and future administrations that many of America's friends and allies are entering a period of political transition with uncertain futures. As John Holbrook observed:

Expanding economic opportunity in the past has helped legitimize non-communist governments in the region and to smother potential unrest in prosperity.... Rapid increases in national wealth are an avenue to at least temporary social peace, but expanded political participation and confidence in governmental structures that can outlast individual leaders are necessary to sustain such stability.[38]

The fall of President Marcos was brought about in part by a failed economy, whereas the current situation in South Korea has come about despite economic success. Thus, even economic success is at times insufficient to smother demands for greater political participation. An American objective is to seek political stability among its friends and allies. Without it, defense planning will at best be crisis planning, and the strengthening of regional coalitions will be difficult to achieve over the long run. The future, as Holbrook notes, is far from bleak, but now is the time to encourage political change and adjustment to popular demands for greater political participation.

With this cautionary note in mind, the issue of the Soviet Union must be faced. There is an ironic twist to US policy here, for while Washington presses Japan to contribute more to the defense of the region and moves steadily toward closer military relations with China, the United States does not seem to recognize that these two strategies have to be viewed in Moscow as a direct and long-term threat to the Soviet Union. Indeed, there is an institutionalized pattern of mutually hostile interaction between the United States and the USSR in which each sees almost any action by the other as threatening to their security interests. Given the USSR's fear of a two-front war engaging its forces in European Russia and the Far East simultaneously, the buildup of Soviet conventional and strategic nuclear forces in the Far East over the past decade should have been anticipated. The Reagan administration is, however, only following past US practice, and there is no sign that this myopia will be corrected.

The American reappraisal of the military situation in Asia began with the Carter administration even before the Soviet incursion into Afghanistan. The Carter administration's pledge to remain a major military power in the Asia-Pacific region was a reaction to the fratricidal conflict between Communist states seen in Vietnam's invasion of Cambodia, China's invasion of Vietnam, and the concomitant tension growing along the Sino-Soviet border. The Reagan administration extended and accelerated the Carter administration's policies for a buildup of American military capabilities and, although shifting its primary focus from China to Japan, ultimately returned to the policy of developing military ties with the PRC while continuing to press Japan for greater defense commitments. The USSR continued its Asian defense buildup but with an added diplomatic effort to execute a rapprochement with the PRC and develop closer, more cordial relations with both North Korea and Japan. There are also uncertain signs that the USSR may be accepting a demarche with the United States.

Soviet embassy officials discussing Gorbachev's restatement of a collective security arrangement for Asia during his visit to India in May 1985, suggested that the United States could be involved. These officials proposed that the United States and the USSR could agree to limit naval operations in the Western Pacific; that Japan and the USSR could sign a treaty of "good neighborly" relations; and that the USSR and China could agree to "confidence-building measures" (CBMs) along their common border. These CBMs could include notification of planned military exercises and possibly a reduction of forces deployed along both sides of the border.[39]

Perhaps prompted by these suggestions, in his August 1985 Helsinki meeting with Soviet Foreign Minister Shevardnadze, Secretary of State George Shultz proposed talks on US-Soviet differences in Asia. Early in September the State Department indicated that Moscow had agreed to high-level discussions and that Paul Wolfowitz, Assistant Secretary of State for Far East and Pacific Affairs, would go to Moscow and meet with Mikhail Kapitsa, the Deputy Foreign Minister for Asian Affairs. Issues to be raised by Wolfowitz were the Soviet military buildup in East Asia, tensions on the Korean peninsula, the advanced weapons supplied by the USSR to North Korea, and the stalemated situation in Cambodia. In regard to the latter, the United States hoped the USSR could be persuaded to urge Hanoi to be more forthcoming in its negotiating position on the future of Cambodia.[40]

These tentative probes by the United States and the USSR do not indicate a major change in either Washington's or Moscow's perception of the causes of their mutual hostility, but rather a willingness to meet and discuss divisive issues at the working level. A desire to raise the diplomatic level of interaction with Asia and the United States is a mark of General Secretary Gorbachev's revised approach to Soviet security problems. It is doubtful that Gorbachev seeks a radical change in Soviet objectives. It is more likely that he seeks to reduce Soviet political isolation in the region. For, even with its growing military strength, the USSR's political position has been weakened.[41]

Given the wariness with which some American friends and allies in Asia view Washington's Manichaean view of the region's security, it is almost certain that they will view Gorbachev's diplomatic forays as far more indicative of potential change in Soviet goals and objectives than will the United States. Thus, assuming a consistent diplomatic offensive by the USSR, the political context of US defense policy will be entering a difficult stage. Currently, the United States is continuing to stress a coalitional and cooperative defense strategy, but such a strategy depends upon close and supportive political relations as much as it does the strength of American arms. Moscow's political strategy is designed to weaken US political relations in Asia and to demonstrate that Soviet arms are designed primarily to deter the United States. At the same time, so long as the USSR continues to fight in Afghanistan, support Vietnam in Cambodia, and sustain its military buildup, a Soviet diplomatic offensive also faces difficulties.

The Reagan administration's defense policy has continued to follow the pattern, with some adjustment, set in motion by previous administrations. The Carter and Reagan policies have proven to be adequate for recovering the American military position in Asia and assuring friends and allies that the United States sustains a strong defense commitment to the region. Where there is weakness it is in the rhetoric used to justify the policy and what appears to be a failure to recognize, at least publicly, that defense relationships in Asia are far more complex than in Europe. Security relations in Asia are far more fluid and politically sensitive to regional and subregional priorities and alignments. This is as true for Moscow as it is for Washington. What, in fact, the United States has achieved is a firming up of a loose coalition of treaty allies and friends in the Asia-Pacific region.

The US military presence must have the capability to restrain any Soviet aggressive behavior threatening friends and allies. This has been, and remains, a major priority of the Reagan administration. For the future, this military capability must be joined by the equally important diplomatic effort to create, in the words of Richard Solomon, "an effective entente of alliance relationships and cooperative ties to friendly, if nonaligned states."[42] While the United States can respond, even if with difficulty, to a continuing Soviet military buildup, it cannot avoid the even more difficult task of developing the political context required for a successful defense policy.

Notes

1. Henry Kissinger, *The White House Years* (Boston: Little, Brown and Co., 1979), pp. 684–87.

2. Zbigniew Brzezinski, *Power and Principle* (New York: Farrar, Strauss, Giroux, 1983), annex I, p. 1.

80   *Paul H. B. Godwin*

3. Caspar W. Weinberger, Secretary of Defense, *Annual Report to the Congress, Fiscal Year 1987* (Washington, DC: GPO, 1986), pp. 55–71.

4. Ibid., pp. 64–66.

5. See, for example, Li Dai, "Independence and China's External Relations," *Shijie Zhishi* (World Knowledge), No. 19 (1981), in Foreign Broadcast Information Service, Daily Report, *China* (henceforth FBIS-China), 19 November 1981, p. A–4; and Xinhua News Agency, 20 August 1981, in FBIS-China, 24 August 1981, p. A–3, where opposition to the policies pursued by the United States toward "certain Third World countries," is clearly stated.

6. Harold Brown, Secretary of Defense, *Annual Report to the Congress, Fiscal Year 1982* (Washington, DC: GPO, 1981), pp. 83–84.

7. Richard Halloran, "Pentagon Draws Up First Strategy For Fighting Long Nuclear War," *New York Times*, 30 May 1982, p. 1; Richard Nations, "Calling all Allies," *Far Eastern Economic Review* 116, no. 25 (18 June 1982), pp. 10–11; Richard Halloran, "U.S. Is Fashioning a New Military Strategy for Asia," *New York Times*, 7 June 1982, p. A–3.

8. Brown, *Annual Report FY 1982*, p. 84.

9. Paul H. B. Godwin, "Soldiers and Statesman in Conflict: Chinese Defense and Foreign Policies in the 1980s," in Samuel S. Kim (ed.), *China and the World* (Boulder, CO; Westview Press, 1984), pp. 221–24.

10. Wang Bingnan, "China's Independent Foreign Policy," Beijing Domestic Service, 30 January 1983, in FBIS-China, 31 January 1983, pp. A–1/7.

11. Mike M. Mochizuki, "Japan's Search for Strategy," *International Security* 8, no. 3 (Winter 1983–1984): 152–79.

12. Ibid., p. 157.

13. Sheldon S. Simon, *The ASEAN States and Regional Security* (Stanford: Hoover Institution Press, 1982), pp. 123–24.

14. Susume Awonahara, "The nice man cometh," *Far Eastern Economic Review* 120, no. 20 (19 May 1983): 14–16.

15. Richard Nations, "Pacific Partnership," *Far Eastern Economic Review* 122, no. 45 (10 November 1983): 18–19.

16. "Japan's Military Chief Meets With His Chinese Counterpart," *New York Times*, 10 June 1984, p. A–70.

17. Bernard Gwertzman, "Malaysia, Seeing a Threat, Urges U.S. to Stop Building Up Power of China," *New York Times*, 10 July 1984, p. A–10.

18. *Yomiuri Shimbun* (Tokyo), 9 December 1981, p. 1.

19. Weinberger, *Annual Report, FY 1987*, pp. 55–71.

20. Ibid., p. 66.

21. For a more detailed discussion of these issues, see Yukio Satoh, ''The Evolution of Japanese Security Policy,'' in Robert O'Neill (ed.), *Security in East Asia* (New York: St. Martin's Press, 1984), pp. 49–53.

22. ''Moscow Upsets Tokyo's Increased Defence Role,'' *Far Eastern Economic Review* 131, no. 5 (30 January 1986): 28–29.

23. Edward Ross, Assistant for China, Office of the Assistant Secretary of Defense, International Security Affairs, ''U.S.-Military Relations,'' a presentation to the Heritage Foundation Asian Studies seminar, 28 January 1986, p. 5.

24. Ibid., p. 3.

25. Ibid., p. 8.

26. Ibid., p. 5.

27. See the press conference of the Defense Minister of the Republic of Korea held on 20 March 1986, reported in Foreign Broadcast Information Service, Daily Report, *Asia & Pacific* (henceforth FBIS-APA), 20 March 1986, p. E–2.

28. Richard Nations, ''Love Boat to Wonsan,'' *Far Eastern Economic Review* 129, no. 34 (29 August 1985): 22–23.

29. See Jonathan Pollack's discussion in ''Peking Stands Back as Moscow Courts Kim'' *Far Eastern Economic Review* 130, no. 48 (5 December 1985): 48–49.

30. The following discussion is taken primarily from William Bach, ''A Chance in Cambodia,'' *Foreign Policy,* no. 62 (Spring 1986): 75–85.

31. Ibid., p. 81.

32. See, for example, James P. Sterba, ''America's Philippine Bases: Vital or Just Convenient,'' *Wall Street Journal*, 20 February 1986, p. 28.

33. Weinberger, *Annual Report, FY 1987*, pp. 64–65.

34. See, for example, Bernard Gwertzman, ''China-U.S. Ties Make Southeast Asia Squirm,'' *New York Times*, 15 July 1984, p. 4–E.

35. Takashi Oka, ''Southeast Asia Wary of Changing Role of the U.S. in Pacific,'' *Christian Science Monitor*, 10 July 1984, p. 10.

36. Agence France Presse (Hong Kong), 27 January 1986, in FBIS-China, 28 January 1986, pp. J–1/2.

37. For a discussion of the reaction among US Asian allies to the fall of Saigon, see Franklin B. Weinstein and John W. Lewis,

"The Post-Vietnam Strategic Context in Asia," in Franklin B. Weinstein (ed.), *U.S.-Japan Relations and the Security of East Asia* (Boulder, CO: Westview Press, 1978), pp. 128–29.

38. Richard Holbrook, "East Asia: The Next Challenge," *Foreign Affairs* 64, no. 4 (Spring 1986): 751.

39. Bernard Gwertzman, "U.S. and Soviet Set High-level Talks on the Far East," *New York Times,* 8 September 1985, p. 1.

40. Cited in Robert G. Sutter, *Soviet Leader Gorbachev Calls for Collective Security in Asia—Possible Implications,* (Washington, DC: Congressional Research Service, 28 May 1985), p. CRS–2.

41. Harry Gelman, "Continuity versus Change in Soviet Policy in Asia," *Journal of Northeast Asian Studies* 4, no. 2 (Summer 1985): 3–17.

42. Richard H. Solomon, "Coalition Building or Condominium? The Soviet Presence in Asia and American Policy Alternatives," in Donald S. Zagoria (ed.) *Soviet Policy in East Asia,* (New Haven, CT: Yale University Press, 1982), p. 327.

AMERICAN-SOVIET RELATIONS: THE RHETORIC AND REALISM

Peter R. Zwick

*D*URING RONALD REAGAN'S FIRST TERM as President, three Soviet leaders served in rapid succession—Brezhnev, Andropov, and Chernenko. By contrast, although the first weeks of Reagan's second term began with Chernenko in charge, it seems probable today that Mikhail Gorbachev will be the Soviet leader well beyond this presidency.

President Reagan has contended that the rapid turnover of aged Soviet leaders made it extremely difficult for him to establish a coherent diplomatic dialogue with his Soviet counterpart until the Gorbachev ascendancy. Fairness, however, demands that we recognize that during this period of unstable and undynamic Soviet leadership, Washington hurled a continuous barrage of ideological rhetoric at the Soviet Union the likes of which had not been heard since the height of the Cold War. The intensity of this rhetoric apparently convinced the Soviet leadership, including Gorbachev, that Reagan was consumed by an irreversible Soviet animus that would make normal diplomatic relations impossible.

It was not just the intensity of Reagan's anti-Soviet rhetoric, which depicted Moscow as the "focus of evil," but also its substance that convinced many political observers, East and West, that Reagan would be true to his conservative anti-Communist commitment throughout his tenure in office. Reagan did not simply revive Cold War "containment" policy, but he resuscitated the chimera of a "rollback" of Soviet power as the result of a shift in the "correlation of forces" in favor of the West. In support of the "rollback" approach, Secretary of State Shultz wrote at the beginning of 1985: "The present political division of the continent (Europe) is artificial; it exists only because it has been imposed by brute Soviet power; the United States has never recognized it as legitimate or permanent."[1]

The enigma of Reagan's first term is that despite the intensity and content of his anti-Soviet *rhetoric*, his *policy* was neither reckless nor especially threatening to Soviet security. In fact, Reagan's Soviet policy was surprisingly moderate. As Adam Ulam observed, "Oratory apart, the Soviets had little reason to complain about the record of Mr. Reagan's administration."[2]

American conservatives could find little in Reagan's *actions* to substantiate their hope that he was abandoning detente in favor of confrontation with Moscow. Reagan lifted the grain embargo imposed by President Carter in response to the Soviet intervention in Afghanistan. He passed up a golden opportunity to initiate a "liberationist" policy in Poland in 1981–82 in favor of efforts to calm rather than exacerbate Polish tensions. He made no major commitments to the rebels (or freedom fighters) in Afghanistan. He condemned the shootdown of the KAL 007, but imposed no sanctions. He railed against the gas pipeline from the USSR to Western Europe, but could not stop it. Even in the case of Nicaragua, Reagan administration support for the Contra effort was minimal (albeit largely due to Congress's resistance). In the context of this "détente-like" policy, the invasion of tiny Grenada only underscored the limits of Reagan's willingness to commit American power against the "evil empire." The so-called "Reagan Doctrine" remained, for the most part, rhetoric untranslated to action.

Ironically, despite this moderation, Western liberals took even less comfort than did conservatives in Reagan's Soviet policy. Liberals shuddered at the prospect of a "second Cold War," and despaired of Reagan's ideological crusade against communism. These liberal concerns notwithstanding, the fact was that the United States and USSR were not brought closer to war.

In fact, although Reagan's first-term rhetoric certainly did not bring the superpowers closer to peace, it is highly unlikely that, even had Reagan been inclined to engage in rapprochement, the ossified Kremlin leadership would have been able to respond.

In other words, although some Reagan critics have bemoaned the "lost opportunities" in American-Soviet relations during the first term, the prospects for improved American-Soviet relations remained extremely low as long as the revolving door to Kremlin power continued to turn.

From Rhetoric to Realism?

The characterization of Reagan's first term as a "rhetorical presidency" raises three interesting questions. First, what explains the gap between Reagan rhetoric and policy toward the USSR? Second, why was there a major shift away from rhetoric in the second term? And, third, does this shift portend a new realism in Reagan policy toward the USSR?

As employed here, the term "realism" implies less reliance on ideological explanations of Soviet behavior and more reliance on factors associated with a *realpolitik* view of Soviet policy. Realism also means a turn toward diplomatic engagement and negotiation to resolve outstanding differences. President Reagan's ideological assessment of Soviet motives and goals could be correct, and, in that sense, his views would be "realistic." However, to the extent that he employs hyperbolic rhetoric as a means of dealing with the Soviet threat (as a substitute for diplomacy) his approach is not realistic.

One answer to the questions posed above is that Reagan had little to lose by engaging in anti-Soviet diatribes. It was unlikely that any long-term American-Soviet relations would develop in his first term until a new generation of Soviet leaders emerged. Not only was he free to indulge his own anti-Soviet feelings and express the ideological beliefs of the conservative wing of his party, but his anti-Sovietism rallied popular support for his defense buildup and generated a genuine post-Vietnam patriotic revival with little risk to world peace. All this was possible because American *actions* were not perceived in Moscow as a direct threat to Soviet security.

As a conservative, Reagan sought to restore both America's *capacity* and *will* to employ force as a means of controlling Soviet behavior. One observer, Coral Bell, has argued that in the age of national technical means of intelligence "ambiguities of the power balance are in the area of will rather than capacity." Reagan's new rhetoric should be seen as a manifestation of America's willingness to stand up to Soviet power. The gap between what Bell refers to as Reagan's "declaratory signals" (rhetoric) and "operational signals" (policy) reflected his recognition of the increasing importance of the *perception of risk* in American-Soviet relations. If Reagan could intimidate the Soviets through his rhetoric, they would be less likely to risk direct confrontation.[3]

The first-term "rhetoric-policy" gap, and the tentative second-term shift to diplomacy has also been explained by reference to Reagan's oft-repeated strategy of "negotiation from strength," which presumably required that he buy time to close the "window of vulnerability." According to this view, Reagan used his first term to build up America's military power so that meaningful American-Soviet negotiations could follow in the second term and beyond. In brief, Reagan's rhetoric kept the Soviet bear at bay until America was again ready to stand up to him.

The problem with this explanation is that despite substantial increases in American military spending, there is little evidence to suggest that the military balance, at both the conventional and strategic levels, had shifted in favor of the United States by the time of the 1985 summit. Increased expenditures for MX and Midgetman missiles, B–1 and Stealth bombers, and the Strategic Defense Initiative (SDI) may have signified Reagan's commitment to American military modernization, but had far more effect on reviving the defense sector than on a shift in the "correlation of forces."

Reagan's tentative turn to summitry in the second term is not, in other words, easily explained as the follow-on phase of the "negotiation from strength" strategy. However, it may have reflected a strategy of "negotiation through *perceived commitment* to strength." Put another way, Reagan's unflagging commitment to increased military budgets in the first term may have been motivated by a desire to convince Moscow of Washington's *will* to sacrifice domestic programs and a balanced budget for the sake of military defense.

Another clue to the cause of the apparent shift from rhetoric to realism lies in the difference in the American popular mood when Reagan first took office in 1981 and that in 1985. Reagan's rhetoric, which described the USSR as the "focus of evil" in the world, simplified the complexities of international relations for a receptive American public, which had become disoriented by Carter's emphasis on human rights and deemphasis of the East-West conflict. Reagan was not only refocusing American foreign policy on the USSR, but re-establishing America's anti-Communist commitment after the Vietnam debacle. In addition, his depiction of the USSR as *the* threat to regional and world peace (and, therefore, American security), mobilized popular support for increases in the defense budget and the hiatus in normal diplomatic relations with Moscow.

In the post-Vietnam era, America's belief in military solutions to international political problems had been abandoned in favor of detente. It was under Carter that the Iran crisis tested American military capacity and found it wanting. Defense spending was sharply reduced, raising widespread concern over American security. In addition, the Sandinista victory in Nicaragua sparked fears of another Cuba in the Western Hemisphere. Finally, the Soviet invasion of Afghanistan convinced even President Carter that Moscow could not be trusted to abide by the "rules of the road" approach to America-Soviet relations. All of this contributed to an overwhelming Reagan electoral victory and to a developing consensus among Americans that the United States had to regain some of its military status if it was going to deal effectively with Moscow and the international community.

Riding the crest of this new mood, Reagan lambasted the USSR and initiated three new military challenges to Soviet power: (1) the "Reagan Doctrine" of active support for "freedom fighters" against communism in the Third World; (2) the deployment of intermediate-range missiles in Western Europe (Pershing II and cruise missiles); and (3) the development of a new nuclear deterrence strategy known as the Strategic Defense Initiative, or "Star Wars."

The Reagan Doctrine was more than hemispheric containment. It involved overt and covert aid to forces attempting to overthrow the Sandinista government of Nicaragua and the Marxist government of Grenada. It was *rollback*. The Reagan Doctrine was a low-cost, low-risk, high-visibility reassertion of America's will to resist Communist expansionism in the post-Vietnam era, and was just what the American people wanted.

Reagan's decision to deploy intermediate-range missiles in Europe was a response to the Warsaw Pact's previously unchallenged military preeminence over NATO, which guaranteed a political status quo in Europe. It would have been absurd for the Reagan administration to reopen the issue of the division of Europe without exerting some pressure on Soviet security. With the Intermediate Nuclear Force (INF) talks stalemated in Geneva, the short-term price of deployment was minimal. Reagan offered the Soviets the so-called "zero option." This proposal would have traded America's planned deployment of a partially tested INF system for Soviet dismantling of its SS–20s, which had been deployed. Further, this proposal did not include British and French nuclear forces.

Without calling into question the realism or sincerity of Reagan's "zero option," it is not likely that American arms negotiators expected their proposal to be accepted. Indeed, it is highly unlikely that either the ailing Brezhnev or the aged Kremlin caretakers who followed were capable of responding to any new arms control initiative. Therefore, the decision to deploy American intermediate-range weapons in November 1983 was another low-cost strategy. Whether that deployment altered the military balance in Europe is secondary because its purpose was to demonstrate America's new-found *will*.

The Strategic Defense Initiative was a response to the perceived Soviet strategic advantage in offensive weapons, which raised questions about the value of America's nuclear deterrence. Given the Soviet lead in land-based heavy missiles, Reagan proposed a new, untested, highly controversial deterrence strategy that would make offensive weapons obsolete, and reestablish American security. Unable to *outrun* the Soviets in an offensive arms race, Reagan decided to *endrun* them with SDI.

Although SDI was publicly touted as "Star Wars," a hi-tech version of the old arms race, arms control experts saw it as something more. The Strategic Defense Initiative represented a fundamental change in America's strategy of deterrence through mutual assured destruction (MAD), to one based on a defensive anti-missile system.

Since SALT I, the United States had rejected any notion of nuclear deterrence based on defensive systems. The provisions of the 1972 Anti-Ballistic Missile (ABM) Treaty had restricted each party to two limited ABM systems each, one around the capital city and one around an ICBM installation. This limit was subsequently reduced to one ABM system each by a 1974 protocol.

All American-Soviet arms control discussions and agreements in the era of detente incorporated this "mutual hostage" principle of vulnerability to nuclear attack. Western critics of the MAD strategy had argued that the Soviets never accepted MAD and were pursuing a "warfighting capability." However, even if true, this was a strategy of "deterrence by denial," which depended on overwhelming Soviet *offensive* superiority.

Although SDI proponents and critics emphasize "space" weapons, the importance of SDI does not lie in the location of the weapons, but in their character. Some perceive that the intent of SDI is defensive in nature, and its purpose is to destroy *all* incoming intercontinental ballistic missiles. (It should be noted, however, that SDI is not a defense against submarine-launched, low-trajectory ballistic missiles, cruise missiles, or conventional bombs.)

If a nation could protect itself against a nuclear attack with an impenetrable defensive shield, one of two consequences could ensue. Either it would no longer need other deterrence systems, such as an offensive nuclear force, or it could launch a first strike against the other side without fear of retaliation.

Either possibility posed a serious challenge to the Soviet system. But, more important, some perceived that SDI offered the American people the hope of a *perfect* defense, without a nuclear arsenal.

Again, in terms of public mood, Reagan's SDI was a palliative to the insecurity of an endless arms race.

Whether the Reagan Doctrine, INF deployment, and SDI were intended as preludes to traditional diplomacy, or as long-term policies, they matched the public mood of the first term. However, abrupt and significant changes in foreign and domestic conditions at the outset of Reagan's second term altered that mood, necessitating changes in both the style and substance of Reagan's Soviet policy.

Reagan's Response to Gorbachev

The most significant change influencing Reagan's approach to the USSR in his second term was unquestionably Gorbachev's ascendancy to power. Unlike the series of aged Brezhnevites who had preceded him, Gorbachev was an unknown quantity. Was he a "hawk" or a "dove"? Was he a reformer or a "Stalinist"? No one knew, but it was essential to know quickly.

Although there was no certainty that Gorbachev would survive the vicissitudes of a succession conflict, actuarially, he was a good candidate for long-term leadership. With Gorbachev in control, Reagan would no longer be able to employ the explanation (or excuse) that he could not meet with his Soviet counterparts because they died before a meeting could be arranged. Reagan had to confront the truth that he was the only postwar President who had not met with a Soviet leader. The imminent prospect of such a meeting demanded a deescalation of the first-term rhetoric.

Further, Gorbachev proved to be a surprisingly skilled "media man." The Western press liked him. He was a new breed of Soviet leader who understood the importance of the media as a means to influence world public opinion. In addition to style, Gorbachev emerged as a man of substance on arms control issues. In the same way that he began to take the initiative away from Reagan in the "media war," Gorbachev also seized the initiative on substantive issues of American-Soviet relations. Suddenly, the Reagan administration found itself in a reactive mode. As Gorbachev took the "peace initiative," the rhetoric of Reagan's first term began to haunt him in his second term. What had been Reagan's strength was transformed into a weakness by Gorbachev's apparent conciliatory attitude. Reagan had to do something substantive to regain the momentum in the intensifying verbal "war of peace."

Reagan's need to know Gorbachev, to confront him head-on in the media spotlight, and to regain the "peace initiative" all account for the reversal, in mid-1985, of the conditions for an American-Soviet summit meeting. Whereas previously, Reagan insisted that a summit would be pointless unless the two leaders had something substantive to discuss, by the summer of 1985 he was willing to attend a summit without even a mutually acceptable agenda. The United States wanted the summit to deal with a broad range of issues, while Moscow wanted the agenda to be limited to arms control. As the summit approached, however, it became increasingly clear that *nothing* substantive would result. Therefore, the Reagan administration adopted the view that even if the summit only afforded the two world leaders an opportunity to get to know each other, it would serve a constructive purpose.

The Geneva meeting in November 1985, which Reagan dubbed the "fireside summit," was a media event. Behind the scenes, there were a series of private discussions, but in the end there was not enough substance or agreement to warrant more than a general joint postmeeting statement on cultural exchanges and the promise to meet again.

Both leaders rushed to the summit because each was afraid of being accused by the other of being the obstacle to peace. In addition, Gorbachev needed the summit to establish his credentials as a strong Soviet leader capable of handling foreign policy, his obvious weak suit going in. Hence, Gorbachev was willing to go to Geneva regardless of the high probability that no substantive agreements would be achieved.

All this pressure on Reagan to engage Gorbachev diplomatically was intensified by American domestic political and economic factors. For one thing, Reagan needed the summit at the beginning of his second term to answer growing criticism of his military buildup. Also, looming massive budget deficits made it increasingly difficult for him to ask Congress for larger military expenditures without making a good-faith effort at negotiating a possible arms control agreement.

With the Gramm-Rudman-Hollings proposal on the horizon, Reagan probably realized that he had played the "negotiation from strength" ploy for all it was worth. Before budget cuts undermined his rearmament efforts, it behooved Reagan to begin serious negotiations with Moscow while the threat of an all-out arms race was still a credible alternative to Soviet recalcitrance.

Another factor that probably contributed to Reagan's response to the Gorbachev challenge is the "second-term" phenomenon. No longer having to be concerned with the judgment of the electorate, and particularly the right-wing elements of his own party, Reagan may have begun to take a longer view of his presidency, especially history's judgment of him as "peacemaker."

Even if Reagan had done little to roll back the Soviet threat, conservatives had supported him in the 1984 election because he had turned his back on the diplomacy of detente and had ideologically, if not militarily, engaged the enemy. Now, in his mid-seventies, with no electoral constituency to be served, Reagan had little to lose by allowing that perhaps it was possible to negotiate in good faith with Soviet leaders.

In combination with the emergence of a new leader in the Kremlin, these domestic political and economic considerations gave Reagan the impetus to shift away from rhetoric and move toward more normal diplomatic relations with the Soviet Union.

Issues in American-Soviet Relations

In view of Gorbachev's brief tenure at the time of his first summit, the ongoing power struggle in the Kremlin, and Reagan's recent conversion to diplomacy, it should not have been surprising that the first Reagan-Gorbachev attempt at summitry achieved very little. It was a premature summit, and should not be taken as a predictor of success of future summits in Washington and Moscow.

The basic issues confronting American-Soviet relations for the remainder of the Reagan presidency and beyond are relatively clear. "Star Wars" will continue to be the centerpiece of Reagan's security policy and the focal point of Soviet criticism. But, other issue areas will also be important, including arms control, regional conflicts, East-West trade relations, and human rights. While none of these issues is new, there appears to be a new willingness on both sides to negotiate with less rancor and rhetoric and a new realism of shared responsibility.

Let us now consider these issue areas and what each portends for future American-Soviet relations.

Arms control. The near-term prospects for any arms control agreement are cloudy. After years of proposals, counterproposals, and unproductive negotiations, both sides came away from the November 1985 summit apparently committed to achieving at least a limited arms control agreement. The preliminary decision to subdivide the discussions into strategic, intermediate, and space-based weapons talks raised the possibility that agreement could be reached in one area without an overall settlement of all arms control issues. This did not guarantee success, but for the first time in the Reagan presidency the arms control process was not doomed to failure by unrealistic requirements on both sides.

The first postsummit arms control negotiating session adjourned in March 1986, amid accusations from both sides that the other was still not serious about arms control. Further, the planned 1986 Washington summit was delayed by disagreements that threatened to derail the entire summit process and make an arms control agreement extremely remote. It was not until late summer that the summit process was back on track, and Reagan publicly acknowledged that the Soviets were making serious arms control proposals. The American and Soviet positions on arms control are summarized in table 1.

The most significant concessions by Moscow in the postsummit period were the uncoupling of the Soviet demand that the United States drop SDI research from a settlement on intermediate-range weapons in Europe, and the partial unlinking of British and French strategic nuclear forces from the INF negotiations. For his part, Reagan's February 1986 INF proposal dropped his previous insistence that Soviet intermediate-range missiles in Central Asia and the Far East be eliminated completely. These items therefore remained the only obstacles to an agreement on INF.[4]

Strategic arms control is closely tied to the issue of space-based weapons and SDI. Reagan's commitment to "Star Wars" research is seen in Moscow as an attempt to secure a "first-strike" capability. Quite understandably, the Soviets find this unacceptable. As long as Reagan persists in this plan to shift America's deterrence strategy from an offensive to a defensive system, the prospects for a strategic arms control agreement remain dim. In fact, the development of SDI could exacerbate the arms race. If the United States hopes to develop a defensive shield, its deterrence effect must lie in its being virtually 100 percent impenetrable. From the Soviet perspective, one logical counter to SDI would be

Table 1
American and Soviet Arms Control Positions: 1986

American Positions	*Soviet Positions*
Strategic weapons. Reduce strategic missiles 50 percent as first step toward total elimination.	*Strategic weapons.* Eliminate all weapons by 2000; 50-percent reduction in strategic weapons over 5 to 8 years.
Intermediate-range weapons. Eliminate intermediate weapons in Europe in two stages by 1990, with a 50-percent reduction in 1987. Also eliminate Soviet missiles in the Far East and reduce those in Central Asia by 50 percent in 1987. British and French strategic forces would not be included.	*Intermediate-range weapons.* Eliminate intermediate-range weapons in Europe in 5 to 8 years. British and French forces need not be eliminated, but cannot be modernized or expanded. Missiles in Far East or Central Asia not included.
SDI and space-based weapons. No limits on SDI or space-based weapons research, but strict compliance with limits on research imposed by 1972 ABM treaty.	*SDI and space-based weapons.* United States must renounce space-based weapons deployment, although some basic research on SDI could continue. Failure to reach agreements in this area should not preclude elimination of intermediate-range weapons in Europe.

a massive offensive strategic force capable of overwhelming America's defensive shield. In short, not only is there little incentive for the USSR to reduce its strategic arsenal, but there is a very strong incentive to accelerate offensive weapons development in order to be ready for SDI if, or when, it is deployed. Another option would be the deployment of "space mines" capable of destroying SDI systems. This would constitute an escalation of the arms race in space.

The question is, under what circumstances would Reagan abandon the Strategic Defense Initiative? Is SDI a "bargaining chip" to be used to force the Soviets to accept deep cuts in strategic weapons systems? Does President Reagan really believe that SDI is an achievable technology? Although he has given no indication that he would give up SDI, the circumstances under which it was initiated—more at Reagan's behest after learning of the theory than in response to demand from military advisers—suggest that "Star Wars" was more a political than a military consideration. Furthermore, serious questions have been raised about the technical feasibility of its deployment within the next quarter century, if at all.[5] The fact that it is not a defense system (even if perfected) against offshore, ship and submarine-launched cruise and low trajectory ballistic missiles and bombers suggests that it could not be a complete substitute for strategic deterrence. However, a partly effective SDI system concentrated on defending American land-based missiles, such as the new MX, could deny the Soviets a "first-strike" capability derived from overwhelming offensive superiority.

In short, if Reagan or his successor could negotiate significant, verifiable reductions of strategic offensive weapons with Moscow (a prospect that appears increasingly likely with Gorbachev), SDI would probably be shelved. Reagan may insist on the right to limited research, but "Star Wars" is too problematic and too expensive to stand in the way of a meaningful arms reduction package in the near term.

A final potential obstacle to arms control agreements is Reagan's belief that meaningful arms negotiations are made more difficult by continued Soviet involvement in regional conflicts. This presummit linkage of Soviet Third World activities, especially in Afghanistan, the Persian Gulf, and Central America appears to have moderated since the 1985 Geneva summit. However such activities are potential sticking points in American-Soviet arms negotiations and relations in general.

Regional conflicts. The heart of Reagan's Third World policy is anticommunism, which means anti-Sovietism. The heart of Gorbachev's Third World policy continues to be antiimperialism, which means anti-Americanism. In short, each of the superpowers depicts the other as the main source of tension in the Third World and the root cause of current regional conflicts.

As noted previously, Reaganism is not the anticommunism of containment. The Reagan Doctrine includes the notion of liberation from communism in addition to the containment of its spread. As the Reagan administration made clear to Congress during the 1986 debates on support for the Contras in Nicaragua, if the "freedom fighters" fail to overthrow the Sandinista regime, it may be necessary for United States forces to take a more direct role. The goal is to overthrow the Nicaraguan government, just as the Marxist government of Grenada was overthrown.

The Reagan Doctrine is legitimized and distinguished from brute imperialism in the President's mind by the conviction that "freedom fighters" are really struggling against the Soviet Union. According to this view, if the USSR, or its Cuban surrogate, had not directly intervened in the affairs of Central American and Caribbean states, the Reagan Doctrine would not be necessary. When it comes to regional conflicts, the Reagan motto is *"cherchez l'Union Sovietique."*

Even former President Nixon, a practitioner of détente, voiced support for President Reagan's policies on the grounds that what Nixon termed the "revised" Brezhnev Doctrine includes "not only defending but extending communism."[6]

Reagan explains the conflicts in Afghanistan, Southeast Asia, the Middle East, southern Africa, and, of course, Central America as the direct result of Soviet "mischief-making." This is not to say he believes that there would be no conflicts but for the USSR; rather he sees the Soviets as troublemakers who take advantage of any opportunity to exacerbate tensions and regional instability. Why is it in the interests of the Soviet Union to promote regional conflict? This comes back to Reagan's view of Moscow as a revolutionary power motivated by Marxist-Leninist ideology.

The President's position on regional conflicts goes to the heart of his perception of the Soviet role in the world. In a very real sense, the "rollback of communism" is synonymous with the "rollback of Soviet power." Reagan is simply unwilling to grant the USSR the status of "global power." At a minimum, Reagan would have the USSR reduced to its earlier, continental power status. This is consistent with the oft-expressed Reagan belief (or, perhaps, wish) that the "correlation of forces" in the world has shifted during his term in office in favor of democracy, and that socialism has had its day.

Finding the USSR under every regional hot bed is the self-fulfillment of Reagan's nightmare. More importantly, it legitimizes, as nothing else could, American interference in the internal affairs of Third World governments with which the Reagan administration disagrees. This, in turn, mobilizes American popular support for a remilitarized foreign policy that is saved from being imperialist by its anti-Sovietism. As Secretary of State Shultz put it: "So long as communist dictatorships feel free to aid and abet insurgencies in the name of "socialist internationalism" why must the democracies—the target of this threat—be inhibited from defending their own interests and the cause of democracy itself?"[7]

In view of Reagan's unwillingness to accept the Soviet Union's legitimate interest in global affairs, including regional conflicts in the Western Hemisphere, the prospects for any meaningful agreements in this area are dim. Therefore, it is unlikely that this issue area will be the focus of any summit conference as long as he is President. Undoubtedly Reagan will raise the issue in international forums, in the media, and in future private fireside chats with Gorbachev.

At the same time, second-term realism, born of economic necessity and political opportunity, may permit Reagan to enter into normalized relations with the USSR *before* any resolution of the major regional problems. Just as Brezhnev did not permit American involvement in Vietnam to block the SALT negotiations or American-Soviet trade agreements, it now appears that Reagan might be willing to move ahead with limited agreements on arms control and East-West economic relations, without insisting on a Soviet withdrawal from Afghanistan or abandonment of the Sandinista regime. Part of Reagan's newborn realism must include a willingness to disaggregate the America-Soviet confrontation into manageable issue areas.

East-West trade. In the West it is generally assumed that the Soviet Union needs trade more than

we do. Technology, consumer products, and grain products are considered by many to be essential to Soviet
economic development. As a consequence, Western
policies have often attempted to force the Soviet Union
into political concessions in exchange for trade: an
approach known as linkage.

The facts that the USSR is "behind" the West in
technology, consumer goods, and food production, and
that they must improve these sectors in order to stimulate productivity, have been well documented. The issue
for American-Soviet relations, however, is not whether
the Soviets want or need Western goods, but what
Moscow is willing to do in order to get them. In the
pre-Reagan years, trade was employed as leverage
against the Soviets in two ways: as punishment for
involvement in regional conflicts, and as an incentive
for reform on human rights.

Contrary to the expectations of many on the left
and right that Reagan's anti-Soviet rhetoric would
surely manifest itself in some form of linkage policy,
this was not the case. In fact, Reagan's views on linkage were ambiguous from the start. At the same time
that Reagan declared himself for linkage in the 1980
campaign, he promised American farmers that he would
lift the grain embargo imposed by Carter; a promise that
he kept when he took office in 1981. No economic
sanctions were imposed against the USSR and its allies
during the Polish crisis, and despite the virulence of the
Reagan attacks against Soviet involvement in Nicaragua
and Grenada, no economic sanctions have been threatened (although Nicaragua itself has been the target of an
American embargo of sorts). In this area at least, neither Reagan rhetoric nor policy stood in the way of normalized economic relations. Yet, American-Soviet trade
sank to its lowest modern levels largely because relations in general were so poor.

American-Soviet trade during the first Reagan administration illustrates the important fact that East-West trade tends to *reflect* rather than *create* an atmosphere of cooperation. The theory that hostile nations are more likely to develop friendlier political relations if they trade tends to ignore the reality of the postwar era. The United States has not been inclined to contribute to the economic well-being of the USSR when levels of tension have been high because there is a perceived connection between Soviet economic and military power. Only when tensions have been low has the United States been willing to engage actively in commercial relations with the Soviet Union.

Furthermore, Moscow has not significantly altered either its domestic or foreign policies for the sake of trade. To the contrary, Washington's attempts at linkage have been consistently repudiated by Moscow and have often backfired (e.g., the Jackson-Vanik amendment). In short, there is no evidence that the Soviets can be threatened or cajoled by trade to adopt policies favored by the United States.

To this calculus of East-West economic relations, the Gorbachev regime has introduced a new element—technological chauvinism.[8] Gorbachev and his associates reject the contentions that the USSR cannot compete technologically, and that it is permanently dependent on the West. In Gorbachev's view, the USSR is no more or less dependent on foreign technology than any other nation. In September 1985, Gorbachev expressed the view that while the USSR "would naturally not like to forgo those additional advantages that are provided by reciprocal scientific and technological cooperation" with the West, the Soviet Union would never become dependent on technology transfer.

Those selling the idea of the U.S.S.R. allegedly being consumed with thirst for U.S. technology forget who they are dealing with and what the Soviet Union is today. Having won technological independence after the Revolution, it has long been enjoying the status of a great scientific and technological power. . . .

We speak openly about our dissatisfaction with the scientific and technological level of this or that type of product. Yet we are counting on accelerating scientific and technological progress not through "a transfer of technology" from the U.S. to the U.S.S.R., but through "transfusions" of the most advanced ideas, discoveries and inventions from Soviet science to Soviet industry and agriculture, through more effective use of our own scientific and technological potential.[9]

This is not simply Soviet braggadocio, à la Stalin, although there is undoubtedly some element of wounded pride. The shift is neither simply the result of Soviet concerns about the political costs of Western imports, nor of the fear of becoming hostage to Western capitalism. Rather, Gorbachev's technological chauvinism derives from two new elements in Soviet thinking. First, some Soviet economists are concluding that technology imports tend to retard rather than stimulate Soviet research and development (R&D). The sectors that have relied most heavily on import substitution, such as the chemical industry, are now the most inefficient and backward because they lack an incentive to improve domestic R&D or management. In other words, Western technology may boost short-term output, but interfere with long-term development.

Second, Gorbachev's seemingly cavalier attitude toward American technology is part of a more profound change in Soviet policy. This shifts the Soviet focus of attention away from the United States, and redefines the traditional Soviet view of the West as an aggregated unit.

If this argument is correct, we can expect the Soviets to emphasize domestic R&D and become less dependent on technology transfer. They will also probably direct their trade more toward the capitalist and industrializing nations of the Third World, Western Europe, and Japan, and less toward the United States. In short, differentiated trade patterns with the West are likely to develop in tandem with technological chauvinism, thereby leading to an increasing emphasis on economic benefits for the Soviet economy and a decreasing emphasis on the politics of trade.

Human rights. The effect of this issue on international relations has traditionally not been well understood by Soviet leaders, a situation that enabled American leaders to manipulate human rights concerns to their advantage in the competition for world opinion. With the ascendancy of Gorbachev, the Soviet Union's position on human rights has been altered for maximum media impact.

Whereas Reagan has generally failed to use human rights to promote his nation's image in the world, Gorbachev began early on to take the initiative in this area. Only when confronted with the inevitability of hopeless situations, and the need to regain the initiative on human rights, did the Reagan administration act by withdrawing its support for the Duvalier and Marcos regimes, and moved in early 1986 toward a majority rule position on South Africa.

Meanwhile, Gorbachev made a number of clever moves that scored points in the Western media at relatively little cost to the USSR. Yelena Bonner, Andrei Sakharov's wife, was permitted to go to the West for eye and heart treatment; American-Soviet married couples, separated for years by Soviet policy, were permitted to reunite in the West; and, most dramatic of all, Anatoly Shcharansky, the symbol of human rights and religious repression in the Soviet Union, was released from prison and exchanged for Soviet bloc spies in Western prisons.

All these events received extensive press coverage in the international media. More important, these human rights cases, which for years had been ammunition in the American anti-Soviet arsenal, were defused. These acts do not portend a reversal of human rights policy in the USSR so much as a recognition by Gorbachev that some repression is more trouble than it is worth when weighed against its effect on world opinion. In fact, many observers contend that Gorbachev is a disciplinarian rather than a liberal reformer and that symbolic acts of humanitarianism belie the underlying repressiveness of the Gorbachev style. From the perspective of Soviet foreign policy, Gorbachev is making it very difficult for his critics to use the issue of human rights against the USSR. The Soviets lost little and gained much by releasing Bonner and Shcharansky. Unique cases such as these will not set precedents, and Gorbachev's actions are unlikely to create a rising tide of activism on human rights among the Soviet people.

It is very unlikely that human rights will occupy an important place in American-Soviet relations as long as Gorbachev is in charge. It also suggests that it will be increasingly difficult for an American President to mobilize world public opinion against the Soviet Union on this issue.

Prospects for American-Soviet Relations

While all of the issue areas undoubtedly influence American-Soviet relations in the near and long term, one crucial factor has yet to be considered. Specifically, Soviet history suggests that leadership changes can have a significant effect on Soviet foreign policy, regardless of what the United States does. The question is: What direction will Gorbachev take in American-Soviet relations?

Under Gorbachev, a new approach seems to be taking shape. Both leadership and policy changes indicate that Gorbachev was moving toward a differentiated view of the capitalist world that was a logical extension of post-Stalinist Soviet foreign policy.

Khrushchev abandoned Stalin's strict two-camp approach when he recognized the Third World (zone of peace), and Brezhnev's "peace campaign" recognized that on some issues American and West European interests did not always coincide. Gorbachev, picking up on a theme first introduced by Andropov, carried this process one step further to suggest that it is possible to differentiate among capitalists and engage in rapprochement with some and cold war with others.

The Gorbachev approach is one of a "differentiated" foreign policy that distinguishes between an anti-American policy and an anti-Western policy. Jerry Hough has described this as a "multipolar" as opposed to a bipolar strategy.[10] Such a policy permits the Soviet Union to normalize relations with West European and Third World capitalist states while continuing to confront the United States.

This is not a break with the Brezhnev approach, but neither is it merely a continuation of the Brezhnev "peace" campaign, which sought to divide the United States and its allies by demonstrating the USSR's peaceful intentions. Gorbachev is apparently prepared to make major concessions on key issues to improve relations with America's allies, which Brezhnev was unwilling to do.

First, let us consider how leadership changes in Gorbachev's first year of power support the theory that a new multipronged approach to Western relations is possible. Admittedly, many of the leaders were old, but replacements in key positions were more than actuarially motivated. The pivotal change was the removal of Gromyko as minister of foreign affairs in July 1985 and his replacement by the relatively inexperienced Eduard Shevardnadze. True, Gromyko did not retire, and he remained on the Politburo and assumed the ceremonial Soviet presidency. Nevertheless, day-to-day control of Soviet foreign policy was taken out of his hands. This signaled a change in the direction of Soviet foreign policy. Then, Gorbachev's leading rival for power Grigorii Romanov, the overseer of the military-industrial complex, was summarily dismissed by the Politburo. He was replaced, first as head of the arms sector and then in March 1986 on the Politburo, by Gorbachev loyalist Lev Zaikov.

In a surprise move at the 27th CPSU Congress, American Ambassador Anatoliy Dobrynin was made Party Secretary responsible for overseeing Soviet relations with nonruling parties and Western nations, replacing the long-time head of the CPSU International Department, Boris Ponomarev, who was retired. A few days prior to the Congress, the head of the Party's Department for Liaison with Workers' and Communist Parties, Konstantin Rusakov, was also retired.

Dobrynin's transfer to Moscow in charge of the party's foreign policy apparatus has a number of implications. First, his presence will bridge the traditional gap between party and government, making the implementation of any new policy easier. Second, it puts a leading Soviet expert on American policy at the center of the new policy-making team who can safely steer Soviet policy away from its American fixation. Third, Dobrynin's replacement, Yuri Dubinin, does not have the stature of his predecessor; hence, this change is a signal that American-Soviet relations will not be as central as they once were from the Soviet perspective.

Other significant leadership changes included the elevation of Aleksandr Yakovlev to the Secretariat.

Yakovlev, the head of the CPSU Propaganda Department, has a reputation as a virulent anti-American. The
appointment of Yuli Kvitstinsky, an arms negotiator in
Geneva, to replace the aged Vladimir Semyonov, as
Soviet ambassador to West Germany in March 1986,
was another important change. This was an indicator of
Gorbachev's intention to revitalize Moscow-Bonn relations and ease the strains that resulted from earlier
Soviet interference in the rapprochement between the
German Democratic Republic and the Federal Republic
of Germany. Also replaced were the ambassadors to
Spain and Japan. In the summer of 1986, virtually the
entire leadership of the foreign ministry was changed,
completing the removal of the Gromyko team. These
changes set the stage for a new cast of actors to implement the reorientation of Soviet foreign policy à la Gorbachev.

Actual policy changes toward the West in the first
year or so of Gorbachev's regime are more difficult to
identify. Some first signs, however, include Italian Premier Craxi's visit to Moscow in May 1985 and Gorbachev's visit to France in October. Foreign minister
Eduard Shevardnadze's visit to Japan in early January
1986 may be viewed as the opening move in what could
be a long-term strategy to restore political and economic
relations with Japan, and more specifically negotiating
the territorial disputes outstanding since World War II.

Gorbachev also took full advantage of the American bombing raid on Libya to drive the point home in
Europe that American actions can be a direct threat to
West European security. Gorbachev was careful not to
lend military support to Libya during the raid or to place
Soviet ships in jeopardy so as to avoid the possibility of
a direct confrontation with American military forces.

It is difficult to assess the damage to Gorbachev's
efforts rendered by the Soviet failure to inform Western

nations in a timely manner of the disaster at the Chernobyl nuclear reactor. Clearly, however, Soviet behavior renewed traditional views that the USSR was not as concerned with the welfare of its Western neighbors as might have been expected.

There are also indications that Soviet Third World policy may be shifting away from support for what Brezhnev called "revolutionary democracies" on the "noncapitalist" road to development and toward an emphasis on relations with the more important, but capitalist, industrializing nations, such as India.[11] If true, this would be the extension of a pattern that emerged in the last years of the Brezhnev regime, when the major recipients of Soviet nonmilitary aid were nations such as Turkey and Morocco. The difference would be that Gorbachev will be less likely to balance this support for capitalist nonaligned nations with support for revolutionary movements.

The problem posed by this shift in Soviet foreign policy for the Reagan administration and its successors is that American foreign policy could unwittingly contribute to the Soviet effort to divide the West by isolating the United States from Third World capitalist-oriented nations. Even though Reagan's efforts to overthrow the regime in Nicaragua received support in the US Congress, this policy has virtually no support among America's allies, and is universally condemned by the nonaligned nations of the world. No matter how bad the Sandinista regime may be, support for Reagan's pro-Contra policy by other world leaders would in fact recognize Washington's right to interfere in the internal affairs of any nation with which it had a disagreement. No Third World leader is likely to risk his domestic support or international stature for such a doctrine.

If Gorbachev takes an arms-length position vis-à-vis revolutionary democratic movements at the same time that Reagan intensifies his campaign against "Soviet-backed revolution," the gap between the myth and reality of Soviet behavior may become so wide that Reagan will find himself totally isolated from the world community while Gorbachev is accepted as a moderate, even liberal leader.

More important, Soviet concessions to West Germany on relations with East Germany, and to Japan on the Kurile Islands could drive wedges into the Western alliance, in particular if Reagan persists in "Stars Wars" and appears to be "dragging his feet" in response to new Soviet nuclear arms control proposals.

Finally, by removing the United States as the centerpiece of Soviet foreign policy, and by redefining Soviet security and economic needs without direct reference to the United States, Gorbachev neutralizes the most powerful leverage that the United States has had with Moscow: the Soviet leadership's own perception of the West as an indivisible unit.

If Gorbachev abandons the "unified imperialist camp" theory in favor of a sophisticated, differentiated world view, it will be all the more imperative that Reagan's rhetoric be transformed to realism. The real danger to American security is not the existence of two nuclear powers with different world views, but the possibility that the two superpowers will act in response to mistaken perceptions of each other's intentions.

To illustrate this point, when President Carter attempted to adopt a foreign policy that was not defined by the East-West conflict, Brezhnev destroyed any chance for a new dialogue when he played according to the old rules and sent Soviet troops into Afghanistan. The Soviets isolated themselves from the community of world opinion by this act and probably contributed to the rising tide of political conservatism in the West.

If Reagan were to involve American forces directly in a regional conflict, use military force in a way perceived by America's allies as contrary to their interests (such as in Libya), or insist on unrealistic conditions for an arms control agreement at the same time that Gorbachev is reorienting Soviet policy away from the traditional East-West confrontation model, the United States could find itself isolated, and actually contribute to a wave of pro-Soviet sentiment in Europe and the Third World. Gorbachev has significantly raised the price of rhetoric and increased the payoff for realism in American foreign policy. It remains to be seen whether Reagan understands and is willing to play by the new rules, which demand a commitment to diplomatic engagement and negotiated settlements based on mutual benefit.

Notes

1. George P. Shultz, "New Realities and New Ways of Thinking," *Foreign Affairs* 63 (Spring 1985): 711.

2. Adam Ulam, "Forty Years of Troubled Coexistence," *Foreign Affairs* 64 (Fall 1985): 29.

3. Coral Bell, "From Carter to Reagan," *Foreign Affairs* 63 (1985): 502–3.

4. In addition, the British government has raised questions about the deployment of shorter-range Soviet SS–21 and SS–22 missiles in Eastern Europe that could stall an INF settlement. And some French defense experts have raised questions about the effects of a complete American withdrawal of Pershing and cruise missiles on the US security commitment to Europe. However, such concerns would likely dissipate rapidly if Gorbachev uncouples completely the American-Soviet INF agreement from British and French strategic systems.

5. See, for example, Harold Brown, "Is SDI Technically Feasible?" *Foreign Affairs* 64 (1985): 435–54.

6. Richard Nixon, "Superpower Summitry," *Foreign Affairs* 64 (Fall 1985): 7.

7. Shultz, ''New Ways of Thinking,'' p. 713. It should be noted that Shultz confuses ''socialist'' internationalism with ''proletarian'' internationalism in this statement. Socialist internationalism only guides Soviet relations with other socialist states.

8. Philip Hanson, ''Technological Chauvinism in the Soviet Union,'' *Radio Liberty Research Bulletin,* RL 138/85, April 30, 1985.

9. *Time,* September 8, 1985, p. 25.

10. Jerry F. Hough, ''Gorbachev's Strategy,'' *Foreign Affairs* 64 (Fall 1985): 33–35.

11. For a discussion of this change, see Jerry F. Hough, *The Struggle for the Third World: Soviet Debates and American Options* (Washington, DC: Brookings Institution, 1985).

TERRORISM:
POLITICAL CHALLENGE
AND MILITARY RESPONSE

John F. Guilmartin, Jr.

> *Let terrorists be aware that when the rules of interna-*
> *tional behavior are violated, our policy will be one of*
> *swift and effective retribution.*
>
> —President Ronald Reagan,
> 27 January 1981

*E*VEN BEFORE HE ASSUMED OFFICE, Ronald
Wilson Reagan scored what many interpreted as a signal
victory over international terrorism; while inauguration
celebrations were still in progress 52 American hostages
held under the auspices of the Revolutionary Government of Iran, if not actually under its control, were
being flown to freedom. Their release came as the result
of negotiations timed so closely with Reagan's assumption of the Presidency as to leave little doubt of a causal
relationship.

During the campaign that preceded his election,
Reagan roundly criticized his Democratic opponent for
being soft on terrorism, scoring him for his handling of
the Iranian crisis. The basic import of Reagan's message was clear: indecisiveness encouraged international
terrorism; conversely, prompt and decisive military
action, if not a cure-all, was an effective antidote. The

decision of the Iranian Government to release the hostages, while ignominiously dropping the bulk of its demands, was widely perceived as de facto confirmation of the validity of this view.

Iranian revolutionary authorities had permitted American TV crews frequent, if not full, access to the streets of Tehran throughout the hostage crisis; their actions suggest they were thoroughly cognizant of the power of the American visual news media and that they used it frequently to communicate their demands and intentions to the American people and Government. A leadership so sensitive to vagaries of American public opinion could hardly have missed the effect of Reagan's campaign rhetoric on the American electorate—and on international opinion.

Whatever one's views of President Carter's effectiveness as a negotiator, the tactical failure of the Iranian rescue attempt was distressingly clear. When American aircraft, American plans, and American resolve dissolved in chaos at Desert One during the night of 24–25 April 1980, the competence of the US military establishment was called into question. The incoming administration would have to address the policy aspects of countering terrorism—and the military means of implementing that policy.

The failure of the hostage rescue focused public attention on the military component of a national policy to counter terrorism. Mounting such a military operation demands leadership, planning, intelligence, and imagination. The rest—firepower, numbers of troops and units, the performance parameters of aircraft and ships, logistic support, and so on—can be counted and evaluated statistically. A survey of such operations over the past decades underlines both the difficulties and the potential benefits of a credible military hostage rescue capability.

As Americans voted on 4 November 1980, ineptitude in the White House use of military force in countering terrorism, as tragically highlighted at Desert One, was seen by many Reagan supporters as a failure which the incoming administration would not repeat. Conversely, many Carter supporters believed he had erred by resorting to force at all and counterproductive bellicosity in America's response to terrorism.

The Problem

> *We have rhetoric on terrorism, we have policy statements, we don't have strategy.*
>
> —Brian Jenkins,
> Rand Corporation

Terrorism, like war, serves political goals. Its manifestations range from the actions of revolutionary groups and externally sponsored organizations attempting to overthrow governments to enforce their rule. "State" terror by totalitarian governments to stifle political dissent beyond their boundaries is, from the point of view of US military response, indistinguishable from nonstate terror. Our focus on the military response to terrorism dictates criteria of location rather than intent—where the act of state terror occurs rather than the purpose which it was intended to serve.

Similarly, the use of terror by internal political and religious groups to achieve their aims is a very real concern to any American Government—abortion clinic bombings are a case in point—but for constitutional reasons this is a police rather than a miliiitary problem. [1]

Our subject is not terror itself, but the use of military force by the United States to counter terror: the employment of American armed forces in a counterterrorist role overseas. [2] The problem includes the planned terrorist action that never occurs; the threat of force occupies a part of the spectrum of policy responses of terrorism, and the intimidating impact of threatened action is extremely difficult to judge. This remains true when the threat succeeds although the terrorist action is aborted. Almost by definition then, the most successful applications of military force against terrorism can never be demonstrated or proved, only inferred.

Clausewitz spent little time analyzing terror, for the technology of his day militated against its practice and terrorism was a minor part of the art of war during the age in which he wrote. Nevertheless, the paradox of the invisibility of success in the application of military force against terrorism is a profoundly Clausewitzian concept, the irony of which Clausewtiz himself would have richly appreciated.

Transnational terrorism's preferred stage is the world's public information media. The terrorist judges success largely by media attention and plans his operations accordingly. Why not judge him by his own criteria? The terrorist action that fails to rise above a given level of media attention has, by terrorism's own yardstick, failed.

Tracking incidents that exceed a given threshold of media visibility must limit and distort any analysis. But such a bias would be present in any event, and at least the data will be consistent. The selection of incidents for analysis was made with reference to a standard world news index, *Facts on File*. Any terrorist or counterterrorist incident involving US armed forces or military personnel reported in *Facts on File* was included in the core data base. This ensured a relatively consistent level of detail covered. *Facts on File* has a slight tendency to give more coverage to events affecting US citizens and interest; the bias is consistent, however, and is in line without emphasis on American military forces and US government policy.

The importance to terrorist organizations of American media reaction as a measure—some would say the measure—of the success or failure of their operations further validates the approach.[3] The froth of English-language signs which almost invariably caps foreign street demonstrations supporting the anti-American actions of terrorist groups verifies the importance of American news to the agitators.

The Threat

Americans don't seem to be able to grasp the politics and psychology of terrorism and hostage taking.
— Vice Admiral James Stockdale, US Navy
28 May 1981

Terrorist actions against American citizens and interests abroad fall into several broad functional categories:

Acts against selected individuals. Assassination and kidnapping, and the less media prominent blackmail and other acts of intimidation are common forms of terrorism. Military advisers, observers, and attachés are particularly targeted. Incidents in this category frequently involve intelligence activities and espionage and are hence removed from terrorism proper. The involvement of US military is almost entirely through the exposure of military individuals as targets; counter-measures are essentially passive and involve such techniques as variations in predictability of travel routes and daily routines, the use of protective equipment, security for automobiles, and so on. Because the perpetrator is normally the agent of a hostile political entity acting in pursuit of discernible political goals, active and aggressive intelligence and counterintelligence procedures have significant potential for identifying probable targets and anticipating specific actions. Although this is a legitimate military responsibility, the ends and means are not often addressed in the open press. Success or failure is difficult to measure based on examination of the public record; a decline in incidents is as likely to represent a change in terrorist strategy as success in the application of preventive measures.

The assassination of US Navy Captain George Tsantes, Jr., Naval Attaché to Greece, on 15 November 1983 is an example of terrorist actions of this type. Tsantes, shot at close range with a large-caliber pistol, may have been murdered in tribute to his effectiveness (he was fluent in Greek and was apparently highly effective in his dealings with Greek authorities) or he may have been killed in a purely symbolic act of anti-American terror.[4] The assassination of Lieutenant Commander Albert Schaufelberger in San Salvador on 25 May 1983 bore, at least superficially, the marks of a terrorist action directed against a particular individual selected for his military significance. Schaufelberger, a Navy special warfare officer, was the second ranking US military adviser to El Salvador at the time.[5] The shooting of US Army Major Arthur D. Nicholson on 24 March 1985 while on an inspection tour of Soviet military facilities in East Germany is an example of direct involvement by hostile military personnel in terrorist actions in this category.[6] Here, a uniformed officer pursuing his official duties was shot and killed by a Soviet soldier. The motivation of the Soviet and East German authorities in ordering Major Nicholson's death (if his shooting was not, as Soviet authorities alleged, accidental[7]) may have been to warn other US military observers to be less diligent, as a general message of intransigence to the American government, as a means of eliminating a particularly well-qualified and capable individual, or, more likely, as a combination of all of these. The only defense against acts of this sort is preventive anticipation through active and effective intelligence-gathering—although even that is frequently impossible.

Symbolic acts against individuals. Terror used against an individual, symbolizing the United States, is usually employed to bring pressure or discredit on the Government. The action against the individual is a means to an end rather than an end itself. This is a particularly difficult kind of terrorism to anticipate since the linkage between the victim's identity and hostile policy objectives is tenuous. Prominent individuals are clearly more at risk, but this is usually due to their symbolic importance rather than any functional threat which they pose to the terrorist organization. As with the previous category, direct involvement of military personnel except as targets is rare.

The difficulties posed by the employment of uniformed US personnel on foreign soil in the absence of a state of declared war has generally precluded exercising military force to secure the release of victims. The military response to this category of terrorist actions is therefore primarily one of individual training and preparation, more a matter of philosophy than of force employment.

The kidnapping of Army Brigadier General James L. Dozier by Italian Red Brigades terrorists is an example of military involvement in this type of terrorist action. Dozier's exemplary conduct in captivity, particularly in his adherence to the Code of Conduct, minimized the damage to US interests. Swift and efficient work of Italian intelligence and counterterrorist agencies not only secured Dozier's release but wrought considerable damage on the Red Brigades and their support infrastructure. The Red Brigades made an earlier, unsuccessful, attempt on a US Air Force general, only to have his apartment door slammed in their faces by his wife. These incidents highlight the importance of imbuing military personnel and their families with the reality of terrorist actions and the efficacy of common sense in countering them.

Symbolic acts against groups. As with symbolic acts against individuals, the terrorist is only marginally concerned with the identity of the target group. Terrorist actions in this category include aircraft hijackings and the seizure of government buildings to secure hostages. Here, direct military intervention has a potentially important role. The terrorist seeks concessions from the target government by threatening deadly violence against his hostages. The use of military and paramilitary units to secure their release by forcible means is an attractive alternative, though difficult to implement.

Although good intelligence can reduce vulnerability to terrorism of this kind, the disjuncture of target and objective limits its value. In effect, all American citizens abroad are at risk and the difficulty in identifying targets in time to take preventive action is immense. This spectacular Israeli success at Entebbe in July of 1976 and West German success at Mogadishu in June of 1977 established a high standard of performance against which subsequent hostage rescue attempts have been measured.[8] Media expectations of what elite military or paramilitary forces can accomplish place enormous pressures to achieve comparable results on public officials and the military units involved.

Acts of destruction against specific targets. Embassy bombings are the most visible terrorist action in this category. The close connection between target and political objectives and the high level of organization and force required place a premium on intelligence efforts to predict attack. Military involvement, though defensive, is direct: US Marine embassy guards are usually the final line of defense. The success of suicide truck bombers has highlighted our difficulty in formulating an effective military response to this category of terrorist threat.

Military Methods and Tactics

> *The maximum use of force is in no way incompatible with the simultaneous use of the intellect.*
>
>   —Clausewitz

Excluding the use of military personnel in an advisory capacity within areas of US civil jurisdiction,[9] military force and military forces may be used to counter terrorism in a number of basic ways.

Intelligence. Intelligence work is perhaps the most basic weapon of all, and one which is essential to the effective employment of other means. A military officer actively engaged in counterterrorist planning put it in these terms: ''The problem is ninety percent intelligence, maybe ninety-seven percent.''[10] In this connection, whatever the relationship between military intelligence resources and those of civilian agencies, any counterterrorist deployment or employment of military forces must be supported by a military intelligence analytical capability and, if possible, a militarily controlled collection capability. The use of intelligence in support of military operations is a special art, especially in support of the offensive application of counterterrorism.

The commander of a counterterrorist force must be supported by an intelligence staff which understands the problems confronting him and speaks his language. The operational intelligence staff must be capable of interpreting, in practical military terms, information made available from a wide variety of sources. Nor should the officers and NCOs involved be narrow specialists in tactical intelligence: they must be sensitive to the intelligence they do *not* have. This requires a broad background in the psychology and culture of the enemy and the population in the operational area.

The pertinent sort of intelligence is manpower-intensive, and people are expensive. First-class intelligence personnel take years to develop, particularly when knowledge of foreign languages and cultures is involved.[11] The application of military force must be undergirded by imaginative and exhaustive analysis of target data; planning for raids must consider anticipated conditions during ingress, egress, and recovery, and an assessment of the human element of friendly and enemy capabilities—all in addition to traditional order of battle analysis. Such factors as topography, moon phase and tidal state, meteorological conditions, and gross behavioral data such as traffic densities on particular roads can be vital. Unfortunately, history suggests this is an easy area in which to cut corners—but the penalties for such corner-cutting can be exceedingly high.[12]

Passive countermeasures. Closely linked to intelligence are such common-sense precautions as instructing military personnel not to travel in uniform and the construction of barricades around embassies and Government buildings. The Code of Conduct has direct applicability to terror hostage situations,[13] and its value in preconditioning individual response to unexpected situations should not be underestimated. The most basic countermeasure of all is instructing military personnel in the nature of the terrorist threat and training them in how to respond; the terrorist works on surprise and there is value in anything which enables friendly forces to anticipate terrorist actions. The traditional focus of our military forces on conventional conflict, reinforced by powerful cultural factors, has made us slow to respond in this area.

The Engagement:
An Analytical Overview

If you stay in the Garden of Flowers, you will smell flowers; if you stay in the Garden of Bombs, you will smell fire.

—Abdul Aziz Muhammad,
Mullah, Kuwait, Shiite
July 1985

It is virtually impossible to defend against if the driver is prepared to commit suicide.

—Lawrence S. Eagleberger,
Undersecretary of State for
Political Affairs
28 June 1983

The following is an analysis of the US military engagement with terrorism during the Reagan presidency to date. It was developed through examination of the public record. Inasmuch as the record on which the analysis is based is incomplete, it is tentative.

One may be winning the war in the shadows, but—at least to a freely elected democratic government—that victory becomes irrelevant if the war in the headlines is lost. Here, we are dealing explicitly with a war in which the enemy's objective is headlines, radio broadcast, and television newscast notice.

The US engagement with terrorism in Latin America is of very different character from that in the Middle East and the reasons are clearly cultural. Our engagements with terrorism in Europe and the Far East have their own distinctive flavors as well, and the roots of the differences go far deeper than the efficiency of European and Asian counterterrorist operations. There is a world of difference between a Salvadorean Communist assassination operation and an Islamic Jihad truck-bomb attack; a similar gulf exists between the collection, analysis, and exploitation of intelligence on the Italian Red Brigades and on the Popular Front for the Liberation of Palestine.

The terrorist dictates the battleground and determines the nature of combat. To assess terrorist operations, even on a narrowly technical, military level requires frequent reference to political and cultural considerations.

The US military engagements with terrorism fall into surprisingly clear-cut categories. Besides the contest between truck bomber and security countermeasure, they are

ASSASSINATION AND INDIVIDUAL KIDNAPPINGS. American military and Government personnel abroad cannot be hermetically sealed in bombproof vaults and bulletproof vests, safe against assault, without destroying their effectiveness.[14] The principal military response is individual training and indoctrination. Here we have done reasonably well. While the prime responsibility is in the hands of the military service, not the administration in power, failure casts blame on the political leadership, and rightly so. No news is good news.

SYMBOLIC BOMBINGS. Whether due to improvements in passive countermeasures at US overseas installations, the efficiency of counterterrorist agencies, or lack of hostile interest in this category of action, "symbolic" bombings of US military installations have been a relatively minor problem during the Reagan administration. The problem is much like that posed by the first category of terrorist action: indeed on at least one occasion the two were combined.[15] The only real counter is heightened awareness on the part of US military personnel and improved coordination with security agencies in host countries.

SEA MINING AND AERIAL ATTACKS. Although we do not ordinarily associate transnational terrorism with antishipping mines and air attack, Muammar Qaddafi and Ruhollah Khomeini clearly do.[16] A series of mining attacks in the Red Sea during the summer of 1984 was attributed to Libya, though the connection was never proven. Nor was the threat limited to conventional attack; in the wake of the Beirut Marine barracks bombing there were persistent press reports of light aircraft purchases by terrorists for suicide attacks.[17]

Here, also a surprise, we have been remarkably effective. Threats that suicide attacks by light aircraft were to be directed against US ships in the Mediterranean followed Navy shelling of shore targets in Lebanon. The Navy countered the suicide aircraft threat by deploying "Stinger" shoulder-held antiaircraft missiles to the Mediterranean and the threat never materialized.[18] A propos the high-performance threat, the Boeing E–3A Sentry is a remarkable instrument which we have used with considerable effect. In February of 1983 and again in March of 1984 E–3As were dispatched to assist in the defense of Sudanese airspace against Libyan-based intruders. Both here, and in deterring attack on Saudi Arabia, they were effective.[19] The fact that it augments the effectiveness of friendly air forces, rather than acting as a direct instrument of US military force, has reduced its media visibility and magnified its strategic impact. A disembodied and unarmed aerial platform orbiting 30,000 feet overhead is hardly a credible target for local anti-US demonstrators. Our success in countering terrorist mining operations was more equivocal, but it is noteworthy that such operations have not recurred at this writing. We are at our best in high-technology contest, and have done well here.

HIJACKINGS. Our concern goes beyond direct terrorist attack on military personnel to encompass all major hijackings affecting US citizens. The use of military force to secure the release of hostages is an omnipresent possibility, one which some of the American news media eagerly anticipate and implicitly demand. The absence of military action to secure the release of hostages can be a major political embarrassment. While hijackings and hostage seizures have presented the Reagan administration with some difficult challenges, the visibility of military action in this area has been low. Consequently, the Reagan administration has suffered little political damage from hostage-holding terrorists (the contrast with the Carter administration is stark), and it is impossible to draw any conclusions about military capacity. We may have effectively encouraged the early, nonviolent, resolution of one or more hostage situations through threatened military action, then again we may not; the public record simply does not make clear which.

There have, however, been a few suggestive glimmers: press reports asserted that US Army Delta Force operatives provided Venezuelan security forces with information from advanced infrared cameras, which enabled them to storm a hijacked Venezuelan airliner on Curacao airport on 31 July 1984, killing two hijackers and releasing 79 hostages unharmed.[20] Senior US Army officers were said to have accompanied Egyptian commandos to Malta prior to their assault on the hijacked Egyptian airliner on 24 November 1985 and to have provided "technical advice."[21]

SUICIDE BOMBINGS. Spectacular success in truck bombing attacks on US embassies, and particularly on the Marine Barracks in Beirut, has given transnational terrorism its greatest victories during the Reagan administration. It is also here that our response is weakest. Analysis of these attacks suggests that we have consistently misidentified the central issue of providing security to potential target installations as a technical rather than a human problem. Public debate has focused on considerations such as the number and placement of checkpoints, barriers, and barricades. This orientation is unproductive. The solution ultimately depends on security personnel who are trained to shoot to kill, who have the authority to do so and the training and judgment to know when. Tentative conclusions from analysis of the 20 September 1984 Beirut Embassy Annex bombing are particularly instructive in this regard.[22] Despite heightened awareness arising from previous such attacks, the truck bomber successfully breached all US security precautions; he was stopped only by the British Ambassador's bodyguards—the British bodyguards trained to shoot to kill, did so without hesitation when the occasion demanded.[23] Whether or not we have learned this lesson remains to be seen. We can take only limited comfort from the fact that there have been no major suicide bombing successes since the Beirut Embassy Annex bombing.

One aspect of this category of terrorist action, however, offers limited cause for optimism. In regarding as commonplace the skills necessary to drive a truck or car, we Americans focus on the fanatical dedication required to mount such an attack, overlooking the considerable technical skill which is also required. This is an indispensable ingredient of success, as even perfunctory analysis of the major car bombing attacks clearly shows. The Marine Barracks and Embassy Annex attacks displayed a particularly impressive level of sophistication in planning and skill in execution. The Embassy Annex attacker displayed a high level of situational awareness and tactical skill in the manner in which he passed the final Phalangist checkpoint. History suggests that the number of individuals in any society who possess the dedication and the technical skills needed to pull off a successful suicide bombing attack is very small. The initial Japanese kamikaze attacks in WWII were mounted by experienced fighter pilots who became frustrated with the lack of success of the inexperienced bomber crews they were escorting. These experienced aviators achieved an incredible success rate: the first five kamikaze attackers got at least four hits. These not only hit aircraft carriers (the preferred target) but hit the carriers' aircraft elevators—the spot calculated to cripple the carrier's operation most.[24]

ATTACKS WHICH DID NOT OCCUR. The categories of terrorist attack which did not emerge from the data were in some ways more noteworthy than those which did. The lack of visible military engagement with North Korean terrorist squads merits our attention, as does the surprisingly low level of terrorist engagement with US interests in the Far East and Africa. Another significant nonevent was the uneventful course of the 1984 Los

Angeles Summer Olympic games. Though visible military involvement in counterterrorist precautions was peripheral to the security effort coordinated by the Los Angeles Police Department and the FBI, the high visibility of the games as a potential terrorist target made the evident success of counterterrorist measures particularly gratifying.[25]

SHOW OF FORCE. In 1986 US naval forces engaged Libyan forces in the Gulf of Sidra frankly to punish the Qaddafi regime for its support of terrorism.[26] In a series of actions which produced remarkably one-sided damage for the size and power of the forces involved, US naval forces were engaged by Soviet-supplied Libyan SA–5 long-range surface-to-air missiles and patrol boats. The US forces were reported to have sunk three patrol boats and put in two antiradiation missile attacks against SA–5 radar installations.

The effectiveness of this type of response remains to be seen. Certainly, it does not yet appear to have had a significant adverse impact on Qaddafi's popularity in Libya. Already highly sensitive to assassination threats before the US show of force, he remains so. Similarly, the flexing of military muscle produced unaccustomed bipartisan congressional support and a surge in public approval for President Reagan.

GENERAL RETALIATION. The Navy's 4 December 1983 raid on Syrian positions in Lebanon and the *New Jersey's* 16-inch guns pounding Syrian positions (or so it was hoped) in the Shouf Mountains have produced generally disappointing results. Some commentators argued, with justification, that these actions were counterproductive. The Reagan administration's evident abandonment of this category of response is perhaps significant.

SPECIFIC ACTS OF RETALIATION. In contrast to the previous category of response, specific US military retaliation against pinpointed objectives have been highly effective. The brilliantly improvised forcing down of the *Achille Lauro* hijackers in Sicily was undeniably a high point of America's military engagement with transnational terrorism. Not only did it produce almost uniformly positive media reaction, it has surely caused problems of morale and motivation among terrorist cadres. Retaliation by capture of the perpetrator is a language universally understood in the Middle East, and even if Mohammed Abbas Zaida succeeded in evading American and Italian criminal prosecution, his aura of invulnerability was badly tarnished.[27] The technical skills and tactical judgment of USS *Saratoga's* air wing and ship's company (and those of the faceless staff personnel who conceived and sold the plan) turned Ronald Reagan's fury over the murder of a wheelchair-bound American tourist from impotent seethings to manifest meting out of just punishment.

The down side of the incident is the image of Carabinieri and SEALS, armed to the teeth and on a hair trigger, confronting one another across the Sigonella airbase ramp while their superiors debated with one another and their political superiors in Washington and Rome issues which might have been dealt with in advance or delegated downward for resolution on the spot. The general impression is that US operational planning and airmanship were brilliant, but that political suavity at the point of contact was (to put it charitably) lacking at the senior line officers present.

United States military forces have an impressive capacity for improvisation in the area of applying conventional forces to unconventional operations. While the Navy has enjoyed the most dramatic success in this area, the counterterrorist use of USAF "Sentry" AWACS aircraft merits favorable comment as well.

HOSTAGE RESCUE RAIDS. Too much should not be made of our failure to duplicate Entebbe or Mogadishu; these were fiendishly difficult operations which succeeded in no small measure because they embodied tactics which had never been tried before and hence took the terrorists by surprise.[28] More to the point would be some concrete demonstration that we have assimilated the lessons of the abortive Iranian rescue attempt and taken measures to prevent recurrence of the command and leadership problems which led to its failure. The author sees no evidence that we have done so.

Conclusion

We've got the scalpel, but we're putting it in the hands of a bear.
> —Colonel August G. Jannerone, USAF
> US Air Force Member
>   Department of State Senior Seminar
> 31 March 1986

Evaluating the success or failure of an American presidential administration in its military engagement with terrorism by tracking the high points of the struggle through news media reports—by definition themselves terrorist victories—gives a distorted picture. Much of the war against terror goes on out of media view; this is particularly true of success.

In two areas there can be little doubts. First, Reagan takes terrorism seriously, and that seriousness is shown by more than words. Under the Reagan administration, the number of troops dedicated to special operations, whose roles and missions include counterterrorism, has increased from 10,000 to 15,000 and the money budgeted for our special operations capability was increased to $1.2 billion from $1 billion from 1985 to 1986.[29] Second, Ronald Reagan and his administration understand the language of the news media very well indeed. Whatever success they may have had in the war of shadows, transnational terrorists have found in Reagan a formidable opponent in the war of headlines. Whatever weaknesses he may have shown in understanding the complex roots of terrorist motivations have been more than compensated for in his confident grasp of America's values, aspirations, and hopes and fears.

The record suggests that the Reagan administration should be given high marks for recognizing the essential nature of terrorism, for taking it seriously, and for being decisive when military action was taken. Conversely, this decisiveness has not, in the author's view, always been backed by a sound appreciation of the operational factors involved in the application of force, nor have our military forces always shown a high level of competence in turning it into action.

Our weakness in planning is most apparent where local political and cultural considerations are a major factor, as they almost always are, and where we as a nation do not understand them, as we almost always do not. The commitment of US Marines in an attempt to stabilize the tangled politics of Lebanon, exposing them to terrorist attack in the process, is the most pointed demonstration of this weakness. However, the Reagan administration is hardly unique among Presidential administrations in its difficulties in comprehending the Middle East and that the problem is at least as much military as political. When the Marines went into Beirut, more than one cynical old soldier of the author's acquaintance commented that we were putting in just enough troops to get us into trouble and not enough to get us out of it. Here we are dealing with a military advisory responsibility of the most basic kind. In this context, the points made earlier concerning the pivotal importance of military intelligence in the struggle against transnational terrorism strike home with particular force.

Another factor which gives cause for concern is the lack of any evidence that the inter-service rivalries which contributed to the Iranian rescue fiasco of April 1980 have abated, let alone been brought under control.[30] There is little doubt that the military units which compose the cutting edge of our counterterrorist raiding capability are very sharp. While the author can offer nothing beyond educated speculation seasoned with a degree of military experience, this comment was particularly prompted by the Navy's SEAL capability and USAF special operations deployment assets; the lack of public visibility of the Army's Delta Force—if that is in fact its name—is also an encouraging sign.

But while the individual components of our counterterrorist order of battle apparently have extremely high standards of competence, how their employment might be planned, by whom, and according to what criteria remain very much in question. Despite professionalism at the raiding team level, the manner of the team's deployment is wanting. Evidence that the Army is committing significant resources in an attempt to duplicate a long-range air-refuelable helicopter capability—which the Air Force perfected over a decade and a half ago—is cause for alarm. Too many cooks spoil the broth. In addition, the author doubts whether the Army fully appreciates the immense planning and logistical differences between sustained long-range air refuelable helicopter operations and the simple use of air refueling to extend tactical radius of action.[31]

The most basic concern, however, is the lack of compatibility of the US military officer promotion system[32] with the requirements of special operations in general and counterterrorist operations in particular.[33] The transnational terrorist is a wily opponent and long tenure is required to develop the requisite skills to combat him.[34] Certainly, the terrorist organizations which conduct attacks on American citizens and property take full advantage of the hard-won experience of their operatives and do not routinely rotate them into assignments in—say—personnel administration or public affairs for career broadening. The military personnel system, particularly the officer promotion system, is a weak link, in this analyst's view, in our military response to terrorism.

In sum, the Reagan administration's visible use of military force to counter terrorism has been reasonably effective. Problems which appeared early have not resurfaced, and in some areas we have done well. But any long-term solution rests on a fundamental reform of the military instrument, and there is no evidence that the Reagan administration has seriously considered this. Clearly, the services themselves have not. Our ability to conduct a long-range hostage rescue seems little improved over that which prevailed during the Carter presidency, additional infusions of funds notwithstanding. The problem is fundamentally a human one of leadership and training, and until our defense establishment appreciates and learns to exploit this, we are at risk.

Notes

1. See Major William R. Farrell, US Air Force, "Military Involvement in Domestic Terror Incidents," *Naval War College Review*, July–August 1981, pp. 53–66, especially pp. 55–56;

Constitutional and statutory law severely restricts the use of military forces in domestic situations, principally through Title 18, Section 1385, of the US Code, which prohibits the use of the Army and Air Force as a *posse comitatus* force; that is, to aid civil authorities in enforcing the law. Stemming from 1878 legislation affecting only the Army, the act was expanded to include the Air Force in 1956; though the applicability of *posse comitatus* to the Navy and Marine Corps was a matter of debate, the Secretary of the Navy applied the doctrine by directive in 1974. The degree to which the doctrine affects the Coast Guard in time of peace is unclear.

2. I have excluded the use of paramilitary forces by agencies other than the armed services. I have also omitted consideration of terrorist groups advocating national independence for Puerto Rico. While these groups have embraced the assassination of US military personnel as a tactic, their suppression is primarily a police and FBI problem rather than a military one.

3. For an extreme expression of this viewpoint which implies active, if unwitting, media abettance of terrorism, see Ernest W. Lefevre, *Revolutionary Terrorism and US Policy* (Washington, DC: Ethics and Public Policy Center, 1983): "The terrorist movement receives considerable aid from the Western media, which provide the visibility that terrorists thrive on. Some terrorist acts ... are timed to get maximum TV coverage via satellite .... Regrettably, the media revel in violence and brutality and they tend to romanticize the terrorist."

4. "US Attache Killed in Athens," *Washington Post*, 16 November 1983, p. 1.

5. "US Advisor Slain in Salvador," *Long Island Newsday*, 26 May 1983, p. 6.

6. *Facts on File* 54, no. 3214 (29 March 1985): 222–3.

7. The Soviet apparatus enjoyed considerable success in portraying Major Nicholson's actions in a sinister light (for example, the widespread repetition in US media reports of Soviet statements which emphasized the fact that he was wearing camouflage fatigues; few American papers bothered to note that this was the standard duty uniform) and to obscure the fact that the inspection visit during which he was shot was guaranteed by Soviet-US agreement. The refusal of Soviet authorities on the spot to permit Major Nicholson's NCO to give him first aid suggests premeditation as well.

8. For a summary of such actions, Richard Halloran and David K. Shipler *(New York Times)* "Terrorism: A War of Shadows," *Houston Chronicle*, 1 December 1985, p. 30.

9. For example, special Forces troopers have been used by the Nuclear Regulatory Agency to evaluate the security of nuclear power plants against terrorist attack, according to Matthew L. Wald, "Green Berets Check Nuclear Plants," *New York Times*, 12 September 1983, p. 1.

10. Personal communication to the author, 14 March 1986.

11. The provisions of DOPMA, the Defense Officer Program Management Act, as mandated by Congress and interpreted by the uniformed services, militates against the long-term stability essential to effectiveness. The insistence of the Army and Air Force, in particular, on selecting officers for promotion on a "best qualified" basis combines with "whole man" evaluation criteria and the up-or-out system to preclude sustained service in a single career field. The officer who insists on remaining in intelligence runs the serious risk of finding himself on the street without retirement benefits after a 13- to 15-year career.

12. Consider, for example, one critical detail among the many overlooked in planning the Iranian rescue attempt. The final chain of events which culminated in disaster was initiated by an unanticipated low-altitude visibility restriction to night flying. The phenomenon in question was well known to aircrews with operational experience in the area, some of whom were readily accessible to US intelligence.

13. The Code of Conduct is a list of six articles, established by Presidential order, to be followed by uniformed military personnel in the event that they become prisoners of war. Originally developed in response to the poor behavior of some US prisoners in Chinese captivity during the Korean conflict, the Code of Conduct was validated by the experience of our POWs in Vietnam. Despite some problems with overly rigid interpretation, the overwhelming majority of our former North Vietnam POWs strongly support the Code of Conduct and oppose attempts to weaken it.

14. For example, Steve Robinson and J. Ross Baughman, "Under Fire in El Salvador," *Life* 4, no. 6 (June 1981), and David Friend, "Embassy on the Front Line of Terror: In Kuwait, US Diplomats Take a Crash Course in Self-Defense," *Life* 8, no. 13 (December 1985): 130–86.

15. In a 9 August 1985 bomb attack on Rhein-Main Air Force Base, Germany, access to the installation was gained by means of documents taken from an Army Sp–4 who was kidnapped and murdered, according to Allen Cowan, "Blast Kills 2 at US Air Base in W. Germany," *Dallas Morning News*, 9 August 1985, p. 1; William Drozdiak, "Car Bombings, Slaying Tied," *Washington Post*, 14 August 1985, p. 17.

16. *Facts on File* 44, no. 2280 (27 July 1984): 542; no. 2281 (3 August 1984): 560; no. 2273 (8 June 1984): 402.

17. "Terrorists Said to Get Aircraft to Hit Marines," *Baltimore Sun*, 21 January 1984; there were reports of highly maneuverable Grumman F–33 trainers being "obtained by groups in Lebanon."

18. Michael Getler, "U.S. Moves to Avert Kamikaze Air Attacks," *Washington Post*, 21 January 1984, p. 1.

19. *Facts on File* 44, no. 2262 (23 March 1984): 197.

20. *Facts on File* 44, no. 2281 (3 August 1984): 560; Miles Latham, "Cameras Doom Sky Pirates," *New York Post*, 4 August 1984, 4.

21. The same reports said that the services of Delta Force were offered but refused, *Facts on File* 45, no. 2349 (29 November 1985): 881–2; Loren Jenkins, "US Officers Gave Support in Raid on Jet," *Washington Post*, 25 November 1985, p. 1.

22. An explosive-laden Chevrolet "Blazer" station wagon navigated concrete barriers and small arms fire before detonating in front of the US Embassy Annex in the Beirut suburb of Aukar at 1144 hours, 20 September 1984, leaving a 15-foot crater. The yield of the bomb was estimated at 400 pounds of TNT equivalent. Damage to the building was heavy and early estimates of a death toll of eight, including the driver of the vehicle, were later raised to 23. US Ambassador Reginald Bartholomew and British Ambassador David Meirs, who was visiting when the attack occurred, were slightly wounded; see *Facts on File* 44, no. 2288 (21 September 1984): 685–6; Robert Fisk, "23 Killed in Beirut Blast," *London Times*, 21 September 1984.

Using false Dutch diplomatic plates, the vehicle passed guards at a Phalangist checkpoint near the annex by a ruse before negotiating concrete barricades on the access road; see "US Beirut Embassy Bombed," *Philadelphia Inquirer*, 21 September 1984, p. 1. Early reports that the driver had exchanged fire with guards were later discounted; however, the Phalangists began shooting and alerted security forces nearer the annex, who also opened fire. The British Ambassador's bodyguards, posted at the front of the building, engaged the vehicle with submachinegun fire and were credited by most observers with shooting the tires out and probably killing the driver; see Charles P. Wallace, "Path of Suicide Bomber Pieced Together in Beirut," *Los Angeles Times*, 22 September 1984, p. 1. The vehicle swerved into a parked car and detonated short of the building. The Embassy Security Chief rushed out the front of the building on hearing gunfire and was blown 20 yards into the snack bar, though not fatally injured. Had the driver succeeded in reaching his apparent target, the underground parking garage beneath the Annex, the bomb would almost surely have collapsed the building, causing far more casualties.

23. Though we cannot be certain who shot out the truck's tires and killed the driver, it is unlikely that either would have happened had the British ambassadorial bodyguards not been present and—a more subtle but equally important point—posted at the point of maximum danger.

24. At the Battle of Leyte Gulf in late October 1945. There is evidence that the fifth attacker hit a carrier previously struck by one of the other four.

25. In 1984, several weeks before the 23rd Summer Games were scheduled to begin, on 10 and 11 July the governments of Malaysia, Singapore, Sri Lanka, South Korea, Zimbabwe, and China acknowledged the receipt of death threats to their Olympic athletes. The threats were contained in letters mailed from Virginia, purporting to be the work of the Ku Klux Klan. On the 11th, State Department Spokesman Alan Romberg pointed out peculiarities in the syntax and grammar of the threat letters which indicated that their authors were not native English speakers; the letters bore, he said, "all the hallmarks of a disinformation campaign." The *Washington Post* reported that the Department of Defense had spent $35 million on security for the games, including the loan of 77 helicopters for surveillance and medical evacuation; see *Facts on File* 44, no. 2283 (17 August 1983). The games opened as scheduled on 29 July and closed uneventfully on 12 August. The closest thing to a terrorist incident reported during the games involved a Los Angeles Police Department officer who confessed to planting a bomb on a bus so that he could take credit for disarming it and be a "hero"; see *Facts on File* 44, no. 2283 (17 August 1984).

26. William L. Chaze, "O.K., Muammar, Your Move," *US News and World Report*, 7 April 1986, pp. 22–25.

27. In the early morning hours of 10 October 1985, Egyptian president Hosni Mubarak announced that the Palestinian hijackers of the Italian cruise ship *Achille Lauro*, who had murdered US citizen Leon Klinghofer, and then surrendered to Egyptian authorities, had departed Egypt. In reality, the four gunmen, joined by Mohammed Abbas Zaida, later identified by US intelligence as their operational commander, were still in Egypt. They had been provided with an Egypt Boeing 737 at Al Maza airfield northeast of Cairo with plans for an early evening departure. American intelligence became aware

of this situation and plans were initiated, apparently within the National Security Council, to intercept the aircraft and force it down at a location where the hijackers could be taken into US custody.

When the Egyptian airliner took off, filed for Algiers, US forces acquired the aircraft on radar and maintained track. In the meantime, US diplomatic initiatives were underway with Tunisian and Greek authorities to deny the aircraft landing rights. At 2330 hours a US navy carrier-based E–3A "Hawkeye" radar warning and surveillance aircraft directed an intercept off Crete by a formation of F–14 Tomcat fighters from USS *Saratoga*. According to subsequent press reports, an accompanying Navy EA–6B electronic warfare aircraft successfully jammed attempts by the Egyptian flight crew to radio Egyptian authorities, leaving the Egyptian captain with no alternative but to follow orders from the US fighters and land at the joint US/Italian NATO airbase at Sigonella, Sicily. The Egyptian aircraft was closely followed on landing by two US C–141s bearing, according to press reports, SEAL Team Six. To preserve security, Italian officials were not informed of the plan until the Egyptian airliner and its escort were in Italian airspace. A short, uneasy, standoff between SEALs and carabinieri took place on the ground at Sigonella while Italian and American authorities debated questions of national sovereignty and jurisdiction. American authorities yielded custody of the Palestinians to the Italian Government on the understanding that the hijackers would be tried for murder; see John Walcott, "Getting Even: How America Did It," *Newsweek*, 21 October 1985, pp. 20–21; George Russell, "The US Sends a Message," *Time*, 21 October 1985, pp. 22–29.

28. For a concise overview, see Halloran and Shipler, "Terrorism: A War of Shadows."

29. Keller, "Conflict in Pentagon"; this, of course, is based on publicly released figures.

30. By all accounts inter-service squabbling over whose pilots would fly the RH–53 helicopters used in the attempt and the ultimate selection of Marine pilots without experience in long-range operations played a major role in the failure; so did the shockingly apparent ignorance of the basic facts of air transport operations of the Army commander of the raiding force, Colonel Charles Beckwith. In published accounts Beckwith expressed surprise at being required to determine the weight of his raiding force and its equipment; see George Christian, "Beckwith and the Iran Raid," *Houston Chronicle*, 27 November 1983, pp. 18, 20.

31. A personal opinion based on experience in long-range air refueling helicopter operations encompassing operations planning, logistic planning, and execution.

32. It would be incorrect to say "the assignment and promotion system." The two are effectively inseparable. Officer assignments in today's armed forces are all too frequently made simply as a necessary means of qualifying the individual for promotion. To assign an officer against a billet simply because it is an important job and the applicant is well qualified for it is all too often simply another way of saying that the job is nonpromotable.

33. While preparing the final draft of this article the author learned that a junior former military colleague, a US Air Force captain, had been passed over for promotion to major for the second time and would be out of the Service by October of 1986 after over 12 years service. The individual in question is the HC–130 standardization/evaluation pilot of a Rescue Wing. The implicit presumption that a wing commander would formally designate as his most highly qualified pilot in a primary unit weapons system an individual who was not deemed of sufficiently high quality to retain in Service is breathtaking. This situation is not unique.

34. This is not a particularly new or novel observation; see Major General Edward G. Lansdale, US Air Force (Ret), "The Opposite Number," *Air University Review* 23, no. 5 (July–August 1972): 21–32.

THE BURDEN OF GLOBAL DEFENSE: SECURITY ASSISTANCE POLICIES OF THE REAGAN ADMINISTRATION

Roy A. Werner

*T*HE ROLE OF SECURITY ASSISTANCE in national security policy is a function of an administration's objectives and recipient states' demand for weapons and other forms of military assistance. Operationally, such assistance is usually provided directly, from suppliers to recipient; this bilateral relationship is the primary mechanism through which we attempt to "influence" other states. But the conditions under which a supplier or a recipient gains influence over the other state are uncertain. The mode of transfer—gift, subsidized credit, or cash—is obviously important in terms of the amount of influence achieved. Other competitive variables include alternative suppliers, threat perceptions, political elites, and objectives.

Any analysis, therefore, must include the interaction between supplier and recipient states, the ambiguity of both "commitments" and "influence," and the effect upon actual military capabilities. The greatest uncertainty is determining the likely consequences of providing, or refusing to provide, such assistance. Hence, there can be no distinct "security assistance policy"; instead, there are many bilateral and regional policies. At best, then, hypotheses regarding security assistance policies have a limited empirical base; more definitive case history comparisons than are available today are required for a theoretically valid model of the process.

Although generalizations about security assistance policies are difficult given the limitations of aggregate data to illuminate specific case histories, some tentative conclusions may be drawn from tracking the budget flows, the declaratory policy of an administration, supplier-recipient interactions, and the evolution of security assistance as an instrumentality of US foreign policy. This essay reviews the record of the Reagan and Carter administrations and defines how security assistance (excluding commercial sales or covert assistance) is utilized by the United States.

Policy-makers believe that security assistance is an essential foreign policy tool. Arms aid helps assure access, a necessary but insufficient precondition to achieving influence. As Lieutenant General Philip C. Gast, Director of the Defense Security Assistance Agency (DSAA), has noted,

The last four years have demonstrated how vital security assistance is in the shaping of our foreign policy, the resolution and containment of conflicts, and the improvement of our relations with a large number of nations around the world.[1]

President Reagan expressed his belief in the importance of security assistance when he signed foreign-aid legislation in 1985:

At a time of defense reductions, we must pay particular attention to our most compelling international security needs.[2]

Armaments, like ideology, follow rather than precede political conflicts and their supply may terminate or lessen as relations change. This is evident in the case of the superpowers: witness the Soviet Union's difficulties with Egypt, Indonesia, and Somalia; or US failures in Iran and South Vietnam. The underlying tensions thus predate the shipment of armaments, but such shipments may exacerbate or dampen these tensions. The essential policy question is whether influence can be acquired or increased through arms transfers, and, if so, can this influence contribute to the achievement of American objectives by such transfers? A review of past transfers suggests several objectives: maximize influence with recipients; arm friends and allies against the Soviets or their proxies; deter aggression; minimize arms shipped and channel transfers into less "provocative" items; improve US power projection capabilities and theater commonality; enhance stability; influence domestic constituencies; and lessen the incentive to acquire nuclear weapons. Obviously security assistance may serve several of these objectives simultaneously.

Reagan Policies

The Reagan administration took office committed to increasing security assistance funds. It rejected the Carter administration's characterization of arms transfers "as an exceptional foreign policy implement" and instead emphasized the role of arms transfers as "an essential element of global defense posture and an indispensable component of foreign policy." Relatively quickly it rescinded the so-called "leprosy letter" which forbade embassy assistance to American sales representatives overseas. Consistent with this change in policy, annual dollar values in security assistance have increased sharply: Military Assistance Programs (MAP) and International Military Education and Training Programs (IMET) grant components grew from $306.3 million for 63 nations in fiscal year 1982 to $861.2 million for nearly 90 nations in fiscal year 1985, a 196-percent increase. Between 1981 and 1985, the three primary military aid programs, Foreign Military Sales (FMS), MAP, and IMET averaged a 20-percent annual increase.

In response to the 1983 Carlucci Commission report, Congress in fiscal year 1985 shifted from a loan guarantee program (that was off-budget and confusing) to one offering both concessional credits at reduced rates and market rate credits. Clearly, the Reagan administration perceived arms transfers as an under-valued tool of diplomacy that it intended to utilize fully. It is important to note, however, that the Reagan team has not returned to the *laissez faire* policies of the Nixon-Ford administrations. Rather, the current policies are a pragmatic and perhaps inevitably *ad hoc* approach seemingly guided by an ideological viewpoint that also expresses concern with such broader policy goals as economic development.

The cornerstone of the Reagan approach is the President's directive of 8 July 1981, which states that, "applied judiciously," arms transfers can deter aggression, demonstrate US commitment, foster stability, and enhance US forces operational and production effectiveness.[3] This document dictates a case-by-case approach to approving arms shipments. These considerations include the nature of the military threat to the recipient state, the receiving state's participation in collective security arrangements, possible effect on US allies that may be hostile to one another, the absorptive capability of the nation (both militarily and financially), and, of course, US security interests. These factors are appropriate; given the shifting sands of international politics, arms transfers may occur more as a matter of opportunity than as a function of a long-term strategic design.

The change in security assistance policy was clearly signaled by F–16 aircraft deliveries to Pakistan, South Korea, and Venezuela. These deliveries of the United States Air Force's inventory fighter aircraft to those allies is the most dramatic early difference between the Carter and Reagan administrations and, one surmises, was designed to underscore the shift in policy.

Earlier, the Carter administration was troubled both by the growing technological sophistication of arms exported and by the increasing aggregate volume of the arms trade. It therefore turned to assessing regional military balances as a significant factor in policy decisions. The official responsible for directing arms transfer policies, Lucy Benson, argued that the desirability of preventing the introduction of sophisticated weapons into a region justified the rejection of advanced aircraft transfers to Pakistan (and by implication to South Korea).[4] A more complete assessment would note that Pakistan believes aerial power is essential to counter India's manpower advantage. Regional stability may sometimes be enhanced by providing technologically advanced weaponry and, in this case, by rejecting the Pakistan request, the United States was openly confirming a tilt towards India on the subcontinent.

Having changed priorities on advanced aircraft, the Reagan administration soon thereafter sought removal of the ban on arms sales to Argentina and Chile and won approval for AWACS (Airborne Warning and Control System) sales to Saudi Arabia. Approval or rejection of an armaments request by another nation will continue to be perceived as an important indicator of the bilateral relationship. This ''fact'' reflects the relative lack of other visible policy tools.

Beyond the obvious political indications, arms transfers have important secondary effects. Increasingly, coproduction and countertrade are important aspects of arms transfers simply because they can help generate additional employment and may enable recipients to acquire technology. In an era when economic benefits are among the most tangible of political assets, foreign leaders carefully evaluate military sales. The new elite in many emerging nations are business leaders and technocrats; thus industrial modernization and trade are significant in any "deal." Finally, in those societies where the military hold important governmental positions, arms transfers may define the status of the bilateral relationship.

Beneath the rhetoric, there is more continuity in American security assistance than many suspect. This is evident in the refusal of successive administrations to export nuclear, chemical, and strategic delivery systems. Further, only the closest of allies have received advanced aircraft. Indeed, this continuity is evident in the behavior of the Carter administration, which quietly moved away from its original policy statements. The former assistant director of the Arms Control and Disarmament Agency during the Carter administration acknowledges that "the implementation was never as pure as the rhetoric."[5] Few now recall that within a month of Carter's Presidential Directive 13 policy declaration, aircraft were sold to Saudi Arabia. International political reality and domestic factors quickly intervened to produce "case-by-case" policy outcomes that were at variance with the 19 May 1977 presidential statement. In reality, the policy of arms restraint collided with growing global market demand for increased armaments. To retain access and influence, actual policies were changed. Thus, both administrations share the conviction that arms transfers are an essential tool of US policy, focus on the perceived benefits more than the dangers, and view the global scene in broad East-West confrontational terms (which admittedly became harsher after the USSR invasion of Afghanistan).

The Reagan administration differences are largely philosophical. It is therefore necessary to outline the Carter administration's policies in order to understand the evolution of Reagan's policies. Initially, some members of the Carter team considered the arms trade morally corrupt, threatening to both domestic and regional stability. The Reagan team, on the other hand, views a country's desires to arm as symptoms of its political insecurity and believes that arms can help to deter and to stabilize. As then Under Secretary for Security Assistance James L. Buckley told Congress, "Weakness attracts the predator."[6] As a result, under Reagan, several Carter restrictions ended, yielding the annual ceiling for arms exports, avoidance of being the first supplier of advanced armaments into a region, restrictions on advanced weapons "solely for export," a limitation on recipients' coproduction opportunities, denial of requests for third-country transfers, and the so-called "leprosy letter" prohibiting assistance to American manufacturers.

The Carter administration's Presidential Directive 13 specified that controls could be waived only through a presidential exception or where the President determined the transfer was essential to "maintain a regional balance." Although these exceptions echo the justifications often cited for arms transfers, few individuals apparently were prepared to argue the merits of such policies with the chief executive. Difficulties with the annual ceiling approach arose quickly, including exemptions for NATO, Japan, and ANZUS nations, commercial direct sales, and exclusion of military construction, training, and other "non-lethal services."[7]

In reality, arms sales increased during the Carter years. Anyone monitoring the congressional notifications and DSAA could discern these increases. This occurred despite the fact that the Carter team's refusal to sell advanced weaponry led to rejected sales and third-country transfer requests, especially the Wild Weasel electronic system proposed for Iran, F–16 fighter aircraft sales to several nations, and the halting of Sweden's sale to India of Viggen aircraft (eventually India bought Jaguars from the United Kingdom). Obviously such refusals had a negative economic effect for the companies that produce these weapons systems and for the localities concerned. Perhaps more important, these examples illustrate the problems of rejecting friends' requests and maintaining influence with foreign governments.

Actual case histories, such as the Rand assessment of lost Latin American markets in the 1960s are not always available when policy-makers must decide.[8] Hence, as in so many security assistance issues, case-by-case judgment is necessary. The ban on coproduction was equally unenforceable given recipient-country desires. Like the denial of advanced technology, both limitations require definitions and rule application, thus permitting the administration relative freedom. Exceptions were readily granted, such as the Republic of Korea F–5E coproduction or Indonesia's production of the M–16 rifle. Striking a balance between national interests, economic gains or losses, political ties, regional interactions, and the availability of other suppliers ensures that such decisions are inherently controversial. The only inescapable fact is the reality of the global arms market. Carter policies, which neglected this aspect of policy, as described by one official, "substituted theology for a healthy sense of self-preservation."[9]

There are, of course, dangers involved in the transfer of armaments. The potential loss of sensitive technology is disturbing, as the classified hearings dealing with the F–14 and the Iranian revolution have demonstrated. Likewise, a ripple effect may spur acquisitions by hostile neighbors, as demonstrated by the Indian-Pakistan arms competition. Some within the Department of Defense worry about the drain on active US inventories. Others worry about unwise transfers, and heightened expectations by buyers. But recent trends—fewer petrodollars, stagnant or declining commodities prices, tightening credit judgments, slower export growth, and domestic priorities—make such fears less marked today. In constant 1982 dollars, global deliveries peaked at $38.5 billion in 1982, declining to $35.1 billion in 1983, and to $32.4 billion in 1984. In fact, the United States market share of global arms transfers has declined from 38 percent in 1976 to 22 percent in 1984, reflecting the growth of the less traditional arms suppliers, the effect of foreign exchange rates on weapons prices, and declining economic resources among potential buyers. These factors help to explain the elasticity of demand for weapons. National economic conditions are probably the most significant single variable in a nation's decision to acquire foreign armaments. Indeed, one can graph a cyclical relationship in arms imports, industrial development, and national economic patterns.

Security assistance decisions also frequently raise human rights issues. Congress is the focal point for such concerns, where such interests enjoy access and can easily mobilize support for denial of transfers or restrictions on use of equipment items. The human rights issue is especially noticeable when military or police forces utilize US equipment during times of alleged widespread violations, such as in El Salvador. The most fundamental problem, the crux of the argument about effect, is the difficulty of controlling use by a recipient state. Even Israel, a staunch friend and the recipient of more security assistance than any other state, regularly encounters these problems.

Budget Flows and Regional Priorities

Prior to the Reagan administration, administration of security assistance programs was based on a regional format with a country focus. Secretary of Defense Caspar W. Weinberger argues that "this obscured the strategic goals we have been pursuing and substituted artificial global groupings for policy-based objectives."[10] Thus, starting with fiscal year (FY) 1983, the Reagan team presented a functional strategic overview.

The overriding priority of the Reagan administration is peace in the Middle East. Indeed, between 1973 and 1983, according to *World Military Expenditures and Arms Transfers, 1985*, 40 percent of the world's arms imports went to six Arab nations, a compelling example of the linkages between economics, security, and arms exports. In terms of US security assistance, Israel and Egypt stand alone as the top recipients. The unique status of Israel and Egypt is confirmed by the "forgiveness" of their FMS loans. The next priority is the southern tier of NATO and the Persian Gulf, specifically Turkey, Greece, and Pakistan. The Reagan administration's FY 1987 security assistance budget proposes $5.3 billion to the Middle East, and $2.8 billion to Spain, Portugal, Greece, and Turkey. These two categories represent approximately 75 percent of all funds sought. The Sudan, Oman, Djibouti, Morocco, and Somalia are presented as essential supporting elements, "making available a range of facilities to enhance the mobility and strategic reach of U.S. forces," according to Undersecretary of State William Schneider, Jr., testifying before the House Appropriations Subcommittee on 6 March 1986. Northeast Asia and Central America are the next major focal points, especially South Korea and El Salvador.

Table 1 depicts the regional priorities under President Reagan until the recent change to functional divisions. It shows the preceding history since World War II, and identifies the principal national recipients during each phase. In effect, it chronicles the historical emphasis of American foreign policy.[11]

Table 1
Security Assistance; Regional Totals (Final FY dollars in millions, 1950–1984)

	1950–1981	*1982*	*1983*	*1984*
AMERICAN				
REPUBLICS	$1,009.9	$622.2	$493.0	$501.3
(Brazil)	264.6	0.0	0.0	0.0
(El Salvador)		195.0	220.0	183.5
AFRICA	422.9	480.9	403.4	486.1
(Zaire)	123.0	10.5	11.5	15.0
(Sudan)		200.0	125.2	165.0
EAST ASIA	2,848.7	400.7	414.0	490.1
(ROK)	1,374.8	166.0	185.0	230.0
EUROPE &				
CANADA	3,122.0	1,232.0	1,502.0	1,925.5
(Yugoslavia)	1,388.0	0.0	0.0	0.0
(Turkey)		700.0	685.0	853.5
NEAR EAST,				
SOUTH ASIA	17,424.0	4,262.0	4,434.7	4,328.2
(Israel)	13,504.0	2,206.0	1,735.0	2,610.0

Data include FMS sales, Credit guarantees, MAP, and Economic Support Funds (ESF). IMET data are excluded.

Source: DOD Congressional Presentation Documents. (FMS direct and guaranty only for 1950–1981.)

The switch to functional organization has not resulted in any significant change in US priorities. In fiscal year 1983, 87 percent of FMS guarantee funds was allocated to seven nations: Egypt, Greece, Israel, South Korea, Pakistan, Spain, and Turkey. The same year, 77 percent of Economic Support Funds were directed at six countries: Egypt, El Salvador, Israel, Pakistan, Sudan, and Turkey. Likewise, nearly 80 percent of the FMS direct-credit funds went to Egypt, Israel, Portugal, Sudan, and Turkey. The triple-crown winners: Egypt, Israel, and Turkey. The prize: the Middle East. The goal: containment and continuing access to the region and its oil resources. The question: aside from partially assisting in stabilizing Egypt, how can security assistance affect the Arab nations that may be most threatened by possible domestic turmoil? Isn't such internal upheaval a more likely danger than overt Soviet invasion? The apparent answer is a military one; prepositioning supplies, retaining access to possible bases, and having a staging area within the region. The issue is whether the imprecise and uncertain benefits of security assistance warrant its costs. On balance, successive American administrations have judged that answer to be affirmative. But questions linger.

Policy Questions

As the current controversy over Central America indicates, the relationship between US arms transfers (covert or overt) and US security interests is endlessly debatable. Only in those circumstances where traditional allies—NATO and Japan—acquire security assistance is controversy muted.

Both sides make assertions about the effects of security assistance, especially weapons agreements and deliveries, that are impossible to verify. A fluid international system does not allow decisionmakers the luxury of indecision. Yet, longer term US security interests are divergent, inconsistent, and contingent. For example, what level and sophistication of armaments represent a US commitment? And since policy is often made on a short-term basis, the trade-offs focus on the immediate costs and benefits. To what extent does the "bilateral focus" become a self-fulfilling mechanism, obscuring possible regional or global interactions and thereby creating near-term policy dilemmas? Are regional guidelines possible for certain weapons technology transfers, given today's market competition? Perhaps the only point of agreement is that we should not arm our enemies—assuming we can identify potential enemies.

Arms markets are, of course, economically significant in the United States. Manufacturers cluster in major urban areas, and particular cities are therefore affected by actual shipments to foreign nations. States receive important economic benefits and tax revenues. And, in aggregate, the country benefits from an economic perspective. An unanswered question is the extent to which recipients acquire knowledge which at some future date may enable them to enter the market and compete against US firms. The only defense against this possibility is to maintain, across the board, an edge in technology, quality, and cost leadership. We can debate the economic losses that might occur from a downturn in security assistance; what is irrefutable is that the short-term economic advantages of such sales often obscure the costs involved. Studies purporting to show transition benefits to an altered economy often neglect the costs of addressing structural problems in converting industry and workers (e.g., steel, shoe, and textile industries). In many cases, then, overall economic gains are illusionary.

On a more hopeful note, the negative precedents of the multilateral conventional arms restraint from the Brussels Act of 1890 to the Carter initiative of the late-1970s Conventional Arms Transfer Talks should not discourage renewed efforts to reduce assistance. Despite the fact that defense spending may help spur economic growth, reduced defense spending may be even more beneficial. It may be that the Reagan administration's perception of eroded strength is so strong that it is over-looking opportunities to reduce assistance. In 1984 total sales of weapons *to* lesser developed countries (LDCs) *by* LDCs ($8.6 billion) exceeded sales to LDCs by the USSR ($8.5 billion), Western Europe ($7.9 billion), and the United States ($6.4 billion) according to calculations of the Congressional Research Service. With both US and USSR deliveries declining (in absolute terms), this is an opportunity to find some common ground.[12] If no attempts are made, the rising ranks of new suppliers, some 30 nations, may preclude any future attempts.

Efforts to limit sales must be multinational, otherwise individual suppliers are happy to sell to a state after denial by another state. The classic example of loss of market share is Latin America in the late 1960s, where unilateral US restraints on military aircraft sales shifted the market to the French. Indeed, if we treat arms exports as part of a global market, the issue of internationally agreed-upon constraint is most unlikely, given potential economic gains. That is the core problem which reformers have yet to solve.

A common misconception, heard in every administration, is that "too much" is being shipped to one or another country X. Statistical flows are meaningful to show patterns but reveal little of the national security calculus that ought to go into such decisions. The purchasing state, not the supplier, must weigh these composite variables: military threat, economic costs, absorbability, drain on human resources, and the effects on bilateral and regional relations. It is possible that a small shipment of M–16 rifles may be as destabilizing as two squadrons of advanced aircraft—depending upon the circumstances and the ratio of power. In effect, the recipient must make an assessment about military capabilities, then relate that to national intentions. The supplier, in turn, must weigh its national security interests in the recipient state, the economic costs at home, and the regional balance, and reach its own conclusions. An example is to be found in Afghanistan. Does anyone doubt that a few hundred precision-guided missiles could substantially alter the existing balance of power in that conflict? But at what price?

If we recognize the reality of the global arms trade, we must also admit that global standards of regulation are exceptionally difficult to achieve. Further, as history reveals, outside suppliers (even when close allies) cannot control or dictate the outcomes of local security situations. Indeed, the unanswerable issue in security assistance policy debates is the degree of direct linkage (influence) between arms transfers and American security interests. As one attempts to answer this for a specific country or region, influence tilts on the seesaw of arms exports.

Reagan's Reasons for Granting Security Assistance

Is there any noticeable difference between administrations in their utilization of security assistance? What accounts for the greatly enlarged security assistance programs for some nations?

For the Reagan administration the answer is more than mere policy shifts. With congressional concurrence, the administration has restructured American foreign assistance. Traditional developmental assistance which focused initially on infrastructure projects and then on meeting human needs is declining, while military assistance and economic support funds are growing. From fiscal year 1981 to fiscal year 1985, the security assistance budget as a percentage of total aid grew by 6 percent ($3.9 billion above fiscal year 1981), while development assistance declined 6 percent (but increased in fiscal year terms by some $1.5 billion). The debate arises not so much on the issue of American security interests in Africa, Asia, Latin America, or the Middle East, but on the relationship between military assistance programs and housing, health care, food, and education for the poor. Former World Bank President and Secretary of Defense Robert McNamara has long argued that security includes military hardware and economic stability. Although this may overstate the short-term reality, it does raise fundamental issues over the longer term. What social forces beget revolutions? An empirical example is now unfolding in the Philippines as President Corazon Aquino attempts to stifle the perceived basis of recruitment for the New People's Army by seeking economic reforms and growth.

Policy differences do emerge when the focus shifts to country-specific programs. This is evident when one arrays, albeit arbitrarily, objectives sought, as stated by the Reagan administration, and specific countries (see table 2). Prolonged debate has occurred on security assistance to Central American nations because many doubt the existence of any grave threat to US security. Many critics argued that the administration's security program for Lebanon put the cart before the horse, a

Table 2
Country-Specific Objectives

Objective	Countries
Diminish conflict/ enhance stability	Afghanistan, El Salvador, Morocco, Republic of Korea, Somalia, Thailand, Yemen
Respond to crisis	Central America, Grenada, Lebanon
Secure base rights or prepositioning	Egypt, Oman, Philippines, Turkey
Influence	India, Peoples' Republic of China

judgment that Lebanon's political collapse seems to vindicate. On the other hand, most Americans applauded the invasion of Grenada and therefore no dispute arose over postinvasion training to the police and to Caribbean security forces. The fiscal year 1985 decision to grant 10-year grace periods for the repayment of 30-year market-rate loans to Greece, the Philippines, Portugal, the Republic of Korea, Somalia, Spain, Sudan, Tunisia, and Turkey was equally noncontentious.

Until recent Greek actions indicating a possible denial of future base rights, most legislative debate revolved around maintaining a 7:10 linkage ratio in security assistance between Greece and Turkey respectively. This artificial device is, of course, entirely independent of either nation's military requirements or even of US security interests, but demonstrates the role US domestic political factors can play in allocation decisions. Resolutions of such splits are always political Band-Aids which may bear little relevance to the actual military needs. It is constituent pressures, honest policy differences, and sometimes disparities in the information made available, that are generally behind congressional attempts to modify security assistance levels and policies.

Presently, it is unlikely that the Reagan administration can find a way to provide large-scale aid to both Israel and Egypt and still fund other nations at near-earlier levels. It would appear that congressionally imposed budget cuts in security assistance are imminent. In 1985, Senator John Glenn offered an amendment requiring congressional notification when "significant upgrading of technology or enhanced mission capabilities are made on previously delivered equipment." This is belated recognition that Congress needs to evaluate actual military effect, rather than dollar amounts, ratios, or policy needs. Senator Joseph Biden and Representative Mel Levine introduced legislation to revise congressional oversight of arms transfers by defining transactions in qualitative terms, eliminating all review for certain classes of exports and recipients. "Sensitive" exports would require an affirmative majority vote by both houses of Congress. If passed, such a provision would intensify congressional-executive conflict.

On a different level, the shrinking international arms market reflects reduced demand because of stagnant economic growth and existing debt-service levels. Yet, increased competition from more suppliers will generate greater utilization of offsets. Recipient offset demands must, of course, reach a level of mathematical impossibility given the inherent limits of both sectorial trade and national trade policies. Long before then, demands will be heard by governments in both supplier and recipient states to "do something about offsets." The persistent rise of new suppliers erodes market stability and will increase the likelihood of joint ventures, technology transfer, and buy-back provisions—all complex but pivotal economic issues that governments have great difficulty reconciling.

Technology sophistication is a great discriminator in armaments. The highest levels of technology are the most closely regulated and the least likely to be subject to the pressure mentioned above. However, basic commodities (rifles, artillery, ships, for example) are widely diffused and available. Further, American companies seldom design systems solely for export, while foreign competitors may offer weapons more "tailored" to the needs of an individual nation, along with lower costs, thereby creating favorable markets.

Presently, indigenous arms industries exist in 22 developing nations and are viewed as "major" producers.[13] Moreover, sophistication of the weaponry continues to increase and the upgrade and refurbish market is emerging as another opportunity. Defense planners pondering possible conflicts outside NATO areas must be alert to the growing potential of regional states to affect outcomes, a lesson made clear to the British in the Falkland/Malvinas conflict.

* * *

Are the old paradigms of American security assistance still relevant? These evolved as military tools in support of containment policies, and as political levers with nonaligned nations, rather than economic programs linked to the balance of payments and trade deficits. Today, the first two elements are present, and many in the administration support the view that our current trade deficits with Japan (in 1985: $49.7 billion) and Taiwan (in 1985: $13.1 billion) could be partially reduced through the sales of armaments. But arms exports are generally not included in such trade statistics, nor are Japanese contributions towards facilities operation and construction in Japan considered. However, the burdensome trade deficits may yet become tied to arms imports for leverage by both sides.

As American foreign policy emphasis has shifted over time, the direction of arms exports has also changed. Finally, the volume of arms trade, the number of suppliers and buyers, and the sophistication of armaments have all increased. These structural changes in the global arms market have yet to be fully recognized by the Reagan administration. The implications of these changes are profound. It may be that neither the Carter policies embodied in PD 13 nor the Neutrality Bill of 1935 were correct responses, but is avoidance of these problems a wise policy?

Arms trade is a unique economic phenomenon because weapons do imply (in theory and often in practice) a special relationship, given the almost universal requirement for government's approval of arms transfers. That being the case, what is the responsibility of a supplier regarding possible recipient uses of such weapons? The intellectual and moral dilemmas of this question remain the crux of arms transfer debates in any administration.

The question becomes acute when one remembers the negative experiences the Untied States has seen with major programs in the recent past, for example, the Republic of South Vietnam, the lack of progress in the cessation of hostilities in the Middle East, and the ongoing stalemate in Central America. There are, of course, positive examples: the emergence from the ashes of World War II of Europe and the birth of NATO. The conclusion one reaches is that the quality of the indigenous government (its authority, legitimacy, and status) is the key. A legitimate government supported by its citizens may benefit greatly from security assistance, but an illegitimate government retaining power by coercion ultimately will fail. But how are we to judge? It is interesting to note that President Marcos was seen as a Filipino version of President John F. Kennedy when he first took office, pledged to reforms.

An incrementalist approach, in response to changing perceptions of Soviet proxy activity, is inescapable. Perhaps the need is for a more proactive policy which envisions future trouble spots and, hopefully, takes earlier corrective action. But securing an American public consensus for such policies is daunting, as Reagan's Central American policy suggests. Nevertheless, recent successful examples include the Special Defense Acquisition Fund (a concept started in the Carter years) signed into law by President Reagan in 1981, which permits the advance procurement of items in anticipation of foreign sales[14] and the pending logistical arrangement with the Royal Thai government.

The aftermath of Vietnam still haunts American foreign policy. As a nation we may be reverting toward the more traditional isolationism, away from the fresh hope of internationalism that followed at the end of World War II. But the notion of anti-Communist containment has remained relatively strong. A "wild card" is the structural alteration of the American economy which must now compete in a global marketplace. Ultimately there are no objective criteria by which to measure security assistance. Although the global containment envisioned in many administration statements may be impossible to achieve, President Reagan has restored a coherence missing since Vietnam, which centers around the notion of defending freedom every-where. The realist's sense of national interest is there-fore subordinate to values or ideology. Whether this is a correct response, only history can judge. Security assis-tance by any standard is only a secondary contribution to the burdens of global defense. Peace, however defined, will ultimately require other international con-flict resolution mechanisms aside from coercion.

Notes

1. Lieutenant General Philip Gast, "Security Assistance: The View from DOD," an adaptation of a speech published in *The DISAM Journal* (Spring 1985), p. 52. See also, Francis J. West, Jr., "The US Security Assistance Program: Giveaway or Bargain?" in *Strategic Review* (Winter 1983): 50–56.

2. The remarks are quoted by Mary Belcher, "Reagan Signs Foreign Aid, Complains of Limitations," *Washington Times,* 9 August 1985, p. 3.

3. *World Military Expenditures and Arms Transfers (WMEAT), 1970–1979* (Washington, DC: The Arms Control and Disarmament Agency, 1982), pp. 13–14.

4. Lucy W. Benson, "Turning the Supertanker: Arms Transfer Restraint," *International Security* 3, no. 4 (Spring 1979): 8–9.

5. Barry Blechman is the official quoted by Richard Whittle, "Arms to the World: Controls on Arms Sales Lifted after Failure of Carter Policy to Reduce Flow of Weapons," *The Congressional Quarterly,* 10 April 1982, p. 797.

6. James L. Buckley, "Security Assistance for FY 1983," a statement delivered before the Subcommittee on Foreign Operations of the House Appropriations Committee, 11 March 1982. Reprinted in the *Current Policy Series of the Department of State,* no. 378, p. 1.

7. Indeed, arms transfer needs careful definition since public perceptions and legal definitions vary. One study found that about 40 percent were not "weapons" but items of supply, logistics, train-ing, and construction. See Senate Foreign Relations Committee, *Arms Transfer Policy, Report to the Congress for the SFRC 95th Congress, 1st Session* (Washington, DC: Government Printing Office, 1977).

8. Luigi Einaudi, Hans Heymann, Jr., David Ronfeldt, and Cesar Sereseres, *Arms Transfers to Latin America: Toward a Policy of Mutual Respect*, R–1173–DOS (Santa Monica, CA: Rand Corporation, 1973).

9. James L. Buckley, "Arms Transfers and the National Interest," a speech delivered to the Aerospace Industries Association, 21 May 1981. Reprinted in the *Current Policy* series of the Department of State, no. 279, p. 2.

10. Remarks by Caspar Weinberger contained in *Hearings before the Defense Subcommittee of the House Appropriations Committee, Department of Defense Appropriations for 1984, Part 1,* 98th Congress, 1st Session (Washington, DC: GPO, 1983), pp. 306–9.

11. Recall that the former Republic of Vietnam received billions of US dollars under a separate MSAF account.

12. Michael Brzoska and Thomas Ohlson, "The Future of Arms Transfers: The Changing Pattern," *Bulletin of Peace Proposals,* no. 2 (1985): 129. For a keen analysis of the choices facing the USSR, see William H. Lewis, "Emerging Choices for the Soviets in Third World Arms Transfer Policy," WMEAT, 1985 (Washington, DC: GPO, 1985), pp. 30–34.

13. Herbert Wulf, "Arms Production in the Third World," *Stockholm International Peace Research Institute Yearbook 1985* (London: Taylor and Francis, 1985), pp. 329–43.

14. *Weekly Compilation of Presidential Documents,* International Security and Foreign Assistance Bills: Statement on Signing S. 1196 and HR 4559 Into Law," 29 December 1981, pp. 1424–25.

☆☆

DEFENSE PROGRAM REQUIREMENTS

DEFENSE BUDGETS
AND SPENDING CONTROL:
THE REAGAN ERA AND BEYOND

Dennis S. Ippolito

*T*HERE HAS ALWAYS BEEN something of a myth about the uniqueness of defense budgeting. As the Congressional Research Service explained a decade ago, the politics of budgeting inevitably affects defense:

Ideally, national security interests are the bases for objectives and commitments which, within policy guidelines, shape strategy. Strategic concepts conditioned by threats generate military force requirements. Budgetary assets then are allocated to satisfy needs. That Utopian sequence rarely occurs in real life. National defense competes with other sectors. The trick is to walk a tightrope between excessive defense expenditures that emasculate [other] ... programs and deficient defense expenditures that actively endanger national security.... Equally important, overallocations in any given military sector can undercut essential capabilities elsewhere.[1]

This situation has not changed. In fact, it has become somewhat more complicated. During the mid-1970s, defense budgets were buffeted primarily by "priorities debates" generated by the new congressional budget process. Today, the Gramm-Rudman-Hollings bill, which requires spending and deficit control targets to be met annually, raises serious questions about future levels of defense spending.[2]

For defense policy analysts, the external constraints imposed by the budget process are undoubtedly frustrating and, at times, seemingly irrational. Regardless, the budget process is one of those inescapable realities that determines the context and structure of defense policy debates. Rigorous analyses of defense policy must take into account the simple fact that at least the highly aggregated defense "numbers," particularly outlays, are decided within a comprehensive budgetary framework. The purpose of this paper is to describe that framework and to offer an analysis of its past and future effect on the defense budget.

It is clear that the Reagan administration's military buildup constitutes a landmark in post-World War II defense budgeting. From fiscal 1981–1985, budget authority for the defense function increased by approximately 60 percent; adjusted for inflation, actual spending rose by almost 30 percent over this period, by far the sharpest peacetime increases under any administration.[3] Whether this growth can be sustained, even at reduced rates, for the rest of the decade is problematical. Congressional resistance has been mounting, and the defense budget is especially vulnerable to the automatic cuts, or sequestration formula, under Gramm-Rudman-Hollings. What is certain is that severe budgetary obstacles must be overcome to preserve the Reagan defense program. Unless "real growth" budgets continue well into the future, significant adjustments in current force plans are inevitable.

Defense and the Budget: Long-Term Trends

The relationship between defense spending and the rest of the Federal budget has changed dramatically over the past several decades. The era of modern budgets, marked by a substantial commitment of economic resources to the Federal Government, can be divided into four stages. The first, initiated during the New

Deal, almost tripled the relative size of the Federal sector. By fiscal 1940, Federal outlays had risen to approximately 10 percent of gross national product (GNP). In addition, spending growth was heavily concentrated in social welfare and other domestic programs. Prior to World War II, domestic spending for the ''human resources'' and ''physical resources'' functions accounted for about 70 percent of Federal outlays; defense was well under 20 percent.[4]

The defense budgets. The second stage in the development of modern budget policy was marked by an abrupt but lasting expansion in defense spending. For nearly three decades after the beginning of World War II, defense dominated Federal budgets. The defense share of total outlays jumped from 17.5 percent to 47.1 percent between fiscal years 1940 and 1941, rising to a wartime peak of 89.5 percent in fiscal 1945. There was a sharp decline in the late 1940s, but the Korean war reversed this, and from fiscal 1951 through fiscal 1970, the defense function never dropped below 40 percent of total Federal spending. Further, defense outlays as a percentage of GNP remained relatively high throughout this period (see table 1).

The 1970s produced a break in defense spending that was markedly different from the post-World War II and post-Korean periods. During the Vietnam war, the defense-GNP level never exceeded 10 percent. The average level during Vietnam was about 8 percent, compared to a *peacetime* average of almost 10 percent for fiscal years 1955–1964.[5] By fiscal 1974, defense outlays were less than 30 percent of the budget, compared to over 45 percent 10 years earlier. Over the same period, total spending was growing quite rapidly.

Table 1
Defense Outlays, Fiscal Years 1941–1986 (in billions of dollars)

	Defense Total Outlays	Percentage of Total Budget Outlays	Percentage of GNP
1941	$ 6.4	47.1	5.7
1946	42.7	77.3	20.0
1951	23.6	51.8	7.5
1956	42.5	60.2	10.2
1961	49.6	50.8	9.6
1966	58.1	43.2	7.8
1971	78.9	37.5	7.5
1976	89.6	24.1	5.3
1981	157.5	23.2	5.3
1986 (est.)	265.8	27.1	6.3

Source: Historical Tables, Budget of the United States Government, Fiscal Year 1987 (Washington, DC: Government Printing Office, 1986), pp. 3.1(1)–3.2(6).

As shown in figure 1, the linkage between defense spending and the total budget was relatively strong during the 1940s and 1950s. With Vietnam, this linkage began to unravel. Defense funding was no longer driving the budget. In sum, a defense decline triggered an overall budget reduction after World War II. High levels of defense spending prevented a parallel decline after Korea. In the latter stages of the Vietnam war and subsequently, a shrinking defense budget contrasted with increased total spending. By fiscal 1976, the budget was 21.9 percent of GNP, the highest level in 30 years; the corresponding defense figure was 5.3 percent, the lowest level in 25 years.

The entitlement shift. The displacement of defense by social welfare spending programs began in earnest

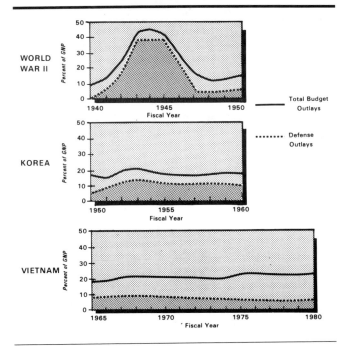

Source: *Historical Tables, Budget of the United States Government, Fiscal Year 1986* (Washington, DC: Government Printing Office, 1985), pp. 3.1(1)–3.1(4).

Figure 1.
GNP Comparisons of Defense Outlays and Total Budget Outlays, World War II, Korea, and Vietnam

during the Johnson presidency. The fundamental source, of course, was the expansion of Federal responsibilities during the New Deal. In the 1940s and 1950s, social security and other income security programs, as well as domestic grants to state and local governments, grew steadily but modestly. Real spending for payments for individuals (income transfers and in-kind benefit programs) and grants to state and local governments increased from $7.6 billion in fiscal 1940 to

$40.7 billion in fiscal 1960.[6] As a percentage of the total budget, this represented an increase from 23.6 percent to 31.1 percent.

Real spending in these categories increased by more than $120 billion over the next 20 years, with their combined budget share climbing to over 57 percent. This extraordinary growth commenced during the mid-1960s and accelerated over the next decade. The combination of liberalized New Deal programs and Great Society initiatives—in health care, education, food and nutrition aid, housing, and a host of major grant programs for state and local governments—radically altered the growth and the composition of the Federal budget.

An important element in this overall trend was the effect of entitlements. The cost of entitlements in fiscal 1967, when the Great Society programs got under way, was less than $60 billion (or slightly more than one-third of total outlays). Changes in eligibility, benefit formulas, and indexing helped to produce a $285 billion increase by fiscal 1980.[7] From fiscal 1967 to 1980, payments for individuals defined as relatively uncontrollable went from $40 billion to $245 billion.[8]

The Reagan retrenchment. When the Reagan administration took office, the spending side of the budget had enormous momentum. Spending growth for the Carter presidency averaged over 12 percent annually (for fiscal years 1978–1981), outstripping economic growth and bringing the spending-GNP level to a 35-year peak.[9] The defense function, however, had dropped to less than one-fourth of total spending, which meant that Reagan was faced with reconciling two competing objectives: restraining overall spending growth and significantly boosting defense. The results for defense have been impressive, but the record on overall growth has been mixed. There has also been a large gap between the administration's stated goals and the programmatic actions Congress has taken.

In its fiscal 1982 budget revisions, for example, the Reagan administration set a target outlay ceiling of $844 billion for fiscal 1985.[10] It also projected defense outlays at approximately one-third of this total.[11] Actual fiscal 1985 spending, however, was more than $100 billion above the ceiling, while the defense share of total outlays was just over one-fourth. Actual changes in budget composition under Reagan, then, have not matched the Reagan budget program. Nevertheless, significant changes have occurred: long-term trends have been reversed (for defense and discretionary domestic spending) or slowed (for entitlements and other mandatory spending).

The budget policy initiatives introduced by Ronald Reagan have not reshaped the budget if the comparison is, for example, pre-Great Society spending. Given the entitlement programs currently in place, this magnitude of change is simply not possible over one or even two terms. The combined weight of defense spending and interest costs, however, means that high growth rates for domestic programs will be difficult to achieve. Decelerating rates of spending growth and changes in composition, then, are likely to have a continuing effect on spending policy.

The deficit problem. Chronic deficits have been a problem since the 1930s, but the gap between spending and revenues has widened drastically in recent years. Almost half of the gross Federal debt (which exceeded $1.8 trillion at the end of fiscal 1985) has been added since fiscal 1980. For fiscal years 1983–1986, the average annual deficits were in the $200 billion range. As shown in table 2, the decade-by-decade growth in deficit levels has been enormous. And the large projected deficits for the latter 1980s are the target for the Gramm-Rudman-Hollings spending reduction formula.

The Reagan defense buildup has not, despite the popular perception, been solely or even primarily responsible for the worsening deficit situation. Defense accounted for only about one-third of the approximately $300 billion in outlay growth from fiscal 1981 to 1985. It currently represents well under 30 percent of total spending.

Defense does not dominate the budget, as it did in the period between Korea and Vietnam. What made defense vulnerable then was its relative size. What makes it vulnerable today is not just relative size (since that has declined significantly) but the practical, political, and legal restrictions that protect most of the rest of the budget. Of the estimated $255 billion in relatively controllable outlays for fiscal 1986, for example, over 80 percent was in defense.[12] With the bulk of the defense budget requiring annual authorizations and appropriations, defense is at a disadvantage when compared to the automatic spending that drives much of the remainder of the budget. It is this disadvantage that helped to produce the imbalances between defense and social welfare during the 1970s. And it is this disadvantage that is exacerbated by the spending cut formulas under Gramm-Rudman-Hollings.

The Reagan Defense Program

The increases in defense budgets under President Reagan have not been uniform throughout the broad appropriation and mission categories into which the budget is divided. There has been throughout the Reagan presidency thus far a relatively consistent ordering of defense

Table 2
Budget Deficits, Fiscal Years 1950–1989 (in billions of dollars)

Fiscal Years	Cumulative Deficits for Period*	
1950–1959	$ 17.4	
1960–1969	56.5	
1970–1979	364.8	
1980–1984	673.8	
1985–1989	719.8	(Office of Management and Budget estimates)
	910.0	(Congressional Budget Office estimates)

*Includes off-budget outlays.

Source: Historical Tables, Budget of the United States Government, Fiscal Year 1987 (Washington, DC: Government Printing Office, 1986), pp. 1.1(1)–1.1(2); Congressional Budget Office, *The Economic and Budget Outlook: Fiscal Years 1987–1991* (Washington, DC: Congressional Budget Office, 1986), p. xiv.

spending priorities. As set forth initially by Secretary of Defense Caspar W. Weinberger, the administration placed its "highest priority on the long overdue modernization of our strategic forces."[13] In addition, Weinberger stressed the need to redress "a major backlog of investment requirements."[14]

By the early 1980s, there was a widespread consensus among defense experts on the necessity for investment increases and the particularly pressing claim for strategic force support. As Leonard Sullivan has noted, "When budgets were cut in the aftermath of the Vietnam war, the investment accounts absorbed the greater share of these reductions."[15] Post-Vietnam defense budgets, which had no real growth over the fiscal 1973–1981 period, were heavily weighted in favor of readiness accounts. Moreover, the fiscal constraints applied to strategic forces were especially severe.

Investment versus readiness. One of the issues that tends to surface during congressional budget debates over defense is based on the division between the ongoing costs of training and operating forces ("readiness") and the costs of modernizing equipment and facilities for these forces ("investment"). There are difficulties in applying this distinction with great precision, but the conventional usage places military personnel and operations and maintenance appropriation titles under readiness. Most of the remainder of the defense budget (procurement; research, development, test, and evaluation; military construction and family housing) is considered investment.[16]

The clear intent of the Reagan defense program has been, and continues to be, to shift spending toward investment. This intent has been partly accomplished: from fiscal 1981–1985, for example, outlay growth for investment was over 90 percent, more than double the growth in readiness. A slightly larger gap characterized budget authority increases.[17] In addition, spending for atomic energy defense activities more than doubled between fiscal years 1981 and 1985.

The net effect of the Reagan budgets has been to balance readiness and investment. Between fiscal 1981 and 1986, for example, the percentage of defense budget authority in readiness accounts declined markedly (see table 3). The budgetary shares for military personnel and for operations and maintenance shrank by about 15 percent, with corresponding increases in procurement and in research, development, testing, and evaluation (RDT&E). The fiscal 1986 allocations, moreover, are expected to continue through the rest of

Table 3
Composition of the Defense Budget, Fiscal Years 1976–1991

	*Percentage of Budget Authority**				
	FY 1976	*FY 1981*	*FY 1985*	*FY 1986***	*FY 1991***
Readiness:					
Military Personnel	34	28	24	24	25***
Operations and Maintenance	30	32	27	27	27
Investment:					
Procurement	22	27	34	33	32
RDT&E	10	9	11	12	12
Military Construction; Family Housing; Other	4	4	4	4	4
	100	100	100	100	100

*   Of DOD military budget.
** Estimate.
***The FY 1991 military personnel figure includes estimated allowances.

Source: Historical Tables, Budget of the United States Government, Fiscal Year 1987 (Washington, DC: Government Printing Office, 1986), pp. 5.1(1)–5.1(3).

the decade. In addition, actual spending is expected to parallel this budget authority pattern through fiscal 1991 (see table 4). For the 20-year period shown, the shifts in spending within the defense budget have been significant.

Mission categories. A second perspective for interpreting the defense budget focuses on mission categories, such as strategic forces and general purpose forces.

Table 4
Composition of the Defense Budget, Fiscal Years 1970–1990

	Percentage of Budget Outlays				
	FY 1970	*FY 1975*	*FY 1980*	*FY 1985*	*FY 1991 (est.)*
Readiness	62	67	64	55	54
Investment	37	32	34	42	43
Atomic Energy/ Other	2	2	2	3	3
	101	101	100	100	100

Source: Historical Tables, Budget of the United States Government, Fiscal Year 1987 (Washington, DC: Government Printing Office, 1986), pp. 3.3(2)–3.3(5).

Here also, the Reagan defense program has had an impact. The fiscal 1982 budget submitted by the Carter administration, for example, was almost identical to the actual fiscal 1979 allocations of budget authority by mission category. The share for strategic weapons was to increase from 6.4 percent to 7.4 percent. By comparison the change from fiscal 1982 to 1985 under Reagan shifted strategic forces budget authority from approximately 7 percent to almost 10 percent (see table 5). In addition, the combined allocation for strategic forces, intelligence and communications, and research and development has risen by over 25 percent since fiscal 1982.

The Congressional Response

In speculating about the long-term prospects for the defense budget, it is necessary to take into account the future congressional response to Reagan defense

Table 5
Defense Budget by Mission Categories, Fiscal Years 1982–1989

Major Mission/Program	Percentage of Budget Authority		
	FY 1982	FY 1985	FY 1989 (est.)
Strategic forces	7.1	9.6	8.4
General purpose forces	41.2	41.3	41.4
Intelligence and communications	6.5	8.8	9.2
Airlift and sealift	1.9	3.0	2.1
Guard and Reserve	4.9	5.5	5.9
Research and development	7.9	8.5	10.1
Central supply and maintenance/ general personnel	28.4	21.0	20.7
Administration and other	2.1	2.3	2.1
	100.0	100.0	99.9

Source: Budget of the United States Government, various years.

policies. Reagan's first term produced important shifts. The defense budget grew more rapidly than the overall budget. Real increases in defense spending accelerated slightly as well. These shifts, while significant, are not nearly as dramatic as media reporting or popular perceptions would suggest. The discrepancy lies in the real versus imagined support the Reagan program has received from Congress. If, in fact, Reagan's influence on defense was at its peak during the first term, the long-term prospects for the defense budget are unfavorable.

Congressional revisions in President Reagan's budget proposals fall into two related categories. After the first round of spending cuts contained in the 1981 Omnibus Budget Reconciliation Act, Congress rejected most proposed domestic spending cuts and, beginning with the fiscal 1983 budget round, greatly reduced the administration's defense requests. Finally, the 1983–1985 defense cuts were used, in part, to boost domestic spending. It was the prospect of continued trade-offs of this sort—reminiscent of funding patterns during the 1970s—that helped make the Gramm-Rudman-Hollings bill acceptable to an otherwise unenthusiastic White House. The automatic spending cut formula written into its final version ensured that defense cuts would have to be matched on a roughly equal basis by domestic cuts.

The fiscal 1983 budget was the first complete submission by the Reagan administration. Proposed budget revisions sent to Congress in March 1981 called for increases over the defense levels recommended by President Carter for fiscal years 1981 and 1982. The fiscal 1981 budget authority increase of approximately $7 billion was enacted with little change, since it was tied to a military pay increase and did not raise a controversial policy issue.[18] The fiscal 1982 revisions were more substantial, calling for an additional $26 billion in budget authority and $4.4 billion in outlays. Congress finally accepted a budget authority level that included a $16 billion increment over the original Carter budget. At the same time, actual outlays for fiscal years 1981–1982 were more than $8 billion below Reagan estimates, although not as a result of equivalent congressional cuts.

Changes in the defense budget prior to 1983, therefore, were marginal adjustments that conformed in large part to congressional spending goals set forth in fiscal 1980–1982 budget resolutions. For fiscal years 1983–1986, by comparison, congressional cuts in defense have been quite large. The annual reductions in budget authority requests have averaged roughly $20 billion

Table 6
Department of Defense Budget Authority and Outlays,
Fiscal Years 1983–1986 (in billions of dollars)

	Budget Authority*		
	Reagan Request	*Enacted*	*Reduction*
1983	$258.0	$239.5	− $18.5
1984	274.1	258.2	− 15.9
1985	305.0	284.7	− 20.3
1986	314.2	289.7	− 24.5
	Outlays*		
	Reagan Estimate	*Actual*	*Reduction*
1983	$215.9	$204.4	− $11.5
1984	238.9	220.8	− 17.8
1985	264.4	246.3	− 18.1
1986	277.5	NA	NA

*Department of Defense: military only.

Source: Budget of the United States Government, various years.

annually (see table 6). The outlay differences have been lower, but still considerable.

Moreover, congressional reductions have been most evident in the administration's priority areas: investment accounts, strategic forces, and research and development funding. In fiscal 1983 and 1984, for example, strategic force budget authority cuts averaged more than 10 percent each year, while budget authority for the research and development mission category was reduced by about 7.5 percent each year. Most important, program cuts within these broad categories have not been uniform. The fiscal 1986 defense appropriations bill, for example, sliced MX missile funding by over 40 percent and Strategic Defense Initiative funding by more than 25 percent. The overall cut in defense appropriations was slightly greater for investment (9.6 percent) than for readiness (7.0 percent) accounts. There was no drastic restructuring of Reagan's basic program nor any termination of major programs.

What has occurred over the past several years is a series of significant congressional cuts in the administration's defense funding requests, with fiscal 1986 an important transition. Until fiscal 1986, cuts could be made while allowing real increases in spending. The fiscal 1986 budget, however, means negative real growth in defense. Current estimates by the Senate Appropriations Subcommittee on Defense show a 2-percent real decline from fiscal 1985 to 1986, with the possibility of this reaching 7 percent under the 1 March automatic spending cuts mandated by the Gramm-Rudman-Hollings bill.[19]

With negative real growth a serious prospect since fiscal 1986, major rollbacks in defense are clearly possible. Despite the size of the defense budget, it is difficult to get immediate short-term outlay reductions of any magnitude without policy changes. Defense spending categorized as "controllable," for example, is almost entirely in readiness accounts, but these accounts are obviously closely linked to troop levels. It is possible to postpone or cancel scheduled pay increases, as has been done in the past, but the only way to preserve large cuts is to lower troop levels significantly. If one accepts the verdict of most defense analysts that readiness and sustainability problems were severe by the late 1970s, it is clearly not desirable to return to the funding patterns that produced those problems.

Focusing on the investment accounts, however, reveals another set of problems. Because procurement funds for any major weapons system are spread out over several years, the outlay rates vary over time. The estimated outlay rate during the first year for procurement funds, for example, is only 13 percent.[20] Cutting *all* of the $86.2 billion in procurement budget authority for fiscal 1984, according to the Congressional Budget Office, would have yielded 1984 outlay savings of only $11 billion. On the investment accounts, the spend-out rates, along with the fact that most spending results from prior-year contracts, make it difficult to achieve significant savings in the short term without massive budget authority cuts.

As we look at the prospects for defense, and the particular problems posed by the specific provisions in Gramm-Rudman-Hollings, it is helpful to keep in mind this relationship between defense policy and budget accounting. It is also of some significance that the positions of the Reagan administration and the Congress will likely differ on where cuts should be made. Thus, one possibility is for automatic cuts that have policy effects no one wants, because there is no agreement on the policy changes necessary to forestall the automatic cuts.

Gramm-Rudman-Hollings and Other Alternatives

Congressional action and a 1 March sequestration reduced fiscal 1986 defense budget authority $8.6 billion below fiscal 1985. It was widely conceded that this reduction could be accommodated largely through reestimating and stretching out spending. Congressional cuts have been in large part offset by inflation rates and oil prices well below estimated levels, along with savings arising from multiyear contracting and other management initiatives.

These offsets, however, did not provide much protection after fiscal 1987. The 30-percent inflation add-on that the Department of Defense has used for major procurement programs in previous budget cycles has been dropped, and Congress may refuse to allow fuel savings to be transferred to other accounts, which negates much of the effect of oil price declines. There may be some residual savings, but these are likely to be minor when compared to the spending cuts currently being projected for defense.

Gramm-Rudman-Hollings provisions. On 12 December 1985, President Reagan signed into law the Balanced Budget and Emergency Deficit Control Act (HJ Res. 372, PL 99–177). The Gramm-Rudman-Hollings bill, as it is known, revises budgetary procedures in the executive branch and Congress and, more important, requires that Federal deficits be eliminated by fiscal 1991. The latter would be achieved either through conventional legislative measures that reduce spending or increase revenues or, failing these, through automatic spending cuts. The new law amends the Congressional Budget and Impoundment Control Act of 1974, greatly accelerating the budget timetable and strengthening procedures to block floor action on legislation exceeding deficit targets.

The starting point for Gramm-Rudman-Hollings is a series of declining deficit ceilings: $171.9 billion in fiscal 1986; $144 billion in fiscal 1987; $108 billion in fiscal 1988; $72 billion in fiscal 1989; $36 billion in fiscal 1990; zero deficit in fiscal 1991. After the President submits his January budget for the upcoming fiscal year, Congress is faced with a series of deadlines. By 15 April, it must pass a budget resolution which includes reconciliation instructions for spending committees on how to bring down projected deficits to specified amounts. Both the presidential budget and congressional budget resolution must keep within the required deficit level for the upcoming fiscal year.

As part of the accelerated timetable, Congress must complete action on a reconciliation bill by 15 June, and the House must pass all regular appropriations bills by 30 June. The unique feature of Gramm-Rudman-Hollings, however, is its acknowledgment that Congress and the President may not be able to agree on how to stay within deficit limits and that neither reconciliation legislation nor appropriations legislation will produce the necessary results.

The Gramm-Rudman-Hollings solution to deadlocks is automatic spending cuts. By August (January for fiscal 1986), the Office of Management and Budget (OMB) and the Congressional Budget Office (CBO) must determine whether the deficit for the upcoming fiscal year will exceed, by more than $10 billion, the statutory ceiling. Their estimates are to reflect projected economic indicators and the spending and revenue legislation then in effect. The resulting spending baseline is used to estimate the deficit and, if the ceiling is breached, to calculate the automatic spending cuts necessary to reduce the deficit below the ceiling. The CBO–OMB report includes the uniform percentage spending reductions to be applied to all Federal programs that are not exempt, by virtue of Gramm-Rudman-Hollings provisions, from the automatic "trigger" cuts under the law.

The next part of the sequence involves the General Accounting Office (GAO), and it is this section that was held unconstitutional by the Supreme Court on 7 July 1986. The GAO was to receive the CBO-OMB report, verify it, and transmit it to the President and Congress by 25 August. This report was to be the basis for actual spending cuts. The President was required to issue, by 1 September, an emergency sequester order reducing non-exempt Federal spending by a uniform percentage, as set forth in the CBO-OMB-GAO report. Unless that order was changed by legislative action over the next several weeks, spending authority was automatically canceled on 1 October, the beginning of the new fiscal year.

Not all spending is covered by Gramm-Rudman-Hollings. There are a number of exemptions, including social security, several low-income programs, and interest on the debt. There are also special rules for automatic cuts in a second category of programs, including unemployment compensation, guaranteed student loans, and the Commodity Credit Corporation farm price-support programs. For defense, special rules exist, but these are not at all favorable.

First, unobligated budget authority from previous years is subject to automatic cuts. Second, the law prescribes uniform percentage cuts in defense accounts and subaccounts (projects, programs, and activities). For the first round of cuts in fiscal 1986, the President had some flexibility within a given account as to percentage reductions among subaccounts. He lacked this flexibility for fiscal 1987 and subsequent fiscal years. Third, the sequestration process is based on outlay savings. For multiyear programs, particularly procurement, a given level of outlay reduction will typically require a much larger reduction in budget authority. Slow-spending programs, therefore, could be especially hard hit by ostensibly uniform percentage cuts in outlays.

The final provision affecting defense is the requirement that spending cuts be divided equally between defense and nondefense programs. The defense category for this purpose consists of military accounts plus half of all Federal retirement cost-of-living adjustments. The inclusion of COLAs reduces the cut in actual defense accounts slightly below 50 percent.

Alternative procedures. One provision of the Balanced Budget Act has been held unconstitutional. According to a three-judge panel of the US District Court for the District of Columbia and the Supreme Court, the Comptroller General, who heads the General Accounting Office, cannot issue the report requiring the President to make automatic spending cuts, so long as he is subject to removal by Congress. The Comptroller General's power, in this instance, has been deemed to be executive in nature, and having executive powers exercised by an official who can be removed by Congress has been held to violate the separation of powers.

The constitutional challenge to the automatic spending cut procedure does not alter certain legal and political realities under Gramm-Rudman-Hollings. The deficit ceilings remain in place, and the law contains procedures for expedited action on a joint resolution, reported out by the House and Senate Budget Committees (acting as a "Temporary Joint Committee on Deficit Reduction") that would make the required cuts. The joint resolution or backup mechanism under Gramm-Rudman-Hollings, then, can still be exercised. There was still a legal commitment and perhaps political pressures associated with the $144 billion deficit ceiling for fiscal 1987. President Reagan will continue to have veto leverage against new taxes and domestic spending bills. Congress will continue to have corresponding leverage over the President's spending priorities, notably defense. The 50-50 compromise on defense and domestic spending cuts will still have considerable support in Congress.

It is entirely possible, in sum, that with Gramm-Rudman-Hollings and the trade-off between defense spending and tax increases on the table, as it has been for the past several years, in fact, the President's hand in these negotiations has probably been strengthened. Without automatic cuts, there will unquestionably be greater administrative flexibility in any defense spending reductions. In addition, it is possible that the President can tie any tax increase directly to defense spending, thereby maintaining the pressure to reduce domestic programs.

The fiscal 1987 budget. The fiscal 1987 Reagan budget called for a substantial defense increase. Budget authority of $320.7 billion had been requested, compared to $286.1 billion that was estimated for fiscal 1986. Defense outlays are to increase from $265.2 billion to $282.2 billion.

Budget authority in the fiscal 1987 budget shows 8.2 percent real growth over fiscal 1986. It is this robust growth at a time when Reagan is recommending a 4-percent real decline in nondefense spending that has led some to dismiss the Reagan defense budget as politically unrealistic. There are, however, some potential strengths in the timing and composition of the President's proposals.

For example, Congress adopted, as part of the fiscal 1986 budget, fiscal 1987 and 1988 defense spending levels that were *higher* (largely because of different inflation estimates) than the President's requests. Because fiscal 1986 budget authority was in fact reduced below fiscal 1985, the administration can argue that Congress is committed to honoring its part of an August 1985 agreement—real funding increases for fiscal 1987 and 1988. Secretary of Defense Weinberger attacked Congress for violating the agreement in fiscal 1986, declaring that "The fact the Congress reneged on its pledge to the President ... is no basis for the President to declare the need is any less. They have violated

Table 7
Defense Budget Authority Increases, Fiscal Years 1985–1987
(in billions of dollars)

	Change from FY 1985		
	FY 1985	*FY 1986*	*FY 1987*
Military personnel*	$67.8	0	+ $9.7
Operations and maintenance	77.8	− 2.9	+ 8.0
Procurement	96.8	− 4.2	− 1.0
RDT&E	31.3	+ 2.4	+ 10.6
Military construction and family housing	8.4	− 0.3	+ 1.7

*Includes pay raise allowances for fiscal year 1987.

Source: Budget of the United States Government, Fiscal Year 1987 (Washington, DC: Government Printing Office, 1986), p. 5–5.

a covenant with the President.''[21] One might reasonably expect this theme to be replayed repeatedly during an election year, and it could provide some political protection for the defense budget.

There is additional protection in the type of defense budget President Reagan has sent to Congress. A number of large procurement programs pushed by the administration (such as the Pershing II missile, B–1B bomber, C–5B and KC–10 aircraft, and the battleship reactivation program) are at or near completion. As a result, procurement budget authority for fiscal 1987 was $1 billion below the fiscal 1985 level. For fiscal 1987, procurement was clearly not as prominent or as vulnerable as in recent years.

The dilemma for defense critics is that fiscal 1987 increases were concentrated in readiness accounts and in RDT&E (see table 7). The former includes funding for almost 14,000 additional personnel, but these are almost entirely dedicated to additional ships the Navy began operating in fiscal 1987. The pay raise then proposed (4 percent) was modest and was tied to protecting the recruiting and retention successes of the past several years. The substantial operations and maintenance increase reflects, among other things, the impact of major procurement programs now being completed. Generally recognized readiness and sustainability requirements should translate into strong support for this portion of the defense budget.

The RDT&E account is probably the most vulnerable part of the Reagan program. The fiscal 1987 increase for RDT&E was about 10 percent in outlays and almost 25 percent in budget authority. Among the more prominent and costly weapons systems included here are the Stealth bomber, the Midgetman and Trident II missiles, the C–17 aircraft, and the Strategic Defense Initiative. The $4.8 billion SDI request, for example, is more than $2 billion higher than the fiscal 1986 appropriation, while the Midgetman and Stealth programs are estimated at roughly double fiscal 1986 levels.[22] The potential fiscal 1987 savings from slowing or even canceling these programs are relatively small, but the long-term savings are enormous. Senator Sam Nunn has estimated the total costs for new weapons the administration proposed to move into full production in 1987 at $250 billion.[23] Five-year costs for the C–17 cargo plane and Midgetman missile alone were estimated at over $40 billion.[24]

Under these circumstances, stretchouts and even eliminations have some congressional appeal. Defense supporters are interested in protecting the "baseline," which means sheltering past programs. Defense critics are naturally tempted to oppose new weapons systems, and they have an advantage whenever debate shifts from the Soviet military threat to deficits. This shift is obvious during the current year and would probably have occurred even without Gramm-Rudman-Hollings. In any case, the President will have a difficult task in moving these weapons systems through Congress, at least without some trade-offs, notably revenue increases.

Protecting the Baseline

On 18 February 1986, the Congressional Budget Office (CBO) issued its economic and budget projections for fiscal years 1987–1991. Its widely publicized conclusion stated, "The outlook for reducing budget deficits has improved dramatically since last summer."[25] The CBO reported that under current spending and revenue policies (the "baseline"), deficits would decline from $208 billion in fiscal 1986 to $104 billion in fiscal 1991. Just one year ago, the CBO projected that deficits would rise to the $300 billion level by the end of the decade.[26]

Long-range projections of this kind are obviously quite uncertain. In fact, however, the comparative optimism of the CBO report makes it more likely that Congress will attempt to comply with Gramm-Rudman-Hollings, since the spending reductions or tax increases necessary to comply are now within the range of possible agreement. According to the CBO, the current policy baseline will lead to a reduction in the outlay level from 24 percent of GNP in fiscal 1985 to 20.6 percent in fiscal 1991.[27] This is extremely important, since the 20-percent level has been considered an acceptable revenue and spending ceiling by this administration. Balancing the budget at or near 20 percent of GNP, therefore, would be an extraordinary accomplishment, one that seemed well beyond reach when this administration took office.

A more favorable budget outlook, however, increases the pressures on defense. The deficit decline CBO projects is based on revised and more optimistic economic assumptions than a year ago and reflects cuts in defense and nondefense spending already enacted. Part is based on outlay control for defense and nondefense in the future.

For defense, the fiscal 1986 sequestration that took place 1 March establishes the base for CBO outyear projections. The $104 billion fiscal 1991 deficit assumes no real growth in defense (or nondefense) appropriations above this base. Thus, with no further cuts but no real growth, the deficit is expected to decline by one-half over the next five years.

The Reagan administration's fiscal 1987 budget requests 3 percent real growth for defense. The outlay difference for fiscal 1987 between the Reagan budget and CBO baseline is nonexistent (as a result of technical estimation differences), but it widens to almost $40 billion by fiscal 1991. Thus, assuming no further attempts to meet the Gramm-Rudman-Hollings deficit targets, there will still be a serious prospect of no real growth in defense.

The more threatening scenario assumes the elimination of deficits by fiscal 1991. This means negative growth for the defense budget. In fiscal 1987, for example, the sequestration formula under Gramm-Rudman-Hollings required, under current CBO projections, a $10.7 billion outlay reduction below the fiscal 1986 base. This means, in turn, an approximately $21 billion reduction in budget authority, with especially large cuts in procurement and RDT&E needed to generate the necessary savings (see table 8). This sequestration would apply to the fiscal 1986 postsequestration base, with no adjustments for inflation or other factors.

Table 8
Projected Fiscal 1987 Automatic Defense
Sequestration (in billions of dollars)

	Spending Authority*	Estimated Outlays
Department of Defense: Military		
Military personnel	$4.3	$4.2
Operations and maintenance	4.7	3.7
Procurement	8.5	1.1
Research, development, test, and evaluation	2.2	1.2
Military construction	0.5	0.1
Family housing and other	0.3	0.2
Subtotal, DOD	20.5	10.5
Atomic Energy		
Defense Activities	0.5	0.3
Other Defense-related Activities	0.1	0.0
Total	$21.1	$10.8

*Includes new budget authority for fiscal 1987 and unobligated balances from previous years.

Source: Congressional Budget Office, *The Economic and Budget Outlook: Fiscal Years 1987–1991* (Washington, DC: Congressional Budget Office, 1986), p. 96.

The total reduction from 1986 appropriation levels would be 10.8 percent for defense programs, and the reduction in real terms would be even greater since there would be no inflation adjustments for fiscal 1987.[28]

The Supreme Court has, in effect, made it impossible to implement a nondiscretionary sequestration. Any sequestration now attempted, barring of course a statutory accommodation for Gramm-Rudman-Hollings, will have to be in the form of a joint resolution passed by Congress and signed by the President. If Congress were to attempt to follow the original sequestration procedure, the cuts for defense, as shown in table 8, would be severe.

A fiscal year sequestration that follows the Gramm-Rudman-Hollings formula would be difficult and painful. It could not be accomplished without major program reductions or cancellations. This prospect, and the general congressional attitude on defense spending, has led a number of defense supporters in Congress to the conclusion that protecting the current baseline over the next several years is about the best that can be done in the absence of budget policy changes in other areas. But even protecting the current baseline will force choices between specific weapons systems.

Budget Policy Options

The future of defense budgets is closely linked to overall budget policy. There is now a realistic prospect that future budget deficits can be reduced or even eliminated, and this prospect provides the starting point for budget policy options. There are, in effect, different routes toward the Gramm-Rudman-Hollings objective, and their political and policy costs vary dramatically.

Option I. The sequestration formula under Gramm-Rudman-Hollings can be implemented by joint resolution, thereby avoiding the constitutional problem of the General Accounting Office. The fiscal year cuts for defense and nondefense spending, however, would be quite severe. It is highly unlikely that Congress would ignore the 50-50 split between defense and nondefense spending cuts that was agreed to last year. It is even more unlikely that the President would agree to the defense cuts that would emerge from any conceivable sequestration package. The joint resolution procedure gives the President additional room to maneuver as far as specific defense cuts are concerned, certainly much more room than is provided by the original sequestration formula. This additional flexibility is probably beside the point, however, since the President is almost certain to veto a joint resolution that cuts defense below the 1986 base.

Deadlock between the President and Congress would not eliminate the defense-nondefense trade-offs. Instead, any presidential effort to move defense above the zero real growth baseline would probably be matched by congressional attempts to get equivalent treatment for nondefense spending. It is possible, then, to get modest real growth in defense, but as long as the bargaining is confined to spending policy, nondefense spending will be hard to control.

Option II. A second option adds revenues to the negotiating table. The President has insisted, of course, on overall revenue neutrality for any major tax bills, but there have been several minor tax increases since 1982. The fiscal 1987 budget estimates that receipts will be approximately 19 percent of GNP by the end of the decade. Under both the President's budget and current CBO estimates, the gap between outlays and receipts, in terms of GNP, will be less than two percentage points by the early 1990s. This would be equivalent to approximately $100 billion.

The crucial point is that budget receipts can be increased without violating the 20 percent of GNP ceiling, which served as the President's original goal.[29] The trade-off in this instance would not be between defense and nondefense spending but between defense and revenues. Congress has an effective veto over the former.

The President has a veto over the latter. An option that combines deficit reduction, modest real defense increases, and an overall "size of government" in keeping with the President's preferences is therefore within reach.

Option III. It is also possible that the President and Congress will use their respective vetoes on annual appropriations bills, rather than trying to fashion agreement on a comprehensive spending (and revenue) package. The consequences for the defense budget in this case are easily predictable. Differential controllability will essentially dictate that short-term cuts be concentrated in readiness accounts, but long-term reductions will be most severe in RDT&E and the weapons systems slated to move into production over the next several years. The best that the President can do in an appropriations war is to protect most of the current baseline, certainly not to expand it in directions identified by the fiscal 1987 budget.

One point that should be stressed is that an absence of budget restraint does not mean that defense budgets will prosper. The 1970s saw unparalleled spending growth; it was also a time when the defense budget did quite poorly. Outlays as percentage of GNP went up by more than 10 percent between 1970 and 1980, but the defense-GNP level dropped by almost 40 percent. Since 1980, the defense-GNP level has risen by almost 25 percent, while the corresponding outlay level has remained fairly stable.[30]

* * *

It is possible to project moderate, sustained defense increases into the 1990s within the context of tightly controlled budgets. In order to do so, however, marginal revenue increases will almost certainly be necessary. The Reagan defense program can be preserved, and the likely price appears much more acceptable than would have seemed possible in 1981.

An agreement between the President and Congress along these lines would have an additional and, according to defense experts, invaluable benefit: stabilizing defense funding. Secretary Weinberger has complained, "Neither the Department of Defense nor anyone else can manage a rational or efficient modernization program when budget resources change unpredictably from year to year, much less so when they do so from month to month."[31] The Army's joint posture statement in 1987 echoed Weinberger's complaint about "the erratic and inconsistent levels of funding [that] complicate the efforts of the Army to provide a consistent and steady program."[32] The simple fact is that erratic defense funding is the direct result of overall budget instability. Reducing that instability makes it possible to sustain modest growth in defense budgets.

President Reagan is in a unique position at this point. He can achieve what was considered impossible back in 1981—long-term growth in defense, along with a reduction in the relative size of the spending budget and a balanced budget. The revenue trade-off would be marginal. By earmarking revenues for defense, moreover, the President will have protected his defense programs against the kind of domestic spending competition that typically prevails in Congress. The result could be a decade of substantial real defense growth. From any perspective, this would represent one of the most important budget policy accomplishments of the modern era.

Notes

1. Senate Committee on Armed Services, *United States/Soviet Military Balance, A Frame of Reference for Congress, A Study by the Library of Congress Congressional Research Service* (Washington, DC: Government Printing Office, 1976), p. 53.

2. The formal title of this legislation is the Balanced Budget and Emergency Deficit Control Act of 1985 (Public Law 99–177). It was signed into law by President Reagan on 12 December 1985. On 7 February 1986, a three-judge panel of the US District Court for the District of Columbia held unconstitutional a portion of the law involving the General Accounting Office. The appeal in *Bowsher, Comptroller General of the United States* v. *Synar, Member of Congress, et al.*, was argued before the Supreme Court on 23 April 1987. The Court agreed that the portion of the law involving the Comptroller General was unconstitutional. As discussed below, the law provides an alternative procedure for reducing spending.

3. For long-term budget data (fiscal 1940–1991), see *Historical Tables, Budget of the United States Government, Fiscal Year 1987* (Washington, DC: Government Printing Office, 1986). Budget authority figures for defense and other functions are reported in section 5.

4. The national defense function includes the budget of the Department of Defense (Military) and atomic energy defense activities conducted by the Department of Energy. The national defense function and "superfunction" are the same. The human resources superfunction includes: (1) education, training, employment and social services; (2) health; (3) Medicare; (4) income security; (5) Social Security; and (6) veterans benefits and services. Physical resources include: (1) energy; (2) national resources and environment; (3) commerce and housing credit; (4) transportation; and (5) community and regional development.

5. *Historical Tables, Fiscal Year 1987*, pp. 3.2(1)–3.2(6).

6. *Historical Tables, Budget of the United States Government, Fiscal Year 1986* (Washington, DC: Government Printing Office, 1985), pp. 6.1(1)–6.1(9). The figures are based on constant FY 1972 dollars.

7. Congressional Quarterly, *Budgeting for America* (Washington, DC: Congressional Quarterly, 1982), p. 48.

8. *Historical Tables, Fiscal Year 1986*, pp. 8.1(1)–8.1(6). There is a good deal of overlap between these payments for individual programs and the general category of entitlements, but the latter is somewhat broader according to most definitions.

9. This includes off-budget outlays, which are technically excluded from the budget under present law but are otherwise indistinguishable from other federal spending.

10. *Fiscal Year 1982 Budget Revisions* (Washington, DC: Government Printing Office, 1981), p. 3.

11. Ibid., p. 127.

12. *Historical Tables, Fiscal Year 1986,* p. 8.1(8).

13. *Annual Report to the Congress, Fiscal Year 1983, Caspar W. Weinberger, Secretary of Defense* (Washington, DC: Government Printing Office, 1982), I–17.

14. Ibid., p. I–6.

15. Leonard Sullivan, Jr., "The Defense Budget," in *American Defense Annual 1985–1986,* ed. G.E. Hudson and J. Kruzel (Lexington, MA: Lexington Books, 1985), p. 57.

16. The atomic energy defense activities are not included in either category for the data and analysis that follow.

17. Budget authority is used here instead of total obligational authority (TOA) for consistency in historical data series. For the military, budget authority is virtually identical to the amount appropriated. Total obligational authority represents the value of the direct defense program in a given year and includes balances available from prior years or resources available from sale of items for inventory.

18. *Fiscal Year 1982 Budget Revisions,* p. 34.

19. *Congressional Quarterly Weekly Report,* 27 (28 December 1985), 2748.

20. Congressional Budget Office, Budgeting for Defense Inflation (Washington, DC: Government Budget Office, 1986), p. 18.

21. *Congressional Quarterly Weekly Report,* 28 (8 February 1986), 233.

22. The estimated totals here are $3.1 billion versus $1.6 billion. *Wall Street Journal,* 13 February 1986, p. 48.

23. Ibid.

24. Ibid.

25. Congressional Budget Office, *The Economic and Budget Outlook: Fiscal Years 1987–1991* (Washington, DC: Congressional Budget Office, 1986), p. xiii.

26. Congressional Budget Office, *The Economic and Budget Outlook: Fiscal Years 1986–1990* (Washington, DC: Congressional Budget Office, 1985), p. xiv.

27. *Economic and Budget Outlook: Fiscal Years 1987–1991,* p. 74.

28. Ibid., p. 98.

29. See *Fiscal Year 1982 Budget Revisions*, p. 7.

30. The fiscal year 1987 level is estimated at 21.9 percent; this was 22.2 percent in fiscal year 1980.

31. *Armed Forces Journal International*, March 1986, p. 50.

32. Ibid.

MANPOWER AND PERSONNEL POLICY IN THE REAGAN YEARS

David R. Segal
Nathan L. Hibler

*R*ONALD REAGAN'S FIRST TERM in the White House followed a decade of dramatic change in the American military. In the wake of an increasingly unpopular and ultimately unsuccessful war in Southeast Asia, support for the defense budget and for military conscription had declined in the American population, although the military institution itself continued to be held in high regard.[1] The willingness of young males to serve in the military had also declined during the 1970s.[2] The GI Bill, which had provided educational benefits to veterans who had served in World War II, the Korean war, the Cold War period, and the Vietnam war, had been allowed to lapse in 1976. Perhaps most important, after decades of debate, America had ended its tempestuous affair with military conscription in 1973 and in its place had chosen to maintain an all-volunteer military system, using labor market dynamics to bring people into the armed forces.[3]

The conversion to an all-volunteer force had numerous implications for manpower and personnel policy beyond the basic change in accession processes. It made the manning of the force dependent upon establishing and maintaining entry-level military pay levels comparable to entry-level pay in the civilian sector for young men and women with the qualifications the armed forces sought, in order to allow the military to compete effectively in the labor market. Entry-level military pay was in fact comparable to entry-level civilian pay in 1973, when the all-volunteer force was born. However, a series of pay caps on general schedule civil service compensation in the 1970s, to which military compensation had been tied, made the armed forces increasingly less competitive through the decade. Indeed, by the end of the decade, entry-level military pay was below the Federal minimum wage.

This unfavorable market posture made the armed forces increasingly dependent for manpower on those segments of the population most disadvantaged in the civilian labor force—women and minority males—who would see military service as a desirable form of employment even if military pay were not truly comparable to civilian pay, since they were in an unfavorable competitive position in the civilian labor market,[4] and on elements of the population with lower qualifications than the armed forces actually desired, who were also in an unfavorable position in the civilian labor market. This latter factor was aggravated by the fact that in 1976 the armed services began using a new selection and classification test, the scoring of which had been miscalibrated at the lower end of the scale. This caused the Services to bring in a far larger proportion of lower mental aptitude recruits during the late 1970s than they were aware of at the time. These recruits, in turn, disproportionately elected to remain in the Service, and are now overrepresented among midcareer personnel. The conversion to an all-volunteer force also shifted the mix of citizen-soldiers and career military personnel in favor of the careerists, increasing the proportion of personnel who would ultimately draw nondisability retired pay.

The initial successes in manning the all-volunteer force were mixed, and the fortunes of the force declined through the decade of the 1970s, accompanied by concerns about the increasing overrepresentation of minorities in the force,[5] the increasing utilization of women,[6] and a decline in the representation of smart high school graduates in the enlisted ranks.[7] These changes in manpower posture were accompanied by a series of incidents that raised questions about whether the force could perform essential military missions.[8] In September 1979, the Carter administration revealed that more than 2,000 Soviet combat troops had been inserted into Cuba, and stated that this was unacceptable. The Soviets refused even to admit that the troops were there. Two months later the US embassy in Tehran was seized and its personnel were taken hostage.

Although US naval forces were massed in the Arabian Sea, the Ayatollah Khomeini's statement that the United States would not engage in a large military operation was borne out, and when a military rescue was ultimately attempted on 25 April 1980, it was aborted with a loss of eight American lives. And in December 1979, the Soviet Union, for the first time since the end of World War II, used its troops outside of Eastern Europe, sending 85,000 personnel into Afghanistan. They are still there.

The month following the Soviet invasion, in an attempt to demonstrate America's resolve, President Carter, who in 1977 had spoken in favor of universal national service, announced in his State of the Union address his intention to reinstate draft registration, which Gerald Ford had put into "deep standby" in 1975, and to register both men and women. The President had the authority to order registration if he deemed it necessary but was dependent on the Congress for the funds to do so, and he did not have authority to begin inductions. The issue of draft registration in general was still controversial in 1980, and the notion of registering women was more so. The Congress did not authorize funds for registration until June 1980, and did not fund the registration of women. The first registration, of males only, did not take place until July. Rallies, teach-ins, and marches against the draft, as well as challenges to registration in the courts, began immediately. Four months later, Ronald Reagan, who had taken a position against registration in the course of his election campaign, was elected President. Candidate Reagan had declared himself opposed to a peacetime draft. He had criticized President Carter's decision on draft registration. His platform had called for the repeal of registration. However, he inherited the mission of improving a weak military manpower posture.

Ronald Reagan's first term as President saw a reversal from his campaign position on draft registration; opposition to and vacillation about the Carter administration's policies regarding the utilization of women in the armed forces; a virtual disappearance of policy debate on the issue of racial representation in the armed forces; vacillation regarding the reestablishment of GI Bill educational benefits; and resistance to strong pressures from the Congress and from within the administration for changes in an increasingly expensive military retirement system. The net effect of the new administration's military manpower policies, such as increased enlisted pay, recruiting resources, and educational incentives for enlistment, coupled with factors external to the military but consequential for it such as declining Federal aid for higher education and increased youth unemployment, produced marked improvements in the quality of recruits and of reenlistments in the early 1980s.

Selective Service Registration in the Reagan Years

For the first year of Ronald Reagan's presidency, policy regarding Selective Service registration was ambiguous. The past President had asked for it, the Congress had funded it, and the newly elected President had won on a platform opposing it. In the face of this ambiguity, compliance with the registration requirements was low, and through most of 1981, no attempt was made to prosecute noncompliers. Antidraft activities continued, primarily on college and university campuses. However, on 1 July 1981, the President established a Military Manpower Task Force, under the chairmanship of the Secretary of Defense, and on 7 January 1982, he announced that he would continue registration, and that after a grace period, noncompliers would be pros-ecuted.[9] The current law simply requires young men to fill out a registration form (available at the Post Office) within 30 days of their 18th birthdays. It does not require them to be examined or classified. Failure to register leaves young men liable to imprisonment for up to five years and up to a $10,000 fine.

During late 1981 and early 1982, compliance was elicited primarily through publicity attempting to remind young men what the legal requirements of registration were. Actual enforcement of the law was "passive," limited to nonregistrants who were reported by others or who defiantly brought themselves to the attention of the authorities. In December 1981, the Congress authorized a more active enforcement program. In June 1982, the Justice Department announced that it was considering prosecution of about 160 young men who had failed to register for the draft, and by March 1983, there had been 14 indictments.[10] In addition, attempts have been made to link citizenship rights to the obligation to register. Since July 1983, for example, under the

Solomon Amendment, registration compliance has been required of students who seek Federal education loans, grants, or employment assistance. This requirement has been one of the most controversial aspects of the system.

Compliance with the current registration system seems comparable to the experience of earlier Selective Service registrations, which were conducted during wartime or Cold War periods. More than 93 percent of those required to register eventually do so although many do not do so within the legally required time limits.[11] And while the rate of compliance appears high, it makes literally hundreds of thousands of young men criminals through noncompliance. Under current enforcement procedures, noncompliers are extremely unlikely to be prosecuted, and if prosecuted, are likely to receive only token punishment.

Most important, while maintaining Selective Service registration, the Reagan administration has continued to assert its dependence upon, and the success of, the all-volunteer military force. Indeed, in early November 1983, Secretary of Defense Caspar Weinberger announced that ''from today it will not be the policy of the Department of Defense to speak about our military as the all-volunteer armed forces. From today, that can go without saying.''[12] Clearly, the strong preference of the administration is to refrain from a military draft.

Women in the Military

The advent of the all-volunteer force (AVF), and in particular the recruiting shortages experienced during the late 1970s, heralded an era of much greater participation by women in the armed forces of the United States. Prior to the AVF, women had been relegated largely to the traditionally female roles of clerical, administrative, and medical support. They had at times been excluded from service or restricted to auxiliary branches or gender-segregated branches. They had been excluded from the military academies and other officer accession programs. They served under a limit on the proportion of the force they could comprise. There were limits on the rank they could attain. They received different family and retirement benefits from men. And they were excluded by statute (for the Air Force and Navy) and by regulation (for the Army) from serving in combat specialties.[13]

In the 1960s, faced with the manpower pressures of the Vietnam war and the domestic turbulence of the women's movement, the Defense Department had created a task force on the utilization of women in the Services, and in 1967, partly on the recommendations of that task force, several provisions of existing legislation were changed. A 2-percent limitation on female enlisted strength was removed. Women for the first time were allowed to be promoted to the permanent rank of colonel and to be appointed as flag-rank officers. Gender differences in retirement benefits were also eliminated.

The 1967 legislation did not create gender equality of service conditions. It left intact gender-segregated promotion systems in all Services except the Air Force, which as the newest Service had only one system from its beginning. It left women in the Army in a gender-segregated corps. It did not redress unequal treatment of dependents of male and female personnel. And it continued to exclude women from the Service academies although the Reserve Officer Training Corps, which is the main source of officer accessions, was opened to women in 1970 by the Air Force and in 1972 by the

Army and Navy. The Gates Commission, which developed the blueprint for the all-volunteer force, assumed that female personnel would not be needed. However, by the time the Congress passed the Equal Rights Amendment in 1972, after rejecting an amendment that would have excluded women from conscription, the military services were planning major increases in their utilization of women. And as recruiting became more difficult during the 1970s, it was necessary to expand both the number of women in the Services and the type of training and assignment opportunities available to them.[14] Thus, major changes in the utilization of women in the armed forces took place in the decade prior to Ronald Reagan's election.

Number of military women. The Department of Defense, and to a great degree the nation as a whole, has historically been opposed to a fully gender-integrated force. Federal statute precludes women from serving on combat aircraft or naval vessels on combat missions, and Army regulations constrain the utilization of women in ground combat operations.[15] This resistance to a gender-blind force has resulted in women in the Army being limited in their opportunity to serve in units or Military Occupational Specialties (MOS) that would subject them to the hazards of direct combat. It is the exclusion of women from units and MOSs that are critical to the conduct of operations within "main battle areas" that has had the greatest impact on the number of women serving both on active duty and in the reserves.

The early years of the all-volunteer force saw a quadrupling of the utilization of women in the US armed forces. At the end of fiscal year (FY) 1973—the year the all-volunteer force was born—there were about

43,000 enlisted women on active duty: about 2.2 percent of the total enlisted force. At the end of fiscal year 1975, there were 95,000 enlisted women on active duty: about 5.3 percent of the force. At the end of fiscal year 1978, 117,000 women constituted 6.6 percent of the enlisted force, and in December 1980, 151,000 women made up 8.8 percent of the enlisted force. The Carter administration's policy had been to continue this increase, which had been projected to reach 12 percent of the force by the mid-1980s, with 223,700 enlisted women and 30,600 female officers serving in the armed forces.

The Reagan administration inherited the plans and programs of the Carter administration that called for increased utilization of women in the armed forces. Under a Carter administration plan, Army female enlisted end strength would have reached 87,500 by fiscal year 1986, up from the fiscal year 1980 level of 60,000. Soon after President Reagan's inauguration, both the Army and the Air Force announced that previous plans to increase female end strengths by 1986 had been shelved in favor of either smaller increases or a wholesale freeze on female force size. The Air Force announced plans to reduce the increase in number of female airmen substantially. The Army announced that it intended to ''hold the line'' or stabilize the recruiting of women in order to maintain a female end strength of 65,000. This freezing of female recruiting levels did not reduce the number of women serving, but terminated the increase in female representation. Subsequently, the Army established the Women-in-the-Army (WITA) Policy Review Group to study the impact that the increased number of female soldiers was having on military readiness.

The first policy change implemented as a result of the WITA study was to eliminate the ''hold the line'' philosophy and call for an increase in the number of women in the Army from 65,000 to 70,000 over a five-year period beginning in September 1982. In fact, by 30 March 1985, there were 77,617 women serving in the Army, comprising 9.97 percent of the force. The increasing number of women in the Army has been used to support the positions of both the Department of the Army, which argues that females are being utilized to the maximum extent possible, and by critics, who argue that the Army has merely increased the raw number of female soldiers without improving their career opportunities.

An investigation of trends in the accession of women in the Army since the beginning of the Carter administration is revealing. If we look at changes in the accession rates rather than total female content rates (because accessions are considered to reflect policy at the time and to produce the desired end strength in future years), during fiscal year 1977 to fiscal year 1985 there was a slight upward gradient in female nonprior service accessions. However, using a least-squares statistical analysis, when we disaggregate this trend to reflect changes under each administration, we find that the line for the Carter years has a steep upward slope, while that for the Reagan years has a moderate downward slope. The slight upward slope of the trend for 1977–1985 is affected by both of these lines, but masks their differences.

It must be remembered that due to pay lags, pay freezes, and a national distaste for military service during the Carter years, the administration found it necessary to increase the number of female enlistees to compensate for shortages in male recruitment, a position that made it appear responsive to demands from the women's movement for equality of opportunity. It would appear that at least for the first five years of the Reagan administration, with military compensation having been increased, youth unemployment on the rise, and military service having become a more desirable form of employment, the US Army has been able essentially to "hold the line" on female accessions and sustain the needed levels of accessions by drawing on its traditional source of manpower.

Utilization of military women. The ease with which women can enter the armed forces and particularly the Army has been reduced during the Reagan administration. Women appear to face two hurdles when attempting to serve the nation in a military capacity: first, they must be among the most highly qualified applicants, and secondly, they are restricted in enlisting for certain types of military occupational specialties.

Throughout the history of the United States armed forces, women have never knowingly been allowed to serve in those jobs that require direct combat with an enemy, or in jobs that might, in the event of hostilities, place them in a position of direct combat with an enemy. The argument has been made that women in a main battle area present a threat to the cohesiveness or "male bonding process" that serves to promote increased combat effectiveness.[16] Empirical evidence has been sparse in support of this proposition, and other researchers have argued that commonality of experience is more important than homogeneity of gender in producing cohesion.[17] Nevertheless, the armed forces have in the past and do still today continue to restrict women to those job categories not likely to expose them to direct offensive combat operations, although they have not been removed from situations in which they are likely to come under enemy fire. Given that the primary task of the armed forces is the conduct of direct combat operations, women are effectively ruled out of the largest number of job opportunities, but not necessarily job categories, and their career opportunities are constrained.

During the Reagan administration, the Department of Defense has reduced the number of job categories in which women are allowed to serve, while proclaiming increased training opportunities for women in the armed forces.[18] During the autumn of 1982, based on the WITA policy review, the Army sought and received Department of Defense support for the closing of 23 MOSs to women. Among those closed at that time were: 54E, nuclear, biological, and chemical warfare specialist; 67T, tactical transportation helicopter repairer; and 17B, field artillery radar crewmember. This action was based upon a Department of the Army study that reevaluated the upper body strength requirements for proper MOS performance and the potential for direct combat exposure by soldiers serving in all MOSs. This type of reevaluation is not without precedent. However, by October 1983, the Department of the Army had decided that 13 of the original 23 MOSs *could* be performed by women. Among those reopened were 54E and 67T, as well as 62G, quarrying specialist, and ten others.

This reversal was not due to a reduction in upper body strength requirements but to two other factors; first, the public response to the closing of career opportunities to women was very vocal and very negative, and secondly, the fact that the Army was experiencing personnel shortages within some of the MOSs that were closed. As Deputy Chief of Staff for Personnel, Lieutenant General Robert Elton explained, ''Some people with the MOSs will be in forward battle areas but jobs are available for women that would not have such a high probability of combat."[19] This would appear to contradict the historical combat exclusion policy and allow for the inclusion of women in combat areas whenever and wherever needed. The Reagan administration throughout its entire term has maintained support for the combat exclusion policy. However, it would appear that manpower requirements rather than gender considerations are the critical factors in decisions regarding the use of women in certain MOSs.

The point was perhaps made more dramatically in October 1983 when more than two dozen Air Force women participated in the invasion of Grenada and landed during the first hours of combat, while US paratroopers were still engaging hostile Cuban soldiers at Point Salinas airport. An Air Force official noted that "To have excluded an aircraft from the mission simply because there was a woman on board would have lessened our response and reduced our effectiveness."[20]

The future of women in the armed forces. The future of women in the armed forces appears to rest on two factors: pressure for equal opportunity of service, and military need. Of these two factors, it would appear likely that due to the decline in the size of the primary military age-eligible male manpower pool into the 1990s, there may in fact be an increased need for women to meet national defense requirements. This could well result in an increased recruitment effort directed at the young women of America. While this increase in need would result in quantitative changes in the use of women, it would not necessarily result in structural changes that would equalize training and career opportunities. As long as the Services are able to recruit enough men to fill those specialties and units most likely to engage in direct combat, there appears to be little chance, under the current administration, for women to enter those traditionally masculine roles necessary for the conduct of combat operations.

In short, as long as women are not needed in large numbers in peacetime and we are willing to overlook the facts that personnel from noncombat roles are frequently used to fill vacancies in combat units under wartime conditions, and that combat support units are likely to find themselves in hostile fire zones in future wars, qualitative opportunities for women will be limited. Most assuredly, women will play an increasing role in the nation's defense, but the rate of increase is likely to be slow enough to negate any structural or policy changes toward women within the Department of Defense, unless we need to mobilize for a major war, in which case we will have to learn how to make effective use of larger numbers of female personnel—perhaps in combat specialties—literally under the gun.

Race in the Military

Ronald Reagan has taken a different approach to the utilization of women in the military from Jimmy Carter's, but issues regarding the utilization of women in combat, and the conscription of women should we return to the draft, have not gone away. Indeed, these were both concerns when the Congress debated the Equal Rights Amendment in 1983. By contrast, the issue of the over-representation and utilization of racial and ethnic minorities in the military, which was a *cause célèbre* during the early years of the AVF, has virtually disappeared in the 1980s.

Like women, blacks have at various times been excluded from the American military, placed in segregated units, excluded from combat specialties, been subjected to quotas, and been restricted in their access to officer commissions and their opportunities to attain positions of command. The armed forces were racially integrated during the era of the Korean Police Action, however, and prior to the advent of the all-volunteer force, blacks had reached a level of representation in the military roughly proportional to their representation in society.

The Gates Commission, which had not anticipated any utilization of women in the all-volunteer force, had also anticipated that the end of conscription would not produce any change in the racial composition of the force. However, between 1972 and 1983, black representation increased from 11 percent of all active duty personnel to about 19 percent, and the overrepresentation was particularly severe in ground combat units that, in the event of war, would take a disproportionate share of casualties and fatalities. Moreover, a large number of reflections of institutional racial discrimination were identified,[21] and attempts were made to correct them. The issue of racial discrimination received a great deal of visibility, and evidence suggests that significant progress was made.[22]

Racial discrimination has been reduced, but not eliminated in the all-volunteer force of the 1980s.[23] Unlike the issue of gender roles, however, it has achieved virtual invisibility in the policy arena in the Reagan years.

The GI Bill

Both the Cold War GI Bill and the "new GI Bill" of 1985 represent a radical departure from the original intent of the World War II and Korean-era Serviceman's Readjustment Assistance Acts—the original GI Bills— which was to provide a means of higher education or training to those citizens who had had their lives disrupted by conscription during wartime. The original GI Bill established a system of postservice rewards for contributing to the defense of the nation. The original GI Bill was not created until after the cessation of hostilities, and played no role in providing an incentive to enlist during the war years.

The Cold War GI Bill was the first educational benefit program offered to personnel who did not serve in wartime (although it was extended through the Vietnam war), and was demonstrated to be a major enlistment incentive.[24] The Department of Defense lost this inducement when the Cold War GI Bill expired in 1977. To compensate for this loss, the Carter administration created the Veterans Educational Assistance Program (VEAP), initially a two-for-one contributory program whereby the Department of Defense would contribute two dollars for postservice education for every dollar the veteran contributed, up to a maximum benefit of $8,100 for a three or four-year enlistment. The Department of the Army had gone on record as wanting a "new GI Bill," a position opposed by the other services, which felt that a GI Bill gave the Army an unfair recruiting advantage. The VEAP did not meet with very much success during its first five years of life. To compensate for the low value of the original program, the Department of the Army began to experiment with additional VEAP programs, such as "Super-VEAP," also known as the Army College Fund, and "Ultra-VEAP."

These programs were able to increase the value of the VEAP up to a maximum of $20,100, an amount commensurate with the Cold War GI Bill. Through these programs, the Army was able to increase the overall VEAP value through the addition of noncontributory bonuses and thereby remain competitive in the recruiting field. It was this program of VEAP, Super-VEAP, and Ultra-VEAP that the Reagan administration inherited in 1981.

The Reagan years. The Reagan administration came into office with a favorable disposition toward a new GI Bill designed to replace the VEAP. Within days of the 1981 inauguration, the Services rekindled their mutual rivalry over the need for a GI Bill. The Army made the reinstitution of the GI Bill its number-one legislative priority for 1981, despite the objections of the Navy, which felt a "recruiting war" might erupt to the detriment of both Services.[25] The Department of Defense mediated this dispute by requesting that Congress delay any GI bill legislation until DOD had an opportunity to experiment with alternative educational incentive packages and to study the fiscal impact that any new GI Bill would have. DOD initially requested that Congress delay any action on a new GI Bill for one year.

In March of 1982, the Department of Defense announced that the administration had determined that the most cost-effective way of recruiting and retaining personnel was through the VEAP system, and not through a new GI Bill. It was also felt that the current and projected pay increases for the armed forces would provide an additional enlistment and reenlistment incentive and thereby reduce the need for any additional postservice educational benefits as a means of recruitment and retention. This policy conflicted greatly with the desires of the House Armed Services Military Personnel and Compensation Subcommittee, which strongly favored passage of a new GI Bill. But the administration did receive tacit support from the Congressional Budget Office, which reported that the most costly type of educational benefit was a new GI Bill with transferability of benefits. Given congressional desires and the Reagan administration's reluctance, little action was taken on a new GI Bill for the next two years, although there was continuous pressure for such a bill.

The New GI Bill. By October 1984, under congressional pressure, the administration had agreed to implement a "New GI Bill" beginning 1 July 1985. As with VEAP, this new program is contributory, with the Service veteran contributing $100 per month for 12 months while DOD varies its contribution based on the length of service of the veteran. Unlike VEAP, this contribution is not refundable if the personnel do not seek postservice training or education. The New GI Bill contains provisions for reduced noncontributory educational benefits for noncollege graduate members of the Selected Reserve. Initially, the program will allow participants to draw a $250 benefit per month for 36 months when enlisting for two years and $300 benefit per month for a three-year enlistment.

Also, at the discretion of the Secretary of Defense, those enlisting in critical-skill MOSs may receive up to $400 per month in additional benefits and those who reenlist for a minimum of five years or serve a total of eight years may receive another benefit of up to $300 per month, or $600 if they serve in critical MOSs. To remain competitive in recruiting, the Department of the Navy, with DOD support, created the "Sea College Fund" to counteract the recruiting advantage the Army realized with its "College Fund." Both of these programs provide the respective Services with the formal authority to award the discretionary $400 per month benefit to those recruits deemed qualified. It is surmised by the Army, and more recently the Navy, that this additional $14,400 in total benefits will provide a sufficient incentive to highly qualified, college-bound individuals to choose one Service over the other and to enlist for training in a critical MOS.

The future of the New GI Bill. It has been estimated by the Congressional Budget Office (CBO) that the cost of the New GI Bill will be anywhere from the administration's estimate of $621 million to the CBO estimate of $435 million over the three-year lifespan of the program.[26] It appears as though the lifespan of the New GI Bill may be cut short due to the budgetary reductions predicated by the requirements of the Gramm-Rudman-Hollings Emergency Deficit Reduction Act. The fiscal year 1987 budget submitted by the Reagan administration deletes funding for the New GI Bill. This appears to be in response to both budgetary constraints and the seeming ease with which mid-1980s recruiting quotas are being met (although the Army was unable to meet its recruiting goals during the winter of 1985/86).

However, both the Army and the Navy have pressed for continuation of the New GI Bill, and key congressional committees seem sympathetic to their position and oppose this element of the President's budget. Moreover, the total budget has failed to receive congressional approval. In summary then, it would appear that the fate of the New GI Bill is dependent on two factors: first, the ability of the Reagan administration to overcome congressional support for the continued funding of the New GI Bill; and secondly, the ability of the Services to meet recruiting quotas while offering fewer postservice education benefits as an inducement to enlist.

The Military Retirement System

Congress began informally promising (although frequently not providing) nondisability retirement pensions for military personnel as far back as 1780.[27] It was not until 1906, after veterans of the Civil War had reached old age, that Congress enacted a nondisability retirement system by defining attainment of the age of 62 as proof of disability under the provisions of the Civil War disability retirement system. Pensions for reasons of disability had been established in 1776. The military retirement system evolved piecemeal thereafter until the late 1940s, when the Congress codified what is today the foundation of the uniformed services nondisability retirement system in the Career Compensation Act of 1949.

The modern retirement system, created during the post-World War II years, provided for the voluntary retirement of enlisted personnel after 20 years of active service and officers after 20 years of service with ten of those years served in a commissioned status. The amount of the pension under this system was to be computed by multiplying basic pay at the time of retirement by the number of years served (minimum of 20) times .025 up to a maximum of 75 percent of basic pay. From 1948 until 1980, only minor alterations to this system were made to allow for adjustments in the method of calculation of the basic pay multiplier, inclusion of the Reserve forces, and provision for semiannual cost-of-living adjustments (COLA) based on the Consumer Price Index (CPI).

The retirement system is very generous by civilian standards for those who serve 20 years or more. It is equally penurious for those who serve less than 20 years. They get virtually nothing. As the military retired rolls swelled with veterans of World War II, the Korean war, and most recently the Vietnam war, the retirement system grew increasingly expensive, and is projected to continue to grow, since military personnel who retire after 20 years of active duty will on the average draw pensions for more years than they served on active duty. During the 1970s, eight major studies suggested drastic changes in the system.[28]

The last few months of the Carter administration saw the inclusion in the Department of Defense Authorization Act of 1981 of a provision that military and Civil Service pensions be adjusted semiannually for cost-of-living increases at the same rate and at the same time. The Act of 1981 also saw a radical change in the method of calculation of the initial pensions. Previously, basic pay at the time of retirement was used for computation, but the 1981 Act stipulated that the average of the highest three years of basic pay be used. It was this basic nondisability retirement system, modified by the Act of 1981, that President Reagan inherited with his first inauguration.

The Reagan years. Candidate Reagan had stated during the 1980 campaign that he did "not favor abandoning the present semiannual indexing" of Federal retirement benefits.[29] This campaign promise proved to be one of the first to fall to the budget axe. The fiscal year 1982 Budget Reconciliation Act, enacted on 13 August 1981, replaced the semiannual COLA for Federal pensions with an annual COLA, still based on the CPI. Along with this major shift in inflation protection adjustments, the fiscal year 1982 act extended the time between COLA increases by varying amounts to allow for increased budgetary savings. The amount of the COLA was also adjusted to correct for the fact that during previous years when active duty pay rates were frozen, retired pay was automatically adjusted to compensate for inflation. This had resulted in pensioners effectively increasing their retirement benefits relative to the active forces.

Fiscal year 1985 saw a second major change in the military nondisability retirement system. Prior to fiscal year 1985, funding for the retirement system was based on an intergenerational (pay-as-you-go) approach, paying for current outlays of retired pay through current appropriations. From fiscal year 1985 on, the Department of Defense is required to fund the retirement system using an advance funding concept and an accrual accounting technique, so that money is "banked" from current appropriations to be used toward subsequent retired pay of personnel currently on active duty. This new method of funding and accounting will allow current budgets to reflect the impact of manpower and force policy decisions on retirement costs. It will also protect retirement benefits from attempts to generate short-term budgetary savings through appropriation cuts. This change appears to be in response to the projected costs of the retirement system for the next 20 years.

The future of the nondisability retirement system. Currently, one out of three enlisted personnel and roughly three out of five officers who reach five years of active service will eventually draw nondisability retirement benefits.[30] The career component of the active force (those with over five years of service) has been growing since the late 1970s. Thus, there appears to be further growth in the career cohort flow similar to the World War II, Korean war, and Vietnam war expansions. Between 1998 and 2006, there will be an ever-increasing number of military retirees relative to the previous 20 years.

This projected increase provoked the Congress to action. Although President Reagan was resistant to changing the military retirement system through his entire first term, the 1986 Defense Authorization Bill mandated a reduction in retirement benefits for future personnel. The appropriation for retirement accrual cost was cut $2.9 billion; a compromise between the House-proposed reduction of $4.0 billion and the proposed Senate reduction of $1.82 billion. The Defense Department and the military services were initially given the task of devising the new system, although the Congress has now reclaimed the initiative.

The Department of Defense has traditionally "grandfathered" any changes to the retirement system, so it seems little can be done to alter the fiscal impact of the increase in retirees in terms of personnel who are already serving in the armed forces. During the Reagan administration, numerous suggestions for change in the retirement system have been made, including a contributory retirement system, partial vesting after ten years of active service, reduced pensions until age 62, reduced multipliers of basic pay to be readjusted upon reaching age 62, and others. Given the political strength of the retired military community both with the Congress and the Department of Defense, there will be great resistance to change. However, the pressure of the budget deficit and projected major increases in the cost of military retired pay are likely to motivate changes that will produce savings when personnel who have not yet been recruited by the armed forces retire at the end of their careers.

* * *

From a manpower and personnel perspective, the US armed forces are far better off in the late 1980s than they were a decade ago. Recruiting goals have been met and personnel quality has improved markedly. This is due in no small measure to increases in military compensation, to the establishment of new educational incentives for military service, to the decline in Federal educational programs not linked to military service, and to increases in civilian young unemployment under the Reagan administration, and we believe that credit should be given where credit is due. At the same time, we feel it unwise to project the recent successes indefinitely into the future.

Attempts to reduce the Federal deficit will most certainly affect the defense budget, and we feel that manpower and personnel accounts are particularly vulnerable because they have the largest proportional payouts in the years in which expenditures are authorized, and can therefore produce the most rapid proportional savings. As we have noted, two important elements of the benefit package are already under the budget knife: military retirement and the GI Bill. These factors may well have an effect on the future recruiting success of the all-volunteer force. To the extent that we maintain a labor market model of military manpower and injure the market position of military recruiters by reducing benefits, the ability of the armed forces to compete in the marketplace will be damaged.

The major differences between the personnel issues in the all-volunteer force in the 1980s and those of the previous decade are in the area of equal opportunity, and these issues intersect with labor market considerations. To the degree that benefits are reduced and the market position of the volunteer force is weakened, it will become more dependent on personnel recruited from the secondary labor market: women and minorities. Increased representation of these groups in the ranks, in turn, will resurrect issues of whether we should send women into combat, and whether disadvantaged segments of the labor force—the poor, the black, the brown—should be asked to absorb a disproportionate share of our combat casualties and fatalities. Should our wars be fought by those who need the work?

The major alternative to depending on volunteers from secondary labor markets is a return to conscription, a policy that has been odious to the Reagan administration from the outset. A fair conscription system may reduce concerns regarding overrepresentation of personnel from the secondary labor market, but it will in all likelihood raise the debate on the role of women in the military to a central position again. Current plans for a draft of medical personnel—an area where the military has severe needs right now—are gender-free, and if we draft women in some occupations, it will be difficult to justify male-only conscription in others. And if we move to a gender-free draft, both the structure of modern warfare and the litigious nature of modern American society will make it difficult to keep women out of combat. For the past three decades, the armed forces have provided a stage upon which the ongoing citizenship revolution which links military service to citizenship rights has been played. The theater has been relatively dark recently, but the show has not closed.

Notes

1. David R. Segal and John D. Blair, ''Public Confidence in the U.S. Military,'' *Armed Forces and Society* 3, no. 1 (November 1976): 3–11.

2. Jerald G. Bachman, ''American High School Seniors View the Military: 1976–1982,'' *Armed Forces and Society* 10, no. 1 (Fall 1983): 86–104.

228 *David R. Segal and Nathan L. Hibler*

3. See David R. Segal, "Military Organization and Personnel Accession: What Changed with the All-Volunteer Force ... and What Didn't?" in Robert K. Fullinwider, ed., *Conscripts and Volunteers* (Totowa, NJ: Rowman and Allanheld, 1983), pp. 7–22.

4. David R. Segal, Jerald G. Bachman, and Faye Dowdell, "Military Service for Female and Black Youth," *Youth and Society* 10, no. 2 (December 1978): 127–34.

5. Morris Janowitz and Charles C. Moskos, "Radical Composition in the All-Volunteer Force," *Armed Forces and Society* 1, no. 1 (Fall 1974): 109–23.

6. Mady Wechsler Segal, "Women's Roles in the U.S. Armed Forces: An Evaluation of Evidence and Arguments for Policy Decisions," in Robert K. Fullinwider, ed., *Conscripts and Volunteers* (Totowa, NJ: Rowman and Allanheld, 1983), pp. 200–13.

7. See Maxwell R. Thurman, "Sustaining the All-Volunteer Force 1973–1982: The Second Decade," in William Bowman, Roger Little, and G. Thomas Sicilia, eds., *The All-Volunteer Force After a Decade* (Washington, DC: Pergamon-Brassey's, 1986), p. 269.

8. See Lawrence J. Korb, "The FY 1981–1985 Defense Program." *AEI Foreign Policy and Defense Review* 2, No. 2 (1980): 3.

9. The final report of the task force notes that an interim report sent to the President on 15 December 1981 "was helpful to the President in making his decision." It does not note what the position of the task force on selective service was. See Military Manpower Task Force, *A Report to the President on the Status and Prospects of the All-Volunteer Force*, Washington, DC, October 1982, p. VI–13.

10. Herbert C. Puscheck, "Selective Service Registration: Success or Failure?" *Armed Forces and Society* 10 (Fall 1983): 5–25.

11. See James B. Jacobs and Dennis McNamara, "Selective Service Without a Draft," *Armed Forces and Society* 10 (Spring 1984): 361–79.

12. Caspar W. Weinberger, "The All-Volunteer Force in the 1980s," in William Bowman, Roger Little, and G. Thomas Sicilia, eds., *The All-Volunteer Force After a Decade* (Washington, DC: Pergamon-Brassey's, 1986).

13. See Martin Binkin and Shirley J. Bach, *Women and the Military* (Washington, DC: The Brookings Institution, 1977).

14. Mady Wechsler Segal and David R. Segal, "Social Change and the Participation of Women in the American Military," *Research in Social Movements, Conflicts and Change* 5 (1983): 235–58.

15. See George H. Quester, ''The Problem,'' pp. 217–235 in Nancy Loring Goldman, ed., *Female Soldiers—Combatants or Non-combatants* (Westport, CT: Greenwood Press, 1982).

16. See David H. Marlowe, ''The Manning of the Force and the Structure of Battle: Part 2—Men and Women,'' in Robert K. Fullinwider, ed., *Conscripts and Volunteers* (Totowa, NJ: Rowman and Allanheld, 1983), pp. 189–99.

17. See M. C. Devilbiss, ''Gender Integration and Unit Deployment: A Study of GI Jo,'' *Armed Forces and Society,* 11, no. 4 (Summer 1985): 523–552. Also see Charles C. Moskos, ''Female GIs in the Field.'' *Society* 22, no. 6 (September–October 1985): 28–33.

18. See Caspar W. Weinberger, *Annual Report to the Congress* (Washington, DC: US Government Printing Office, 1986).

19. See Rick Maze, ''Strength Test No Bar to MOS Entry,'' *Army Times,* 31 October 1983, p. 1.

20. See ''Air Force Women Participated in Grenada Invasion.'' *Minerva* 4, no. 1 (Spring 1986): 67–69.

21. See for example Peter G. Nordlie, James A. Thomas, and Ezequiel R. Sevilla, *Measuring Changes in Institutional Racial Discrimination in the Army,* Arlington, VA, US Army Research Institute for the Behavioral and Social Sciences, Technical Paper 270.

22. David R. Segal and Peter G. Nordlie, ''Racial Inequality in Army Promotions.'' *Journal of Political and Military Sociology* 7 (Spring 1979): 135–42.

23. See for example Gary J. Zucca and Benjamin Gorman, ''Affirmative Action: Blacks and Hispanics in U.S. Navy Occupational Specialties,'' *Armed Forces and Society* 12, no. 4 (Summer 1986): 513.

24. See David R. Segal and Jere Cohen, ''Educational Benefits and the Legitimacy of Military Service,'' in Reuvan Gal and Thomas C. Wyatt, eds., *Legitimacy and Military Commitment* (Fairfax, VA: Hero Books). In press.

25. See Larry Carney, ''GI Bill Bid Ready for Hill,'' *Army Times,* 2 March 1981, p. 4.

26. *Budgetary Costs of Military Educational Benefits,* Congressional Budget Office, Staff Working Paper.

27. See David R. Segal, ''Military Personnel,'' in Joseph Kruzel, ed., *American Defense Annual 1985–86* (Lexington, KY: DC Heath, 1986).

28. See Robert L. Goldich, ''Military Nondisability Retirement 'Reform,' 1969–1979.'' *Armed Forces and Society* 10, no. 1 (Fall): 59–85.

29. See Tom Philpott, ''COL Hike Cut Urged,'' *Army Times,* 23 February 1981, p. 1.

30. US, Department of Defense, *Fifth Quadrennial Review of Military Compensation* (Washington, DC: Government Printing Office, 1984).

DEFENSE POLICY
AND PROGRAMS IN
THE GRAMM-RUDMAN ERA

Dov S. Zakheim

*D*EFENSE PROGRAM PLANNING in the United States has always responded to two exogenous variables. The first and more conventional factor common to defense planning is the nature of the threat against which forces and systems are planned. The second is more peculiar to the American system of government, namely the constraints imposed by Congress, within which all planning must operate.

These variables, however, create pressures in opposite directions. Potential threats to US interests tend to induce more demand for defense resources, while congressional activity traditionally has reduced the levels of resources available to the Defense Department for coping with those threats. The effect of these counterpressures has led some observers to consider that there is a permanent mismatch between ''strategy'' and ''resources.'' Moreover, many of these observers have also concluded that Department of Defense planners must alter their ''strategies''—presumably making them less ambitious and thereby less demanding of defense resources.

From the vantage point of another partly overlapping group of analysts, the forces that have pulled defense planners in virtually opposite directions were not as strong as might have been thought. During the

1970s, these analysts argued that the threat to US interests posed by the Soviet Union and its allies had been overstated by those who sought higher levels of defense expenditure. Moreover, proponents of this view contended that the threat could be further reduced through arms control agreements. Reduction of the potential threat, in turn, would permit still lower defense expenditures. In this regard, the supposedly independent threat variable was indeed subject to alteration as a result of US activities.

An entirely different set of considerations appeared to refute the contention that the "congressional variable" was independent. For many years it was reasonable to assume that Congress was subject to influence on the defense budget. Budgets, after all, were—and are—submitted by the administration, and constant interaction between the administration and congressional committee members and individual legislators clearly influenced legislative outcomes in response to those proposed budgets. Indeed, opponents of greater defense spending argued that administration use of that influence actually lessened the supposedly "objective" requirement for more efficient defense strategy and planning.

Developments during the recent past belie both assumptions about the liability of either the "threat variable" or the "congressional variable" to manipulation by any administration. With respect to assumptions about the threat to US interests worldwide, events over the past decade have demonstrated that, far from shrinking, Soviet power actually has grown, despite (and many argue because of) arms control efforts. Indeed, far from being constrained by arms control or any other similar factor (i.e., freer economic and cultural relations), Soviet capabilities have expanded both qualitatively and quantitatively, and have manifested themselves over a wider geographic expanse than ever before. Requirements for US capabilities have grown commensurately.

Recent events have shown that the "congressional variable" is no less independent than the "threat variable." The passage of the Gramm-Rudman-Hollings (GRH) budget reduction legislation further complicated the task of program planners by minimizing the degree to which they might hope for congressional relief from budgetary constraints. Indeed, by virtue both of the automatic spending cut formula and its disproportionate penalizing of the defense budget (which would supply half of all outlay reductions despite accounting for less than a third of all outlays), the Gramm-Rudman-Hollings enactment places the defense budget hostage to congressional action on all other budgetary accounts, unless the administration's budget is sustained intact. The Supreme Court's ruling regarding GRH may, if anything, have created even greater uncertainty in the defense budget process.

Clearly, these two developments are still pulling the defense budget in different directions. Soviet developments call for greater defense resources; Gramm-Rudman—however it may be modified by Congress—holds out at most a promise of limited growth at or near 3 percent annually. Clearly, the defense budget cannot fully respond to either development, though it cannot ignore either.

The threat environment and the congressional environment should not be confused; only those who forget why they are defending the Republic, or never realized why they were doing so in the first place, could consider the Congress their primary adversary. Nevertheless, the changes in these two component parts have therefore tightened the vise that constrains and complicates defense program planning. Program planning, however, cannot come to a dead halt. It is incumbent upon planners not only to continue their seemingly hopeless efforts to reconcile threat requirements with congressionally imposed constraints, but, more important, to build upon their current procedures and abilities to fashion a defense program that accomplishes that reconciliation.

The program planning effort, to be successful, must address four key principles that reflect the essence and ideal of both defense policy-making and the program process.

1. Defense planning is about defense against external military threats, not against internal budgetary foes.

There has always been a fringe element, both within and outside Government, that has forgotten (or never learned) that Congress is not the enemy. It is the ebb and flow of congressional debate, and the vicissitudes of the outcomes that debate engenders, that is the hallmark of the freedom we are all pledged to defend. The most unenlightened congressional critic is not the less loyal a citizen for the error of his (or her) ways.

There will never be unanimity over the levels of resources that should be applied to the nation's defense, particularly when the issue is being debated in peacetime. Once this truism is recognized, other principles follow as corollaries.

2. Defense planning cannot be constrained to an assumed budget level, since the nature of congressional action indicates that level will never be exactly realized.

Continuing congressional line item management of the budget on an annual basis, and influences upon congressional behavior that stem from sources other than those generated by, or even related to, administration concerns will ensure that no budget proposed by the administration will emerge as law untouched by legislative modification. There will be times when external events, such as the invasion of Afghanistan, will galvanize Congress into action far beyond that anticipated by a phlegmatic administration. There will be other times, such as congressional action over the fiscal year 1986 defense budget, when the administration's *cri de coeur* for support will go unheeded. As a result, no determination of requirements can be adjusted to fit expected resource availability. The resources are never what they are expected to be.

The Packard Commission's report and the National Security Decision Directive (NSDD) signed by President Reagan on 1 April 1986, both attempt to provide more rigorous fiscal constraints to the planning process. The NSDD goal, with respect to national security planning and budgeting, is to "improve the integration of national security strategy with fiscal guidance provided to the Department of Defense." The Secretary of Defense is asked to recommend to the National Security Council and to the Office of Management and Budget, procedures that include

- The issuance of provisional five-year budgets for the Department of Defense.

- A military strategy to support national objectives within the provisional five-year budget.

The Department of Defense is responding to this directive by reviewing its current procedures and proposing initiatives that will further realize the President's goals. Lead responsibility for DOD's efforts with respect to planning and budgeting has been assigned to the Under Secretary of Defense for Policy, together with the Assistant Secretary of Defense (Comptroller) and the Director of Program Analysis and Evaluation.

In the end, it is the Congress that imposes the ultimate budget constraints. Moreover, congressional reductions in any given year not only affect spending levels for that year, but, due to the cumulative effect of multiyear obligations and obligation requirements, also depress spending levels for future years. This phenomenon can best be understood by recalling that reductions in any year's spending levels result in lower absolute spending for the following years even if predicted percentage increases in real growth are retained intact. Put another way, a decrease in base-year spending creates a decrease in out-year spending unless additional real growth is applied. It is noteworthy that the Department of Defense's current (fiscal year 1987) request calls for real growth sufficient to offset last year's harsh reductions. In sum, congressional actions will continue to be the ultimate arbiter of defense resource availability. Only with Congress's cooperation can efforts such as those recommended by the President and the Packard Commission prove successful.

In this regard, Congress has launched a major and promising initiative leading to the formulation and possible adoption of multiyear defense budgets. This initiative hopefully could provide more stability to the defense planning system and realize significant cost savings by fostering more stable acquisition programs. Congress took the first step in this direction by enacting section 1405, General Provisions, of the Fiscal Year 1986 Defense Authorization Act. The act directs the President to

include ... for fiscal year 1988 a single proposed budget for the Department of Defense and related agencies for fiscal years 1988 and 1989.

The Department of Defense has already begun to implement the terms of the fiscal year 1986

Authorization Act's directive on budgets. On 31 December 1985, for the first time ever the Secretary of Defense signed a two-year Defense Guidance for the department. This guidance, covering the five-year program for fiscal years 1988–1992, is the Department's primary program planning document and represents a first major milestone in the department's (previously annual) Planning, Programming, and Budgeting System. In March 1986, the department's Comptroller issued preliminary instructions for preparation of FY 1988/FY 1989 biennial budget estimates.

3. Commitments are as unchanging as resources are variable.

Although the availability of resources can never be totally predicted from one year to the next, much less for a five-year span, commitments appear to remain fixed for years on end. All US treaty commitments stem from the early post-World War II period. These commitments have survived two Asian wars, countless minor military skirmishes, Republican and Democratic administrations of both liberal and conservative stripes, and Congresses led by both parties. No one has advocated renouncing a single treaty that the United States has signed with any of its allies, however wayward they might have been at times. Moreover, the United States has taken on commitments to "friends" that often have even greater force in practice, and in the vocal support they receive from Congress and the American people, than treaty commitments.

The relationship with Israel is one example. The United States has no formal treaty relationship with Israel, only a series of Executive Agreements on security cooperation. Nevertheless, US support for Israel has been manifested not merely in massive levels of military assistance ($1.8 billion had been proposed for fiscal year 1987, and a slightly smaller amount was granted in fiscal year 1986) but also operationally, i.e., the airlifted resupply of Israeli forces during the 1973 Middle East War. Since 1979, in the aftermath of the Camp David accords, the relationship with Egypt has been virtually coequal in importance in the eyes of many legislators and opinion leaders.

Finally, the relationship with Saudi Arabia has had many strong proponents both in the administration and in key sectors of the informed public for a period that antedates the creation of the State of Israel.

4. Support for commitments, even if costly, can be no more variable than the commitments themselves.

Commitments are meaningless unless they are consistently supported. For example, the United States consistently has rejected Soviet attempts to sever the US nuclear relationship with the North Atlantic Treaty Organization (NATO), whatever guises those attempts may have taken at various times and in spite of tempting opportunities to reduce defense expenditure as a result.

Thirty years ago the Soviets, with the assistance of Poland, pressed the Rapacki Plan for a denuclearized Europe. The resulting landscape would have witnessed the preponderance of Soviet conventional forces, unchecked by the American nuclear umbrella, which at the time supported the policy of massive retaliation. Later years witnessed proposals for nuclear free zones. The Nordic nuclear free zone proposal was a classic example of an attempt to update and, in Soviet terms, suboptimize, the Rapacki Plan. Under the latter plan Soviet nuclear forces could have dominated the Nordic area without ever leaving port. Most recently, the Soviets have sought to achieve their long-standing goals by means of the various proposals they have put forward in Geneva at the Intermediate Range Nuclear

Forces (INF) talks. Nevertheless, whether their offers are geared to reductions commensurate with British and French missiles or warheads, or are suggestions that the Allied forces not modernize at all (thereby soon eliminating those independent deterrents), the goal is the same: to create a gap in the progressive American nuclear deterrence doctrine that continues to underpin the Atlantic Alliance.

The temptation to accept a variant of these Soviet proposals is difficult to resist at a time when pressures from a variety of arms control advocates are merged with the fiscal pressures imposed by a need to control American deficit levels. Yet succumbing to that temptation would lead to a more basic questioning of the American commitment to NATO, and particularly, to its vulnerability to fiscal vicissitudes on Capitol Hill. Moreover, it is unlikely that European reaction in turn would stop at mere questioning. All latent impulses to press for lower European defense expenditures would merge with emerging neutralist strains, creating tremendous fissures in the very fabric of the Alliance. Only the Soviets would stand to benefit.

Consistency, moreover, is not in demand in Europe alone. In the late 1970s, for example, both Northeast and Southwest Asia witnessed a wavering of the purposefulness with which America stood by friends in those regions. In one case, that of the aborted Carterite proposal for the withdrawal of the 2d Infantry Division from South Korea, the outcome was not an unhappy one. The proposal itself was said to stem from a desire to trim defense expenditures. It had been foreshadowed in studies by various think tanks prior to the 1976 election. Nevertheless (and this case provides an excellent parable to those who might employ Gramm-Rudman as an excuse for major adjustments to American military posture) the Carter administration could not implement this policy. Congress itself objected strongly to the proposed action and the idea was unceremoniously dropped.

Far less felicitous was America's inability to prevent the fall of the Shah, or at least to foster a peaceful, democratic transfer of his power. The reverberations of America's lack of commitment to Iran were felt equally in Riyadh and Jerusalem. Furthermore, Southwest Asia became a region of anguish for Americans as Iran's taunting retention of American hostages took place virtually simultaneously with the Soviet invasion of Afghanistan.

Consistency need not mean blind support for regimes that themselves have changed their behavior, or which no longer can claim the support of the majority of their populations. It does, however, mean a readiness to support those forces most likely to produce a more democratic society for their people. Such support, and the readiness to exert it, may or may not require military means. Yet those means must be available in case they are called upon, as in the case of Grenada.

Previously noted examples of the need for consistency, whether with respect to intermediate nuclear forces in Europe or infantry units in South Korea, only begin to hint at the variety of resources required day-to-day to render credible America's commitments to her allies, friends, and overseas interests.

At one end of the spectrum of military forces is America's strategic nuclear deterrent. Paradoxically, the combination of land- and sea-based ballistic missiles, strategic bombers (including cruise missile carriers), and the command, control, and communications (C^3) that support them, are the subject of never-ending criticism from budget cutters, even though they comprise less than 15 percent of annual defense budgets. Moreover, if effectiveness were measured on the basis of firepower alone, strategic nuclear forces would outstrip all other systems in cost effectiveness. To be sure, debate about these forces frequently takes place within the context of efforts to implement an arms control regime. Nevertheless, there is a persistent undercurrent of discussion relating to the cost of these systems. Measured in absolute per-unit costs, these systems are indeed expensive, though, as noted above, taken together they comprise a far lower percentage of the budget as a whole.

At the other end of the spectrum of military capability lies a set of forces that likewise has been the center of controversy: special operations forces (SOF). As in the case of strategic nuclear forces, the cost of SOF is nowhere near commensurate with the capabilities they engender. For example, in fiscal year 1987 less than 2 percent of the Department of Defense budget was expended on these units.

Nevertheless, as with strategic nuclear forces, questions of cost are interwoven with questions of policy in SOF budget debates. In some quarters, they are anathema. They conjure up images closely associated with Vietnam, as if SOF were in some direct way responsible for the course of events that took place there. In other quarters, they represent an inordinately large expenditure on inordinately small forces. Again, as with strategic forces, this second argument is couched in terms of absolute per-unit cost. Both perspectives overlook the critical values of SOF—their cost-effectiveness in ensuring that conventional conflicts are contained at the earliest possible stages, as well as in acting as a significant multiplier for the capabilities of conventional forces.

If strategic nuclear forces suffer from a surfeit of analysis and measurement—in the absence (and hopefully, continuing absence) or empirical evidence, SOF suffers from the opposite. Unconventional forces confer benefits that defy conventional measurement. That SOF may be the bane of systems analysts in no way diminishes their importance.

In the past few years, special operations forces played a very important role both in British operations in the South Atlantic and in US combat on Grenada. The common element in both these operations was the brevity of time available to planners, the military's unfamiliarity with local terrain, and a resulting need for small units to provide reconnaissance and other special mission capabilities. These needs are likely to grow in future; there is still no tried-and-true method for predicting where US forces might next have to operate. The most reliable prediction about future contingencies is that they will be unpredictable. Special operations forces represent one hedge against the inevitability of uncertainty.

Other forces, of course, also provide a hedge against the uncertainty of future scenarios. Naval forces are a prime example of the type of hedge that flexibility confers. Carrier-based firepower has long been recognized as a source of mobile support to alliance commitments. For this reason the carriers of the 6th Fleet embody the US commitment to deploy carriers to assist in the defense of Europe within 48 hours of the onset of a conflict. The origins of that conflict, its time and locale, cannot be foreseen. Carriers are sufficiently mobile to be available, in whatever context military planners deem necessary, at the appropriate locale, within the allotted time. In effect, their flexibility is the antidote to the uncertainty of the contingency to which they would respond.

Flexibility is not for that matter limited to carriers or to the US Navy. Battleships, escorts, submarines, support ships, and auxiliary units all embody different aspects of the Navy's flexibility, while light divisions, airlift and sealift forces, and tactical aviation constitute other forms of US military flexibility. Light divisions are most amenable to rapid transportability by air. The two new active Army light divisions, as well as their reserve counterparts, have been tailored to facilitate airlift not only by C–5s, but by the smaller and far more numerous C–141s. The airlift fleet is growing due to the acquisition of additional C–5s and KC–10 tankers, both of which will enhance the transport of the "outsize" equipment associated with armored and mechanized divisions, as well as with various support units. Finally, the additional sealift capability, including the acquisition and modification of fast shipping to a roll-on/roll-off configuration, supports a more rapid resupply of major items of all sizes and volumes. The responsiveness of all of these units is critical not merely for assisting an ally under attack or threat of attack. Flexibility is a powerful deterrent to a would-be aggressor, and, as such, underwrites multiple US commitments to a host of friends and allies worldwide.

Acting Upon the Four Principles: The Policy-Program Linkage

For US defense policy to be credible, it must have forces and weapons adequate to its military needs. Flexible forces certainly ease the absolute burden of military requirements, but only to a limited extent. For example, the commitment to support NATO Europe with 10 divisions with 10 days of warning of an impending attack includes, in part, prepositioned materiel (POMCUS) and forward-based land units, neither of which are particularly flexible. Similarly, US land forces in East Asia are theoretically redeployable from one theater to another; operationally, however, they must be considered stationary within the Northeast Asian theater.

In practice, therefore, US forces must combine elements that are flexible, in terms of deployability and adaptability to different types of scenarios, and others that are more (though not necessarily exclusively) oriented to the demands of a single contingency. Moreover, both types of forces require well-trained and motivated personnel, provided with hardware that is no less capable than that which a potential adversary might deploy. Obtaining the requisite personnel calls for pay and benefits to attract and retain them and sufficiently superior training to ensure they can operate effectively on the battlefield. Obtaining the requisite hardware involves a never-ending research and development effort for more effective equipment; procurement of the most modern systems in adequate numbers; acquisition of spares and war reserves to ensure sustainability; and maintenance of an integrated logistic system to support their operation.

The ingredients that contribute to effective forces remain valid even in the Gramm-Rudman era. Every one of those ingredients, for example, contributed to the successful operation on 15 April 1986 against Libyan military facilities associated with terrorist activities. The naval aircraft that undertook suppression missions, as well as the A–6s that struck targets on Libya's northeast coast, were part of a larger naval force that included carriers, escorts, and other ships. The pilots of the F–18s and the A–7s, as well as of the Air Force F–111s that struck at targets in northwest Libya were highly motivated and well trained professionals. The aircraft required first-rate mechanical and logistic support—in the case of the F–111s, they had to be aerially refueled four times during their mission. Again, the personnel involved in these activities required motivation and training of the highest order. The weapons that were fired at the targets were products of America's most recent successful development efforts: the HARM anti-radiation missile and Paveway II laser-guided bombs. The systems that provided airborne support for the attack aircraft included carrier-based F–14s, which, with their own highly sophisticated AWG–9 radars and fully active Phoenix missiles provided air cover; Navy E–2Cs, which furnished additional early warning and battle management; and Navy EA–6Bs and Air Force EF–111s for electronic support. The 6th Fleet remained protected, as in the earlier Libyan operation, by its own shipborne systems, including the sophisticated AEGIS air defense system, which, like Harpoon, is unrivalled in any other fleet. Integrating these operations and systems required excellent command, control, communications, and intelligence (C^3I). Nothing less could have sufficed to ensure precision coordination of a two-pronged attack by aircraft originating at different points and transiting vastly different ranges.

The Libyan engagements also highlighted two other policy-related factors that Gramm-Rudman has not, will not, and cannot change. First, as already noted, threats requiring a military response cannot entirely be foreseen. Moreover they need not involve the Soviet Union directly. The Libyan threat to US interests emerged at short notice; Soviet forces in the Mediterranean remained quiescent. Second, all other potential threats to those interests remained undiminished even as the 6th Fleet and the F–111s engaged the Libyans. Put another way, the Libyan encounter represented both a key example of the need for credible and responsive forces, and a microcosm of the different sorts of expenditures that comprise the defense budget.

The defense program in the Gramm-Rudman era must of necessity remain roughly similar to the one that existed prior to the introduction of deficit reduction legislation. US forces remain bound both to support commitments that have not changed and to defend against threats to those interests that continue unabated. Unless the United States is prepared to renounce commitments decades old, and thereby fundamentally overhaul the entire political basis upon which its defense strategy has been built since World War II, Gramm-Rudman will not bring about changes in the defense program planning commensurate to those it is likely to engender in other areas of US Government activity.

☆☆

Part III

US FORCES
AND WEAPONS

THE DECISIVE ROLE OF LANDPOWER IN US NATIONAL SECURITY

William O. Staudenmaier

*I*T HAS BEEN CLEAR, at least since America's entry into World War II, that unified military action is necessary to success in modern warfare. Joint or unified military operations—the coordinated direction of land, sea, and air forces toward a common objective under a single military commander—has been national security doctrine for over 40 years. The importance of an individual Service in a given military operation varies depending upon the mission that must be accomplished. For example, the Air Force and Navy have been used often in situations short of war, but when the President wishes to signal the irrevocable commitment of the nation, then Army forces are indispensable.[1]

In the event of war, the decisive element is the Army supported by the Air Force and Navy. Hanson W. Baldwin stated the case this way:

the ultimate objective in war is man himself. You may approach his final citadel by sea or air or land. But it is man you must conquer. If you do not conquer man—his body, his mind, his spirit—your control of great sea spaces and vast air spaces may be futile.... The ultimate objective of wars between men is men. The penultimate objective is land—the other fellow's land—and what is on and beneath it.[2]

Admiral Joseph C. Wylie, in his treatise on strategic theory, agrees that the soldier is the crucial element in the strategic equation:

there is offered as a fourth basic assumption for strategic planning foundation the following: *The ultimate determinant in war is the man on the scene with a gun.* ... He determines who wins ... after whatever devastation and destruction may be inflicted on an enemy, if the strategist is forced to strive for final and ultimate control, he must establish, or must present as an inevitable prospect, a man on the scene with a gun. This is the soldier.[3]

Yet, the Army's decisive role in war is currently being underestimated in the deliberations that lead to the allocation of resources to the Services. In a period of expanding defense resources, the Army's share of the defense budget has contracted. In 1975, when the Army's stabilized end strength was about 780,000, where it still remains today, the Army's share of the defense budget was about 25 percent. In fiscal year 1984, the Army's share had dropped to 23 percent, despite an increase in Soviet land forces and an expansion of US strategic commitments.[4] Further, the decline in the Army's share of defense resources occurred while the Reagan administration was making every effort to strengthen general-purpose forces in particular and Congress was a willing partner in the trillion-dollar-plus program to revivify defense in general. Now that the nation seems less willing to allocate the funds the administration believes are needed for defense, it is appropriate—indeed urgent—to argue for the resources needed to ensure that US landpower remains adequate as the decisive element in warfare.

To put the essential requirements for an effective landpower capability into strategic context, the following analysis reviews the strategic environment, identifying major US national interests and the threats to them. Next, the US national military strategy is examined, focusing on the role of the Army in that strategy. Then, we consider the land force programs needed to support the strategy. Finally, this paper offers some thoughts on how to alleviate the major shortfalls that inevitably arise from a consideration of requirements and capabilities.

Strategic Environment

The national security debate that has been prominent throughout the Reagan administration is, in the final analysis, caused by the imbalance between strategic capabilities and strategic needs. Strategic needs, or requirements, are established through an analysis of the strategic environment, which leads to the identification of US national interests and commitments. To establish how much military capability is required to secure these interests and commitments, threats must be assessed and strategies and defense policies formulated to deal with them. The dynamic interaction of these factors leads, in turn, to judgments on the size of the armed forces required to carry out the strategies. Typically, this approach results in a gap between what is needed and what is available.

The development of defense policy and of military strategy should not be based on the premise that a particular Service should be dominant. Neither should policy or strategy strive for balanced forces if that is taken to mean that each Service should receive an equal share of the defense budget. Equally, policy and strategy should not be based on some estimate of what we think we can afford at some nebulous level of risk. Rather, the size and structure of each Service should derive from the strategy itself, which, in turn, is a function of the threat to US national interests. As Secretary of Defense Weinberger has argued,

the logic of defense planning should be clear. The need for military forces arises from U.S. security interests and commitments. These interests are threatened by adversaries in ways that create contingencies that U.S. forces must be able to meet. Defense policy judgments about the manner and method of U.S. responses are translated into requirements for specific forces that are designed to provide the necessary capability at the lowest cost.[5]

In common with other nations, the United States has four basic national interests it must protect.[6] First, the United States must ensure its survival both as a nation and as a people with their fundamental political values and institutions intact. The United States is no longer superior to the Soviet Union in strategic nuclear capability.[7] However, neither superpower currently or in the near future will have the capability to launch a strategic nuclear attack without the prospect that it would receive a devastating nuclear counterattack in return. This balance of terror not only stabilizes the strategic nuclear balance but also increases the importance of conventional forces. While the Soviets can threaten US survival with their nuclear arsenal, there is no compelling evidence to suggest that they believe it in their interest to risk nuclear war. Deterrence should therefore remain stable as long as the United States ensures that the Soviets do not attain a first-strike advantage and do not achieve a unilateral breakthrough in ballistic missile defense technology.

Second, at present, our territorial integrity is not seriously threatened. The oceans that separate the United States from the Eurasian landmass remain effective barriers to conventional invasion, if not to nuclear attack. As long as the nation does not neglect its armed forces, it need have little concern for the safety of its base area. Recent developments in the Caribbean together with the increase in international terrorism targeted at US interests are worrisome, however.

Third, maintenance of a high standard of living requires access to trading partners and critical resources.

The West is dependent on strategic raw materials, generally located in areas where they are subject to interruption by insurgencies, intraregional conflict, and terrorism. Threats to the West's supply of critical minerals are frequently sponsored by or taken advantage of by the Soviet Union. Many of these threats, however, are indigenously inspired or caused by the instability in the Third World and have no relation to East-West rivalry.[8] The loss of access to these vital resources, however, and for whatever reason, would have a damaging effect on the US economy and national security.

The fourth national interest is the maintenance of a favorable world order in which contemporary American values cannot only survive, but can flourish. This translates into policies and strategies that will assure that no nation or group of nations can establish hegemony over Western Europe or Japan. This task is complicated by the erosion of the simple bipolar world of the recent past with the emergence of regional and subregional centers of power that attempt to manipulate superpower relationships to their advantage. This has also resulted in greater political, economic, and military interdependence among nations.

Two other emerging trends also influence the development of strategy and force structure in the near term. The first is the export of militant Islamic Fundamentalism by clerical leaders in Iran. Islamic revolutionary fervor in the Middle East threatens to provide a transnational vehicle for the overthrow of legitimate secular regimes from Morocco to Pakistan. The second trend of strategic significance is the increase in politically inspired terrorism in Western Europe, the Middle East, and the Caribbean, with its probable extension soon to North America. The terrorist threat is made more dangerous by its use as a violent tool of foreign policy by governments such as Libya, Syria, and Iran.[9]

The challenge to US policy-makers and strategists is to protect vital interests in Europe and Japan without jeopardizing interests elsewhere that are more seriously threatened, and to do this in such a way so as not to increase the likelihood of nuclear war. The Soviet Union is and will remain the principal threat, although not the only one. Moreover, the Kremlin has increased its military capabilities with an unprecedented buildup over the last 20 years, making it difficult for the United States to narrow the gap in some important areas despite the Reagan defense budget increases.[10]

Because of geopolitical and historical factors, however, the Soviet Union has structured its forces in ways that mitigate some of their apparent advantages. For one thing, the USSR is a continental power, and it has shaped its armed forces to fight in Europe. This European-oriented force structure is characterized by

its emphasis upon armored divisions and mechanized, com- bined arms teams ....; the large, readily mobilized reserve force it maintains to augment subpar divisions; its reliance on preplanned, tactical air strikes to extend the range of artillery ... its poor ratio of fleet-support ships to combatants, which adversely affects Soviet naval sustaining capability; and a navy that still needs land-based air units to protect its ships.[11]

Obviously, this force structure, together with the proximity of the Soviet armies to NATO's vital areas, provides it with major advantages in Europe. But the same heavy armored formations will be difficult to deploy to theaters far removed from Central Europe. Moreover, these ponderous armored formations are not effective against insurgents, who launch their attacks from inhospitable terrain—a fact that the Soviets face daily in Afghanistan. Hence the paradox that faces Soviet global strategists. The Soviet Union is well organized and equipped to fight wars that have a very low probability, in areas like Central Europe, Northeast and Southwest Asia, where the Red Army can walk to work. But it has a limited capability to project force in the more likely areas of superpower confrontation in the Third World. In those areas, consequently, the threat to US interests is posed by indigenous forces, perhaps supported by Soviet economic, political, or military aid. It is clear then that the US strategy must have capable and flexible forces to meet threats, Soviet and indigenous, across the spectrum of conflict on a global scale.

The Changing Nature of Military Strategy

To the demands that the international environment makes on the strategist striving to field armed forces effective against a wide array of threats at the lowest possible cost must be added the complications brought on by the changing nature of war. The modern experience with war has been within the great-power system, in vogue since the Treaty of Westphalia in 1648. The international system that evolved as a result of that treaty recognized that war was an instrument and a monopoly of the state. Wars were waged between regular professional armies; civilian noncombatant casualties were generally low. This system worked fairly well until Napoleon democratized war with the *levée en masse,* which tended to make wars total. When the managerial genius and technological advances of the industrial revolution were added to this democratic fervor, wars became much more deadly affairs.[12]

Even with these evolving changes in the nature of war, the aim of strategy—the defeat of the enemy army—remained steadfast. Although wars became more dangerous to those in uniform, the civilian population was largely exempt from its more lethal tolls.[13] But, with World War I, the convention that protected civilians from the more extreme hazards of war began to break down. In 1928, Winston Churchill wrote,

The entire population in one capacity or another took part in the war; all were equally the object of attack. The air opened paths along which death and terror could be carried far behind the lines of the actual armies, to women, children, the aged, the sick, who in earlier struggles would perforce have been left untouched.[14]

About the same time that Guilio Douhet, Hugh Trenchard, and Billy Mitchell were developing their theories of strategic air bombardment, Mao Tse-tung was developing his theory of guerrilla warfare, also designed to attack the fabric of society. So, in a matter of 20 years, two of the fundamental pillars of the "war system" were undermined. War was no longer a monopoly of the state, and society was no longer exempt from the ravages of war.

If this were not enough to complicate the lives of strategists, new technology in the form of thermonuclear weapons married to supersonic intercontinental ballistic missiles made matters worse. For the nuclear superpowers it became difficult to fight wars even over vital interests. The threat to use force—rather than its actual use—became the *sine qua non,* leading to the emergence of coercive diplomacy or crisis management. This type of "warfare" is characterized by its strong political and diplomatic content, its use of limited means in measured ways, and the close control of strategic (and very often tactical) options by civilian policy-makers.[15]

As a result of the changing nature of war, the modern state must be prepared to pursue three main themes of strategy to secure its national interest. First, since nations still use war to resolve political disputes, the strategist must have plans and forces that will enable his country to participate in classical wars in which the objective is the destruction of the enemy armed forces. The Iran-Iraq War, the Falklands War, and the several Arab-Israeli wars are examples of this type, which we shall call conventional strategy. Second, the strategist must also be able to counter activities aimed at destroying the social fabric of the nation. This category includes, paradoxically, both strategic nuclear war and unconventional war—terrorism and guerrilla war—both of which have as their target society or the social structure. Examples of this type of strategy are US efforts in Vietnam and El Salvador, insurgency in the southern Philippines, and French operations in Algeria. These we will call social strategies, because their focus is on society. Finally, the strategist must be able to orchestrate the use or threatened use of force in situations short of war. Actions by the United States during the Cuban Missile Crisis in 1962 and the US operations against Libya in 1986 are examples of coercive diplomacy—the use of force in situations short of war. These three strategic typologies and the force structures they imply clearly affect the size and composition of the landpower component of the defense establishment.

The United States has also changed the way in which it seeks to secure its national interests. In the past 85 years, the United States has evolved from being a young nation asserting itself, seeking perfection in its society and institutions, to one that is more mature, chiefly concerned with maintaining its place in a more violent, complex, and interrelated world. The initial condition necessitated bold action, initiative, and opportunity; present circumstances require caution and reaction in maintaining the status quo. As evidence of this

shift US national strategy in the post-World War II
world has emphasized containment and deterrence. The
United States has sought to deter nuclear and conventional war in Europe, and Northeast and Southwest
Asia. Its role in guerrilla and terrorist campaigns has
been confined to counterinsurgency—and defensive
actions to prevent terrorism—assisting friendly governments to resist such threats. In the case of using force
short of war, the evidence is mixed. In some cases, the
United States has acted boldly and quickly, as in the
Cuban Missile Crisis in 1962 and Grenada in 1983.
Other times, caution was the rule, as in the *Pueblo*
affair in 1968 and Angola, 1975.[16]

The current military strategy of the United States is
deterrence—both of strategic nuclear war and of major
conventional war in Europe and the Far East. Nuclear
deterrence is achieved by maintaining survivable
nuclear forces able to retaliate and devastate any
attacker. Concomitantly, the United States seeks,
through arms control negotiations, a more stable nuclear
balance at lower force levels. The conventional military
strategy is based on a strong network of alliances, with
special emphasis on Western Europe and Northeast
Asia, where US forces are forward-deployed to demonstrate American resolve. These forward-deployed units
are backed by reinforcing elements located in the United
States that are critically dependent on the Reserve Components to round out the active forces. This strategy
involves a high level of air and sea mobility, prepositioned equipment, intermediate staging bases, and host-
nation support to allow reinforcement of forward-
deployed forces and quick response to contingencies in
the Third World. In addition to forward-deployed air
and land forces, the Pacific and Atlantic fleets facilitate
for the United States and its allies access to global

commercial markets and permit reinforcement of the two main centers of deployed military strength. Freedom of space, survivable command and control systems, particularly at the national level, and timely strategic warning of threats to US interests are also important strategic elements.[17]

Landpower Force Programs

The national military strategy described above has been remarkably stable over the past 20 years. The Army program to support this military strategy, however, evolved in the years following American withdrawal from Vietnam. Of all of the services, the Army may have come out of that war in the worst shape. Its morale was low, its equipment was old—showing the effects of hard use in Vietnam and a decade of neglect of needed modernization—and its doctrine was in a shambles. In 1973, the Army turned its back on its Vietnam experience and concentrated its attention on conventional war in Europe. For the time being, it gratefully left the problem of terrorism and guerrilla warfare to the special forces.

For the next 10 years, the Army planned, trained, and reorganized to fight the Soviet Union and its allies, in a high-intensity war. Its major concern was to implement conventional strategy in Europe, Northeast Asia, and Southwest Asia using heavy divisions that would fight mounted and lighter infantry divisions that would fight dismounted. In 1976, the Army promulgated its new doctrine, called the Active Defense, which was oriented to division-level operations. Active Defense envisioned a tactical defense that would win the first battle through attrition. The requirements of social strategy would be met by special forces and the 82nd Airborne

Division would be used by the Army in situations short of war.[18]

At about the same time, the Army embarked on its most ambitious equipment modernization program since World War II. Its new equipment included the Abrams tank, the Infantry Fighting Vehicle (the Bradley), the Patriot Air Defense System, and Apache and Black-hawk helicopters. Then, two events occurred that changed the entire thrust of the Army programs to support the national military strategy.[19] The first was the development of AirLand Battle doctrine. First announced in 1982, the new doctrine shifted the way the Army would fight in high-intensity combat. The new doctrine is designed to defeat Soviet forces in a European conflict, although it has applicability in other situations that require the Army to destroy an opposing army. The strategy has been described this way:

Forces, under AirLand Battle, will seize the initiative through a violent disruption-destruction sequence and then defeat enemy forces in detail. Relying on rapid seizure and retention of the tactical initiative, AirLand Battle seeks, through maneuver, to confront the enemy's engaged forces with unforeseen threats more rapidly than they can react to them, while simultaneously disrupting and destroying the reinforcing echelons upon which he depends for victory.[20]

AirLand Battle has shifted the emphasis from the division commander as the primary warfighter to the corps commander, which effectively moves the commander's level of interest from the tactical level to the operational.[21] The doctrine is maneuver-oriented and considers the close battle as well as the deep battle and the rear battle. Although it considers both offense and defense of equal importance, its preference is clearly for offensive operations.

The other major event affecting the post-Vietnam Army occurred in 1983. In response to the changing strategic environment and the perception that low-intensity conflict in the Third World areas was increasing, senior Army leaders saw a need for rapidly deployable light infantry forces. The result was a decision to increase the number of light divisions, including two new divisions that would be added in the midst of the ongoing modernization program. These changes were to be accomplished while holding Army end strength at 781,000.[22]

The new light infantry divisions—units that could deploy quickly to trouble spots to put out brushfire wars before they expanded—helped satisfy the needs of social strategy and coercive diplomacy. The 10,000-man unit was designed to be rapidly deployable in 500 C–141 sorties. The light division has the capability to fight extensively at night; its missions include defense of key mountain passes, antitank defense in restricted terrain, raids and heliborne operations, rear-area protection, and clearing and defense of urban areas or restricted terrain. Normally, a light division will be employed as part of any army corps or joint task force, although it could be used independently.

The light division's strategic flexibility and mobility are accompanied by several limitations. First, the light division's battlefield mobility is restricted, although it can move the assault elements of one of its nine infantry battalions by either wheeled vehicles or Blackhawk helicopters. Second, it has limited artillery support (105mm howitzers and mortars) when operating independently. Third, it carries only enough supplies for 48 hours of operations, after which it must be resupplied by some outside agency. Finally, it does not have a forced-entry capability. Either it must be employed in a permissive environment or it must be part of the follow-up echelon, deploying after amphibious or airborne troops have secured landing or entry areas. None of these limitations is fatal, but the combat versatility of the Light Infantry Division is much less than that of other Army divisions.

Even before it pursued its light infantry initiative, originally justified on the basis of a capability to fight in low-intensity environments, the Army began to strengthen its special operations forces (SOF). These forces can be employed under circumstances in which large conventional forces may be a political liability. As currently organized in one special operations command, SOF consist of eight Special Forces Groups, four Psychological Operations (Psyops) Groups, and two Special Operations Aviation Battalions. There is also one Ranger Regiment, consisting of three battalions and one Civil Affairs Battalion from the active forces and three Civil Affairs Commands in the Army Reserve. Overall, the reserve components provide 50 percent of the special forces and 90 percent of the Psyops and civil affairs units.[23]

The Army is currently structuring a 28–division force. These units can operate throughout the spectrum of conflict and the special operations force is especially well suited for low-intensity warfare. Divisional units include 14 heavy armor and mechanized divisions tailored for use in Eurasia, 6 multipurpose infantry divisions, 5 light divisions able to respond quickly in crisis situations, and 1 each airborne, air assault, and high-technology division. The latter combines a high degree of tactical mobility with strong firepower.

The restructuring has been achieved without an increase in active-component end strength, which has allowed the Army to pursue modernization and sustainability programs that have improved readiness. Still the new force structure requires greater reserve component participation than before. For example, of the 28 divisions, 10 are Army National Guard units (1 light, 5 infantry, 2 armor, and 2 mechanized). Moreover, 5 of the 18 active divisions are assigned 1 National Guard ''round-out'' brigade. There are also other separate brigades and cavalry squadrons provided by the reserve components. Within this overall structure, the reserve components provide more than 50 percent of the combat and combat support function of the Army.[24] This integration of active and reserve functions—the Total Force Concept—has changed the way the Army does business. Since the concept was introduced in 1973, the Army has relied on the availability of its reserve components when developing Army support for joint or combined contingencies.

This transfer of missions and functions from the active component to the reserve component has several important implications. First, if ''roundout'' or support forces are not mobilized, the Army will not be ready to perform its combat missions. Crisis situations will therefore require an early mobilization decision by the National Command Authority. This may or may not send the proper signal in a crisis. Second, if the reserve components must deploy to combat rapidly, then these units must be highly trained and equipped to the same level as the active forces. That is not the case today. Third, it will be important to exercise mobilization procedures to ensure that the reserve units can meet their deployability dates. All of this demands time and money, time on the part of the reservists and money from the active army to provide the equipment and training necessary to achieve and maintain the requisite level of readiness.[25]

Of equal importance to the force structure changes is the Army's equipment modernization effort. (See table 1.) The central thrust of equipment modernization is to provide what is needed to make AirLand Battle doctrine work. The modernization pace slows under the fiscal year 1987 budget, which will delay fielding of some of the weapons needed to make AirLand Battle fully effective. The Army is only about midway in its modernization of the forces that would first confront a Soviet blitzkrieg and is only beginning to buy the systems that will disrupt the reinforcing echelons.[26]

Modernization is also concerned with warfare at the lower end of the conflict spectrum. Although recognized as a vital issue, doctrine for low-intensity warfare, which includes counterinsurgency and counterterrorism operations, is not as well-developed as AirLand Battle. As a consequence, the equipment needed to support such operations has not been completely defined. Nevertheless, some items that would assist in countering terrorism and insurgencies have been identified. Lighter equipment that is more easily deployable, vehicles—both armored and wheeled—that are extremely mobile, equipment that will enable the soldier to acquire targets at night, and heavy mobile mortars—all are currently under development or already in procurement. Some systems needed for this important Army mission, however, have either been deleted from the budget or delayed. The Armored Gun System, which would have mounted a gun capable of killing tanks on a light armored vehicle, was cancelled during the Department of Defense fiscal year 1987 budget review. This would have been an excellent capability for light infantry forces fighting against more heavily equipped Third World forces. Another item equally useful in counterterror or counterinsurgency situations, as well as in more conventional operations, is the LHX (Light Helicopter Experimental). The Army's light helicopter force, used

Table 1
Ground Force Systems Modernization

System	Description
ABRAMS Tank	Main Battle Tank
M60A3 Tank	Main Battle Tank product improvement
BRADLEY Fighting Vehicles	Infantry and cavalry fighting vehicles
UH–60 BLACKHAWK	Utility helicopter
AH–64 APACHE	Attack helicopter
PATRIOT	Surface-to-air missile system
Multiple-Launch Rocket System	Artillery
Army-TACMS	Conventional ballistic missile
Copperhead	Precision-guided artillery
JSTARS	Airborne radar battefield management/target location system

Source: OJCS Military Posture, fiscal year 1987

for observation, reconnaissance, and command and control, is rapidly becoming unable to meet the Soviet threat. But reduced funding levels have pushed back the initial fielding of LHX from the early to the mid-1990s.

Another Army concern is its ability to sustain the battle for as long as it takes to win. Sustainability requires forward positioning of equipment for early deploying units, stockpiling of adequate war reserve stocks overseas for use until they can be replenished from the United States, and sufficient strategic mobility assets, both sea and air, to deploy and support ground forces. The greatest deficiency in sustainability is the lack of a "hot" industrial base that can expand quickly in times of crisis to meet the surge demands caused by active military operations. That capability does not exist today.[27]

Army Future Directions

Even with the greatly increased effort that the Reagan administration has mounted since its election in 1980, the Army fully realizes that funding constraints will not allow it to obtain the force structure that its leaders believe is justified by the threats now facing the United States. Given the experience of the past several fiscal years, the Army should not expect suddenly to have its budget increased significantly relative to the other Services. Hence, it must accept a smaller force that relies on the reserve component to compensate for deficiencies in the active structure.[28]

The problem that faces Army force planners was aptly explained in this way:

The real issue is this: Given no expected increase in manpower, primarily tasked with fighting against heavy Soviet-style forces in all major theaters, faced with tight budgets and a traditionally small piece of the DoD pie, and being in the middle of a major modernization effort, should the Army pay the enormous price associated with a major expansion of light-infantry forces?[29]

This is certainly a reasonable question when the prospects for budget cutbacks seem probable.

The following seem relevant to the future direction of the Army should severe program cuts be realized:

1. The Army now emerging will be the Army of the twenty-first century. Equipment lead-times are such that the weapons systems being procured today will still be in the inventory 15 years from now. Moreover, modernization of today's scope can be supported only once in a generation. Although product improvements and evolutionary changes to the force structure can be expected, the unique circumstances that were the engine of Army modernization will not reoccur in the near future.

2. The Army equipment modernization program is consistent with AirLand Battle doctrine, which dictates

how the Army intends to use its force in executing conventional strategy. The new weapons that are coming into the inventory will enable the Army to fight the close and deep battles demanded by its doctrinal imperatives. The same cannot be said of the equipment needed by light infantry divisions to fight effectively against Soviet clients or surrogates in the Third World. The lack of an adequate antitank capability will restrict the employment possibilities of this division.

3. The strategic rationale of the light infantry division is also suspect. Perhaps the case can be made for fielding one or two such units, but four active and one National Guard division strains credibility, particularly since some will have "roundout" brigades. Given its need for augmentation in high-intensity scenarios and its limited antitank capabilities, the light infantry division concept—or at least their number—should be a candidate for reevaluation if severe budget constraints (beyond those currently in effect) are imposed on the Army. Whatever the fate of the light division concept, the 82nd Airborne Division should be retained for use in coercive diplomacy situations. Similarly, Special Operating Forces should be relied upon for counterinsurgency and counterterrorism missions. With severe budget restraints, the Army may also wish to reevaluate the role of the 2nd Infantry Division in Korea. One senior Army officer has compared the stationing of a US infantry division in Korea, which has 20 active and 23 reserve infantry divisions in its force structure, to "sending coals to Newcastle."[30]

4. To man a balanced 18-division force adequately, the Army needs 860,000 soldiers. It therefore faces a choice between a "hollow Army" or a substantial cut in its force structure if severe budget cuts are forced on it.[31] But neither the Army nor any other Service should

be forced into unilateral cuts given the strategic logic outlined earlier. Budget allocations in times of fiscal poverty as well as in more prosperous years should be in accordance with national priorities and unified military strategy.

5. When the four basic US interests are examined in the context of strategic trends and threats, they suggest that US strategic priorities should be ordered in the following manner. First, the United States must deter the outbreak of nuclear war. Second, regional priorities should be Western Europe, Japan and Korea, Southwest Asia and the Middle East, Central and Latin America, Southeast Asia, and Africa. Given these priorities and the evidence that deterrence and defense in NATO are firmly in hand, a national military strategy may be advanced. Nuclear deterrence would remain the highest military priority. Next, economy of force would be practiced in those areas where deterrence was stable, such as Western Europe and Northeast Asia, or where the US interest was low, as in Southeast Asia and Africa. The United States would retain the capability to intervene in Central America, the Middle East, and Southwest Asia to combat terrorism and revolutionary insurgency. In appropriate circumstances,[32] primary reliance in situations short of war would fall on air and naval forces, along with the Army's rapid deployment capability.

6. This strategic concept would require some shifts in defense budget allocations. It has been estimated that the budget has been allocated in the following manner: 23 percent for nuclear forces; 42 percent for general-purpose forces oriented on NATO; 15 percent for Asia; and 20 percent for other conventional contingency forces.[33] The strategy outlined above would leave the nuclear forces as is, but reduce general-purpose

NATO-oriented forces 6 percent. These savings would be applied to contingency forces, raising that category to 25 percent. For the Army, this would continue the emphasis on social strategy and slightly deemphasize conventional strategy.

Indisputably, twentieth century warfare requires unified military action, whether the strategy is conventional, social, or coercive diplomacy. Landpower will require extensive sea and air support to come to grips with an enemy wherever he is located. But it is certain that success will be achieved only when the soldier with a gun is on the scene.

Notes

1. Barry M. Blechman and Stephen S. Kaplan, *Force Without War: U.S. Armed Forces as a Political Instrument* (Washington, DC: The Brookings Institution, 1978), pp. 38–49.

2. Association of the United States Army, *Landpower: The Decisive Element* (Arlington, VA: Association of the United States Army, 1984), p. 118.

3. Joseph C. Wylie, *Military Strategy: A General Theory of Power Control* (New Brunswick: Rutgers University Press, 1967), p. 85.

4. AUSA, *Landpower,* pp. 106–7.

5. Caspar W. Weinberger, *Annual Report to the Congress, FY 87* (Washington, DC: GPO, 1986), p. 31.

6. Donald E. Nuechterlein, *National Interests and Presidential Leadership: The Setting of Priorities* (Boulder, CO: Westview Press, 1978), pp. 1–18.

7. John M. Collins, *U.S.–Soviet Military Balance, 1980–1985* (Washington, DC: Pergamon Brassey's, 1985), pp. 53–65.

8. Ibid., p. 45.

9. William O. Staudenmaier, "Options for U.S. National Strategy in the 1980s and Beyond," *Naval War College Review* 34, no. 3 (May–June 1981): 3–14.

10. Collins, *U.S.–Soviet Military Balance,* pp. 152–57.

11. Keith A. Dunn and William O. Staudenmaier, "Strategy for Survival," *Foreign Policy*, no. 52 (Fall 1983): 37.

12. Martin Blumenson, "The Changing Nature of War: Old Parameters Are Vanishing," *Army*, February 1982, pp. 11–13.

13. There are obvious exceptions to this generalization to be found in military history. The Thirty Years War, with its large toll in civilian lives, and the military operations of the Mongols spring immediately to mind. However, during the great power period, this generalization is valid.

14. Winston S. Churchill, *The Gathering Storm* (Boston, MA: Houghton Mifflin Company, 1948), p. 39.

15. Gordon A. Craig and Alexander L. George, *Force and Statecraft: Diplomatic Problems of Our Time* (New York: Oxford University Press, 1983), pp. 189–203 and 206–7.

16. This is not to pass judgment on the wisdom of the response in each case, it is only to show that our approach to the three strategic typologies is not necessarily the same in each instance—nor should it be. The fact that our response to deterrence and terrorism is often retaliatory and reactive respectively will, of course, have force structure implications.

17. Organization of the Joint Chiefs of Staff, *United States Military Posture for FY 1987*, pp. 7–9.

18. John C. "Doc" Bahnsen, Jr., "The Kaleidoscopic US Army," *Armed Forces Journal International*, November 1985, pp. 9–15.

19. MG Sam Damon and BG Ben Krisler, "Army of Excellence: A Time to Take Stock," *Armed Forces Journal International*, May 1985, pp. 86–94. The authors' names are pseudonyms.

20. John O. Marsh and John A. Wickham, Jr., *The Posture of the United States Army for Fiscal Year 1987* (Washington, DC: GPO, 1986), p. 15.

21. Bahnsen, "The Kaleidoscopic US Army," p. 12.

22. Damon and Krisler, "Army of Excellence," p. 86.

23. Marsh and Wickham, *Army Posture Statement, FY 87*, pp. 18–19.

24. Ibid., p. 16.

25. AUSA, *Landpower*, pp. 82–83.

26. Marsh and Wickham, *Army Posture Statement, FY 87*, p. 10.

27. AUSA, *Landpower*, pp. 96–100.

28. Damon and Krisler, "Army of Excellence," p. 92. The authors hit the mark in their review of the Army's recent budget

experience. They wrote: "The track record on Army budgets over the past five years would indicate limited growth when compared to other Services—barely adequate to support modernization initiatives already on the books.... In terms of real growth, the Army is dead last in DOD, with 10% gain since 1980.... All of this would suggest that money for the Army is tight and will get tighter as the deficit issue squeezes future Federal budgets."

29. Ibid., p. 87.

30. Ibid., p. 90.

31. In fiscal year 1987, the Navy will add 12,000 personnel to its force, while the Army will add 100.

32. Dunn and Staudenmaier, "Strategy for Survival," pp. 39–40.

33. Earl G. Ravenal, "Defending Persian Gulf Oil," *Intervention* 1, no. 2 (Winter, 1985): 12–15.

THE US NAVY UNDER THE REAGAN ADMINISTRATION AND GLOBAL FORWARD STRATEGY

John Allen Williams

*R*ONALD REAGAN'S 1980 election victory was interpreted by many as a mandate to ''rearm America.'' Despite small increases in military spending every year of the Carter presidency, and a significant promilitary reorientation of administration priorities in 1979, there was a widespread perception that not enough was being done to reverse a decade-long reduction in US military capability relative to the Soviet Union and to potential opponents in the Third World.

With the important exception of the Strategic Defense Initiative (SDI), the Reagan administration did not greatly alter the basic defense programs of its predecessor. It did, however, increase the resources given to them—and in this way made previously underfunded policies more likely to succeed.[1] This trend was particularly evident in the dramatic expansion of the Navy's budget.

Many individuals have assisted my understanding of the issues discussed here, including James R. Kurth, John J. Mearsheimer, Peter M. Swartz, John L. Byron, Donald C. Daniel, and Robert S. Wood; however, the responsibility for the analysis and conclusions remains mine.

At the same time, strategic guidance was evolving from within the Navy that directs how the increased capabilities would be used. Known variously as the "Forward Maritime Strategy" or just the "Maritime Strategy," this guidance outlines the campaigns of a global conventional war with the Soviet Union and serves, in the view of its critics, primarily as a rationale for the expanded forces the Navy has long desired. Whether or not this is its purpose, the Maritime Strategy offers a distinct strategic alternative to the plans of the Carter administration, and deserves evaluation on its merits. Because the strategy presupposes a large number of highly capable forces, its premises and conclusions must be examined carefully during a period of budgetary retrenchment.

The purposes of this analysis are threefold: first, to examine the Maritime Strategy as a basis for deterring and, if necessary, fighting a global conventional war; second, to review the naval force structure investments that have been made during the Reagan administration in support of that strategy; and third, to explore future Navy directions in the light of projected threats and budgetary realities.

The Maritime Strategy

Before discussing the details of the current Maritime Strategy, a review of some historical factors is in order.

Historical background. The end of the Second World War found the United States with absolute maritime supremacy, without any need for allied assistance. The primary opponent was domestic, as the Navy and the newly created Air Force struggled over the role each would play in naval aviation and strategic attack.[2]

With regard to potential foreign opponents, the need for a coherent strategy was less compelling at a time of absolute maritime dominance.

The introduction of tactical nuclear weapons into the Soviet fleet caused some concern about fleet vulnerability, but even this development did not provide the impetus for a thoroughgoing strategic reexamination. Three factors combined to cause such a rethinking in the 1970s, however: the growing maritime power of the Soviet Union, the block obsolescence of the ships of the World War II Navy, and the declining national commitment to defense resources.

By the 1970s the Soviet Union was becoming a world-class maritime power. It is now hard to imagine that it was not until the 1960s that the Soviet Navy regularly deployed out of home waters[3] and became a formidable ''blue water'' force.

At the end of World War II, the US Navy was a newly constructed, balanced force, prepared for and experienced in wartime operations ranging from amphibious assault to air attack and fleet defense. Even as recently as 1970, the Navy operated over a thousand ships, including 22 aircraft carriers. Unfortunately, many of these ships were approaching the end of their service lives. These old ships were increasingly expensive to operate, and decisions were needed about the forces that would carry the Navy into the next century. Rather than continue to operate these ships, the Navy retired them in large numbers, with the expectation that the money saved could be used for new construction of the sophisticated new vessels needed for modern warfare. With a much smaller number of larger and more capable ships, the Navy needed to rethink how maritime superiority could be maintained in this new situation.

A complicating factor in all of this was the diminishing willingness of the American people to provide the resources necessary for a strong defense. The resolution of US military involvement in Vietnam satisfied neither hawks nor doves, and the disclosures of the Watergate era further increased the popular distrust of national leaders. These developments combined with a tendency to put the most favorable construction on Soviet activities during the period of ''détente'' and greatly diminished support for maintaining US naval supremacy.

The naval strategy of the Carter administration. The Carter administration accurately reflected this national mood. Defense resources increased an average of only 1.5 percent per year, clearly insufficient to support the Navy's restructuring goals.[4] Of even greater concern, however, were the administration's strategic priorities and the roles assigned to the Navy in meeting them.

The most important military priority for Carter defense planners, apart from deterring strategic nuclear war, was the defense of the Central Front in Europe against a land attack by the Warsaw Pact. Defense Secretary Harold Brown noted the growth in Warsaw Pact combat potential in his last annual report, particularly the qualitative improvements in their forces.[5] The result of this concern was a ''continental strategy,'' emphasizing forces immediately useful on the Central Front and a continuing flow of supplies from the United States to support them.

There is no disagreement about the importance of such forces, and the Navy does not dispute the requirement to keep open an ''Atlantic bridge'' to Europe. No one wants a US President to be confronted with the need to use nuclear weapons to defend Europe because the battle there cannot be sustained on a conventional level, but there remains much disagreement about the best way to keep the vital sea lanes open. Under the Carter administration the Navy, greatly reduced in numbers because of the ship retirements noted earlier, was left with a strategy of ''defensive sea control.''[6] Although certain forces, such as an indeterminate number of attack submarines (SSNs), would be permitted to move to forward areas north of the Greenland-Iceland-Norway line, the bulk of the Navy's forces would be reserved for barrier operations and for close-in defense of the sea lanes.

Evolution of the Maritime Strategy. Not surprisingly, Navy leaders were unhappy about being relegated to a defensive/reactive role in the event of a major war, and they were painfully aware of the effect of such a status on budget priorities. The turnaround in naval strategy dates from Admiral Thomas Hayward's tenure as Chief of Naval Operations (CNO), which bridged the Carter and Reagan administrations. The Maritime Strategy that eventually emerged (the ''official'' version) owes a large debt to the strategic concepts put forth in 1979 by Admiral Hayward.[7] He emphasized the need for offensive strikes against Soviet forces wherever they may be found, even in their home waters. The budgetary implications of this are apparent, but they should not obscure the even more important strategic ones. If it is possible for US naval forces to operate north of the Greenland-Iceland-Norway line successfully, their activities would tie down Soviet naval assets that otherwise could be employed along the sea lanes farther south. A credible threat against these forces could reinforce the Soviet inclination to pull back into a defensive posture from which they would pose a lesser threat to the United States and her NATO allies.

If Admiral Hayward and his successor as CNO, Admiral James Watkins, provided the intellectual foundation of the Maritime Strategy, Secretary of the Navy John Lehman provided much of the political muscle. Lehman took office with clear ideas about what he wanted to accomplish. A commander in the Naval Reserve and a naval flight officer, Secretary Lehman was a strong supporter of a forward, offensive strategy and of the forces necessary to carry it out. He castigated the Carter administration's strategy of defensive sea control as ''defeatist'' and a ''Maginot Line'' approach,[8] and pressed for an offensive strategy that placed the Navy in forward areas early in a conflict. In a significant departure from previous policy, Lehman argued that battle groups centered around aircraft carriers could be used to attack Soviet forces in their home waters, and even, at some stage of the conflict, in port or on the runway.

These offensive principles, refined through Naval War College analyses and war games and inputs from Navy and civilian analysts, were incorporated in a series of briefings prepared by the Strategic Concepts Group of the Office of the Chief of Naval Operations (OP–603). These briefings became, in turn, the basis of the Maritime Strategy. Classified ''hard copies'' of the briefing slides and text are updated yearly and circulated widely within the Navy. In addition, Admiral Watkins had an unclassified version published in a January 1986 supplement to the U.S. Naval Institute *Proceedings*.[9]

The Maritime Strategy is important for two reasons. First, it has become the baseline Navy strategy, guiding the employment of naval forces in a global conventional war with the Soviet Union. It also affects naval operations short of global war, that is, in peace-time presence and crisis control.[10] To the extent that the Maritime Strategy is seen by potential opponents as a credible warfighting strategy, deterrence will be enhanced and the probability of war lessened.

Second, the Maritime Strategy is also the CNO's Program Advisory Memorandum (CPAM) that deter-mines what forces should be purchased in the future. As one head of the CNO's Strategic Concepts Group explained, the Maritime Strategy is "the triggering ele-ment in the Navy's Planning, Programming, and Budgeting System (PPBS). It is the first 'P' in the PPBS cycle."[11] The following examines the relationship between the Maritime Strategy and naval force structure below, after considering the Maritime Strategy itself.

Characteristics of the Maritime Strategy. Although as noted, the Maritime Strategy began as a framework for waging a global conventional war with the Soviet Union, it has expanded to include peacetime presence and crisis response operations. Judging from Admiral Watkins' article, however, it still deals primarily with a global war situation. Such a war, although fraught with immeasurable dangers and difficulties, is conceptually much simpler than the less demanding but more varied crisis situations that could arise. It is also the most dan-gerous situation, apart from strategic nuclear war, and one for which the United States must be prepared if war is to be prevented. The Maritime Strategy has several characteristics:

DETERRENT. The overarching goal of the Maritime Strategy is deterrence, and Navy strategists are con-vinced that the best way to avoid fighting a war is to be perceived as able to prevail if one should occur. The second best way is to increase the uncertainty on the part of a potential adversary that he could gain anything from an attack. Raising the level of Soviet uncertainty is the basis of the nuclear deterrent now in place in Europe, and the Maritime Strategy has a similar effect—but at the safer and more relevant conventional level. Naval forces are also believed to add to deterrence in that the Soviets would be unable to preconfigure the conflict to occur at places where they have an advantage.

GLOBAL. If the Soviets expected that a war could be confined to Central and Western Europe, it would be easier for them to calculate the correlation of forces and the risks of launching an attack. The Navy believes that inherently mobile maritime forces, which can attack the Soviet Union from many directions, are useful as forces in being which tie down Soviet forces. The Navy argues that the global dimension of the Maritime Strategy is important for the defense of the Central Front in Europe, even though the direct contribution of naval forces would not be significant in the early days of a war.

FORWARD. The "forward" characteristic of the Maritime Strategy is emphasized for military and political reasons. Militarily, the offensively minded Navy is convinced that it makes more sense to attack Soviet forces directly than it does to sit back and await their attack. Politically, the demonstrated willingness of US forces to share the risks of a forward defense and the increased likelihood of success is thought to shore up the willingness of our allies to continue to resist Soviet encroachment.

JOINT AND ALLIED. Unlike the Soviet Union, the United States can defend its borders far from home, and has the assistance of several wealthy allies in doing so. Secretary Lehman emphasizes the importance of allied contributions in carrying out the Maritime Strategy, and says the US Navy ''is prepared to bet that US allies will continue to maintain modern, effective navies.''[12]

Although the Navy is reluctant to surrender its freedom of action—and has resisted reorganization proposals to strengthen the Chairman of the Joint Chiefs of Staff and the civilian Defense Department—it is aware of the fact that it cannot expect to ''go it alone'' in a global war and successfully complete its missions. This is reflected in a 1982 memorandum of understanding with the US Air Force which provided for joint maritime operations. (Since that time, the Air Force has assumed this as a major mission, including it in their Manual 1–1, *Basic Aerospace Doctrine of the United States Air Force*.[13]) Among the missions for which Air Force assistance is useful are antiair and antisurface warfare, maritime reconnaissance, minelaying, and airborne warning and control (AWACS) support.

SEQUENTIAL. Despite the interpretation placed on early statements by John Lehman,[14] published accounts of the Maritime Strategy show no requirement for an immediate movement of surface forces into the highest threat areas. While such actions are not ruled out by the strategy, they are by no means required. Navy strategists agree that particular operations must depend on the tactical situation, but there is less unanimity on the feasibility of sending surface forces close to Soviet defenses early in a conflict.

Sequentiality also means that the US Navy cannot be everywhere at once, and priorities will be established among the areas of operations. Still, as Secretary Lehman wrote early in his term of office, naval operations "could well involve a number of significant and widely separated regions, probably simultaneously, and for this the forces must be fully prepared and trained."[15]

Navy planners divide a hypothetical global war into three phases.[16] Phase I is "deterrence or transition to war." Although the primary purpose of this phase is deterrence, forces must also be positioned properly for wartime operations. This may mean an early forward movement to areas of crisis or to areas of Soviet fleet operations. For example, antisubmarine warfare (ASW) forces, including P–3 aircraft and SSNs, would deploy as far forward as possible to be ready to attack Soviet SSNs and, it is now clear, their ballistic missile-firing SSBNs. By 1989, as many as 13,000 Marines and more than 150 aircraft could be deployed in a matter of days to marry up with materiel prepositioned in Norway, to prevent the Soviets from turning the northern flank of NATO by seizing the airfields and harbors of that country.[17] Also, carrier battle forces would be moved forward to support Norway, Greece, Turkey, and Japan.

In practice, of course, the goals of deterrence and proper positioning for war would conflict if forward naval deployments caused the Soviets to escalate a crisis into a confrontation or an attack. For example, they might well interpret early carrier force movements to Norway as precursors to an attack on their own Northern Fleet based on the Kola Peninsula and take preemptive action. US Navy concern about such criticisms is apparent from Admiral Watkins' statement that such a prepositioning "does not imply some immediate 'Charge of the Light Brigade' on the Kola Peninsula or any other specific target."[18]

Phase II is "seizing the initiative." In this phase, war has broken out and the US Navy will take offensive action against Soviet targets "as far forward as possible."[19] Admiral Watkins's article is the clearest expression to date of the US Navy's intention to attack Soviet SSBNs in their "sanctuaries" near the Soviet Union and under the polar ice, although that intention could also be inferred from previous statements by the CNO and Secretary Lehman. That, of course, has caused a great deal of anguish among critics, who accuse the Navy of being unnecessarily provocative.[20] Admiral Watkins also implies that the Soviet Union itself could come under attack in this phase as the threat from Soviet Naval Aviation is eliminated.[21]

Phase III is "carrying the fight to the enemy." This is a continuation of Phase II, with attacks closer to the Soviet homeland as Soviet defenses are attrited. The goal of all these phases is "war termination on favorable terms," including no use of nuclear weapons and the destruction of the Soviet Navy.

Evaluation of the Maritime Strategy. The purpose of a military strategy is to guide the employment of force so as to achieve a political objective. Strategy should be distinguished from tactics, the methods of employing military force in particular engagements, and from campaigns, the theater-level engagements designed to further the goals of strategy and are fought using appropriate tactics. Tactics and campaigns support strategy, but are not subordinate to it.

By these definitions the Maritime Strategy is true strategy, as distinct from campaign planning or tactics. It is, in fact, the most developed and integrated expression of a national military strategy that currently exists. Both the Army and the Air Force have "doctrine," but the highest level at which this exists is the campaign level. The Army, for example, has developed a doctrine for fighting a land war in Europe under modern conditions called "AirLand Battle," and the Air Force is concerned with "Follow-on Force Attack," but neither of these approaches offers an integrated approach to fighting a global war. There is, in fact, a feeling among some Army and Air Force officers that the individual Services have no business planning at the strategic level, arguing that this should only be done by the Joint Chiefs of Staff (JCS) or in the Office of the Secretary of Defense (OSD). In the view of Navy strategists, such planning was not adequate, and the Navy simply filled the intellectual void. That the resulting strategy has a distinct blue-and-gold coloration should surprise no one.

The Maritime Strategy is not without its detractors. Critics name four deficiencies: first, it is not effective; second, it is dangerous; third, it detracts from higher-priority forces needed on the Central Front; and fourth, the forces required for its implementation are unnecessarily complex (and therefore costly).

Effectiveness. I agree that an overly aggressive implementation of the Maritime Strategy that would involve, for example, early movement of surface naval forces near Soviet home waters, is not likely to be effective. It is not clear that any surface force could last long against the massed raids the Soviets can mount close to their shores, and aircraft carriers are far too valuable to be lost in the Arctic early in a war.

A less aggressive version of the Maritime Strategy, however, promises important advantages. Forward operations of submarines, and perhaps later in a war of surface units, force the Soviet Navy back into its bastions, reinforce a pronounced tendency for caution in military affairs, and, together with mobile amphibious forces, pin down Soviet forces that could otherwise be used against US allies. I call these missions "forward area sea control."[22] They contrast with the "defensive sea control" orientation favored by the Carter administration, which was clearly inadequate for a nation as reliant upon sea lane defense as is the United States. Forward area sea control also contrasts with "offensive sea control" missions that envision the early use of surface forces to project power against the shore of the Soviet Union.

Danger. All military operations are potentially dangerous, and the possibility of a violent end is ever present. At issue is whether the Maritime Strategy is unnecessarily dangerous. Certainly some of the forward operations envisaged by the strategy are quite risky for the forces involved, and anti-SSBN operations pose additional problems of escalation control and strategic stability.

A particular concern is the possibility that certain US naval actions could trigger a nuclear response. No one can say with certainty how the Soviets would respond to a discovery of a carrier battle group nearing striking range of the Kola Peninsula or to an American campaign against Soviet SSBNs in their sanctuaries. It is possible the Soviets would regard the carrier battle group (CBG) as a nuclear threat, in view of its nuclear potential, and launch a preemptive nuclear attack of their own in response.[23] Navy analysts are reluctant to discuss this possibility, but it is rendered more likely by the clearly military nature of the target.[24] (Such an attack might also depend on the status of the ground battle, and the United States might want to link Soviet nuclear restraint at sea, where they are relatively weak, with US nuclear restraint on land, where NATO is at a conventional disadvantage.) Even if the US Navy were to sink all of the Soviets SSBNs, the result might then put their remaining land-based systems on a very dangerous "launch on warning" posture. The anti-SSBN mission may be one which becomes more dangerous the more "successful" it becomes.

The foregoing comments do not mean that the Navy should return to the days of defensive sea control only, or that forward operations, even of surface forces, should never be attempted. Certainly the Soviet perception of the US Navy's ability and willingness to perform these tasks should bolster deterrence. The same is also true of prospective attacks on their SSBNs; the knowledge that such attacks are possible may have a deterrent effect, but US leaders should consider long and hard before actually ordering such attacks. Nor should it be assumed by the Navy that it would automatically receive authority for such attacks.

Priority. At issue is whether resources devoted to the Navy might better be spent building up NATO's conventional defenses. To be sure, the defense of Europe remains a vital commitment of the United States, and its loss would be catastrophic. Still, the argument that European defenses are extremely weak cuts both ways. If so, they should surely be strengthened. But if Europe were lost, maritime superiority would be crucial to defend what would be left of US interests, and even to protect a "fortress America" that had fallen back to the Western Hemisphere. If this should come to pass, the Navy will be very happy not to have lost the use of its carriers early in the war.

It may be, on the other hand, that the conventional balance is not as unfavorable as has been assumed. Although a sharp critic of the Maritime Strategy, John Mearsheimer has written that NATO forces have a good chance of "thwarting a Soviet blitzkrieg" and forcing the Warsaw Pact to fight a war of attrition.[25] If that is so, expenditures on maritime forces that can attack the Soviet Union from many directions also make sense for their deterrent effect as well as their warfighting relevance on the NATO flanks. For deterrence to be fully effective, the Soviets must realize not only that they cannot achieve a blitzkrieg, but that they cannot expect to win a war of attrition either.[26]

Complexity. Only the most sophisticated and complex forces would have a chance of survival near the Soviet Union in wartime. Increasingly, however, this is true for "low threat" areas as well. The British recovery of the Falklands Islands was purchased at a high price in lives and ships—a price that would have been lower with airborne early warning and higher performance aircraft. Similarly, the periodic "freedom of navigation" exercises by the US 6th Fleet in the Gulf of Sidra are much safer because of the sophistication of US defensive and offensive weapons. Libyan efforts to disrupt these operations have been notably unsuccessful. Sophistication can be both a force multiplier and a lifesaver.

Summary of the Maritime Strategy. Changes in US Navy plans for fighting a global conventional war were well underway before the Reagan administration came into office, but the increased emphasis on offensive operations was fully consistent with administration priorities. Secretary of the Navy John Lehman supported this new direction strongly, and it was further elaborated by the first Chief of Naval Operations appointed by Reagan, Admiral James Watkins. Reagan's appointee as Chairman of the Joint Chiefs of Staff, Admiral William Crowe, is also well versed in the Maritime Strategy, although he may not promote it as hard as he would if he were CNO instead of the Chairman of the JCS.

Strategically, the Maritime Strategy assumes that a war with the Soviet Union would—and, from the United States' perspective, should—become global, although it may not involve the use of nuclear weapons. (The contrary assumption, that nuclear use in war is inevitable, is a self-fulfilling prophesy, since one would not be prepared to fight a conventional war.) Maritime Strategy supporters argue that money spent on the Navy to implement the Maritime Strategy is more beneficial than money spent in support of forces to defend the Central Front directly, and Secretary Lehman was extraordinarily successful in convincing Congress and the administration to support naval force investments.

Naval Force Structure

The key difference between the defense policies of the Carter and Reagan administrations is the much higher level of funding by the latter, particularly when the comparison is made with the first three years of the Carter presidency.[27] Secretary Weinberger acknowledged this in his fiscal year 1987 report to the Congress, saying, ''The principal difference between the Reagan Administration's defense program and its immediate predecessor's is our determination to ensure a balance of forces adequate for credible deterrence.'' The differences are not, he said, caused by strategic disagreements, but by differing judgments about the proper level of funding.[28]

Reagan administration priorities. But with respect to naval forces, the increased resources are not simply attributable to a policy of "more,"[29] but flow from the requirements of the Maritime Strategy. Since surface engagements near Soviet defenses were not contemplated, the Carter administration strategy could arguably be implemented with a smaller number of less capable ships than would be necessary for a forward strategy. The result was a deemphasis on sophisticated naval units in favor of a smaller number of less costly alternatives, plus nonnaval forces usable on the Central Front. Specifically, Carter believed the Navy needed only 12 deployable aircraft carriers and 90 SSNs to carry out his defensive strategy.

Secretary of Defense Caspar Weinberger made it clear in his first annual report to the Congress that the global strategy of the Reagan administration presented "a clear need for increased U.S. naval power." Consistent with this belief, his procurement program contained "a significant increase in the number of new ships, aircraft, and weapons procured for the Navy."[30] The goal of the new administration was "maritime superiority over any likely enemy.... This goal dictates an increase in U.S. naval power."[31] In a discussion of "defense in depth" for surface forces, Secretary Weinberger clearly adopted the offensive emphasis of the Maritime Strategy:

Our preferred approach [to fleet defense] is to destroy enemy bombers before they can reach ASCM [antiship cruise missile] launch range by striking their bases or by destroying them in transit.[32]

Secretary of the Navy John Lehman strongly supported this shift in strategy, and pushed hard for the forces necessary to carry it out. As a naval aviator, Secretary Lehman could be expected to support aircraft

carriers, and those familiar with his earlier writings
were not surprised by his emphasis on carrier procurement.[33] Lehman called for a fleet of 600 ships, including 15 deployable carrier battle groups. Because at any
one time one carrier will be in extensive overhaul until
the end of the century under the Service Life Extension
Program (SLEP), a total of 16 carriers is required to
support this goal.

Testimony by Admiral Hayward soon after the new
administration took office showed a clear understanding
of the force structure implications of the Maritime
Strategy. He viewed the fiscal year 1982 budget submitted by the outgoing administration as ''wholly

Table 1
Deployable Battle Forces, Fiscal Year 1980
and Fiscal Year 1987

Ship Type	1980	1987
Ballistic Missile Submarines	40	39
Strategic Support Ships	8	6
Aircraft Carriers (Deployable)	13	14
Battleships	0	3
Cruisers	26	35
Destroyers	81	69
Frigates	71	115
Nuclear Attack Submarines (SSNs)	74	99
Diesel Attack Submarines	5	4
Patrol Combatants	3	6
Amphibious Ships	66	62
Mine Warfare Ships	3	5
Underway Replenishment Ships	48	57
Support Forces Ships	41	53
Total	479	567

Source: Secretary of Defense, *Annual Report to the Congress,
Fiscal Year 1987.*

unsatisfactory in terms of its impact on the naval balance.'' Needed was a Navy of

at least 15 carrier battle groups, the capability to lift one-and-a-half Marine amphibious forces, a force of 100 modern attack submarines and all the auxiliary and support forces necessary to sustain such a large fleet.[34]

The new administration began immediately to implement its ''naval recovery program.'' A comparison of Reagan's first five-year defense plan with Carter's last one shows 2 carriers, 4 renovated battleships, and 11 amphibious ships to none, and 17 SSNs to 7.[35] Table 1 shows the result of this buildup strikingly: from fiscal year 1980 to fiscal year 1987 there is an increase from 479 to 567 in the number of deployable battle-capable ships; moreover, many of these are larger and more capable than the ships that have retired in the interim. Much of this increase is due to the completion of ships ordered in the Carter administration (due to the long lead time in ship construction) and to the delayed retirement of some older ships, so the effect of the Reagan ship construction program is just beginning to be felt. Table 2 indicates the force level goals of the Reagan administration, compared to the fiscal year 1987 end strength. Clearly the ''naval recovery program'' is not yet complete.

As a result of this emphasis on construction, the Navy will reach its goal of 600 ships either in 1989 (according to the Secretary of the Navy) or in 1992 (according to the Congressional Budget Office, which assumes an earlier retirement for some older ships). As important as numbers, however, is the need to modernize the fleet—and this will be increasingly expensive given the larger number of the more sophisticated vessels required by the Maritime Strategy. The modernization shortfall will be particularly acute in the guided missile destroyer (DDG) category, ships which are necessary to protect the fleet from air attack.[36]

Table 2
Navy Force Goals for Fiscal Year 1987

Ship Type	Goal	1987
Ballistic Missile Submarines (SSBNs) and Other Strategic Ships	20–40*	39
Deployable Aircraft Carriers	15	14
Reactivated Battleships	4	3
Principal Surface Combatants	238	219
Nuclear-Powered Attack Submarines	100	99
Mine Countermeasures Ships	14	5
Amphibious Ships (MAF + MAB Lift)	75	62
Patrol Combatants	6	6
Underway Replenishment Ships	65	57
Support Ships and Other Auxiliaries	60–65	59
Total	597–622	563***

* Not determined; depends in part on arms reduction agreements
** Includes strategic support ships
***Plus four diesel-powered attack submarines

Source: Secretary of Defense, *Annual Report to the Congress, Fiscal Year 1987.*

Future Navy budget requirements. The US Navy budget has done well under the Reagan administration, increasing 43 percent from fiscal year 1980 through fiscal year 1985 (in constant 1986 dollars).[37] Despite the emphasis on procurement, however, Navy budgets have not been as heavily weighted toward procurement relative to operations and maintenance as has the Defense Department budget as a whole. From fiscal year 1980 through fiscal year 1985 Defense Department procurement increased 105 percent, compared to an operations and maintenance increase of 37 percent. Navy procurement, however, increased 62 percent, with a 39-percent increase in operations and maintenance.[38]

Construction expenses are only the tip of the budget iceberg. New ships must be manned, and they are expensive to operate. The result is that procurement funds in one year generate substantial operations and maintenance requirements once the ships are commissioned. The Congressional Budget Office believes these expenses, coupled with the requirements of force modernization, point to budget increases of from about 3 to 5 percent per year (in constant dollars) until 1994.[39] Secretary Lehman is more optimistic, but he concedes that a 3-percent growth rate will be necessary to sustain the 600-ship Navy.[40]

The remaining questions deal with the likelihood of achieving such an increase in a period of budgetary austerity, and the difficult choices faced by a Navy convinced of the effectiveness of the Maritime Strategy, yet faced with the prospect of severe budgetary retrenchment that would make the strategy more difficult to execute.

Future Navy Directions

President Reagan's fiscal year 1987 budget showed a 3-percent growth per year through 1991 and a shift toward operations and maintenance at the expense of procurement. Comparing defense expenditures as a percent of gross national product or of total Federal expenditures, it is clear that the capacity for defense growth is there; whether the political willingness to provide it will also be there is less certain. The administration cannot be pleased, however, at strong indications of congressional unwillingness to fund defense increases. Considering the sequestrations required by the Balanced Budget Act (''Gramm-Rudman-Hollings''), defense appropriations actually declined in fiscal year 1986.[41]

The impact of budgetary retrenchment. Even without the Balanced Budget Act, the political momentum for increased defense expenditures has become increasingly difficult to sustain. Only President Reagan's determination and enormous personal popularity has spared defense from further cuts. Despite Secretary Lehman's expressed optimism that defense budgets can and will increase, and despite the good arguments he and others have made in support of this position, it seems more likely that a period of moderate to severe budgetary retrenchment is at hand for defense. As the Service which has benefited most from the defense buildup, the US Navy will find itself with severe financial problems.

Navy alternatives. Assuming that cutbacks will come, and this analysis is not arguing they should, the Navy has several alternatives:

MODIFY THE MARITIME STRATEGY. Even if resources are cut back severely, the Navy is unlikely to abandon or greatly modify the Maritime Strategy—and it should not do so. Notwithstanding the disagreement in naval circles over how the Maritime Strategy should be implemented, there is a strong consensus among Navy strategists that the broad outlines of this forward global strategy best support US national interests. A change in the "strategic culture" to emphasize defensive operations, for example, is unlikely, and would require years to take root.

CUT BACK THE PROCUREMENT PROGRAM. One way to reduce costs while maintaining desired force levels is to delay retirement of older ships. As noted above, this is one way in which the Reagan administration is meeting its goal of 600 ships. If this philosophy is applied to attack submarines (SSNs), and new procurement is reduced from four to three, a total of $4.7 billion could be saved in the next five years.[42]

With respect to carrier procurement, the *George Washington* will replace the aging *Coral Sea* when it, in turn, replaces the *Lexington* as the aviation training platform in 1991. A post-Lehman Navy could decide to economize and not construct a replacement carrier for the *Midway,* now scheduled to retire sometime in the 1990s. (The Navy is vague in its public statements as to when.)[43] This would save the expense of building and operating the other ships in the battle group and an air wing but would leave the Navy with 14 deployable carriers, as it had at the end of fiscal year 1987. Fear of just such a decision may motivate the Navy to push for an additional carrier to be authorized before the Reagan administration leaves office.[44]

Whatever alternative is chosen, one hopes the Navy will accelerate its development of vertical/short takeoff and landing (V/STOL) aircraft. These can be operated from a large number of Navy platforms, including the helicopter-capable amphibious ships that are available or on order.

REDUCE THE TEMPO OF OPERATIONS (OPTEMPO). The Navy has already made significant changes in its deployment cycle, with the goal of limiting peacetime deployments to 6 continuous months out of 18. The other 12 months are to be spent near home ports doing maintenance, on local operations, and on refresher training and workup for deployment. The motivation for this change is that the current OPTEMPO is actually higher than during the Vietnam war, and has adverse effects on crew morale and retention.[45] With a larger number of ships and with the substitution of battleship "surface action groups" for carrier battle groups, some reductions in OPTEMPO are possible.[46]

But large reductions are not possible without a significant change in operational philosophy. Carriers have proven very useful in their "peacetime presence" role, and both national and Navy leaders have thought it important that as many as possible be forward-deployed to reduce reaction time. With 15 deployable carriers and a one-in-three deployment cycle, only 5 can be forward-deployed regularly. In the event of hostilities it is preferable to operate two or three carriers together to permit around-the-clock flight operations and to increase the ratio of offensive to defensive aircraft. The alternative is to retain a greater proportion of the fleet in home water, and surge forces forward in the event of a crisis. This obviously requires excellent intelligence about developing crises and the political will to act promptly. The disadvantages to this posture are not having forces where they can affect developments and having only a limited number of ships "showing the flag" in noncrisis times. If budgetary constraints force this option upon the US Navy, however, there are some compensating advantages. The effect on crew retention would be positive, and when the fleet did sail in response to a crisis, it would be a stronger demonstration of national resolve.

INCREASE THE ROLE OF THE NAVAL RESERVE. This is, in fact, already happening. If current administration plans are approved, the Naval Reserve would increase from 142,000 to 156,000 and the Marine Corps Reserve would increase from 43,000 to 44,000 by the end of fiscal year 1987.[47] Compared to the 3 percent overall defense growth requested, the administration proposed to increase reserve funding for all the armed services by 10 percent in fiscal year 1987.

As manpower expenses climb, the transfer of additional functions to the Naval Reserve makes sense, so long as the reservists are supported with the proper equipment and training. It must be remembered, however, that this alternative is not cost-free: if reserves are given obsolete equipment, their warfighting potential will be degraded accordingly, and even Naval Reserve ships have crews of approximately 65 percent active-duty personnel.[48] The Reagan administration has transferred 11 of a planned total of 26 relatively modern guided missile frigates (FFGs) to the Naval Reserve, and will continue to provide the reserves with modern planes such as the F/A–18 fighter-bomber and the A–7E light attack aircraft. Such plans may have to be expanded, as must the legal authority of the President to mobilize particular reserve units (and individual reservists) quickly in an emergency.

One possibility that has been discussed is to put three entire carrier battle groups into the Naval Reserve, in a special category of ships that would not go to sea unless mobilized. Reservists assigned to these vessels would be those recently released from active duty whose skills can be assumed not to have degraded significantly. If the ships are properly maintained for deployment on short notice and continuously updated with modern equipment, the estimated savings over five years would be on the order of $1 billion.[49] There is concern, however, about the combat effectiveness of personnel who have not operated their equipment until mobilization. In addition, the carriers would not be available for routine deployments or for crisis operations.

REDUCE OPERATIONS AND MAINTENANCE FUNDING
(FOR ALL DOD). It is tempting to cut "O & M" funds
because such large reductions can be made in this area.
Additionally, the result of these cuts in reduced readiness is less apparent, at least during peacetime. The
CBO has suggested two alternative cutbacks that could
save from $50 to $80 billion over the next five years.[50]
The smaller figure could have been achieved by reducing President Reagan's fiscal year 1987 request 10 percent, then allowing O & M to grow in future years as
he requested. The larger sum results from holding the
growth of O & M to the rate of inflation. Whether
either of these options is wise in view of the increased
force levels is a matter for further study, but savings of
this magnitude are difficult to resist.

MANAGE PROCUREMENT CONTRACTS MORE EFFI-
CIENTLY. This is an area where efficiencies do not
degrade force levels or their readiness. Secretary Lehman pointed to several initiatives, including increasing
competition among suppliers, controlling changes in
programs after they have commenced, creating a
"career path" for materiel professionals, and maintaining program stability to avoid costly "ups and
downs."[51] Much has been accomplished in this area,
and doubtless much remains to be done.[52]

The Post-Reagan Navy

Changes in capital-intensive forces such as the US Navy
do not occur quickly, and the changes wrought by the
Navy starting late in the Carter administration will
affect forces and missions well into the next century.
The Maritime Strategy is the basis of current Navy missions and procurement choices and will provide the
beginning point for decisions by future administrations.

Nevertheless, changes on the margins are possible, and over time these will affect the Navy significantly.

Two factors are not likely to change in the short term, however: the threats to national commitments and the declining willingness of political leaders, perhaps even Presidents, to fund defense at a level sufficient to meet them. How this contradiction will be resolved is unclear, but the time of relatively painless adjustments is over. There are several choices, all unpalatable: reduce commitments, accept a greater risk to national interests, reduce necessary domestic spending, or raise taxes.

But changes do occur. President Eisenhower's desire to limit military spending led to the "New Look," emphasizing strategic nuclear forces in a policy of "massive retaliation." President Kennedy's "Flexible Response," emphasizing forces across the spectrum of conflict, made sense at a time when the Soviet Union was believed able to respond in kind to a US strategic attack, and is still the basis of US military policy. Increased Soviet strategic and theater nuclear capabilities, however, have caused a renaissance of thinking about how to fight an extended conventional war. The Maritime Strategy is part of that reassessment. Future challenges in the Third World, especially those close to home in Latin America, may combine with other trends such as increased terrorist activity to alter defense priorities once again. The greatest change would occur in the event of the political neutralization of Europe and the subsequent degradation or dissolution of NATO.

Still, it is risky to predict the future. Few people anticipated the about-face by President Carter in 1979 in response to the Soviet invasion of Afghanistan, the Soviet intimidation of Poland, and the Iranian seizure of

American hostages. Events in the Middle East, Central America, or elsewhere will surely affect the future course of the US defense policy, including the Navy's force structure, in ways that cannot now be known. As this course is determined, Navy leaders hope that the American people will bear in mind the 1780 advice of George Washington: "Under all circumstances, a decisive naval superiority is to be considered a fundamental principle, and the basis upon which all hope of success must ultimately depend."

Notes

1. John Allen Williams, "Defense Policy: The Carter-Reagan Record,"*Washington Quarterly* 6, no. 4 (Autumn 1983): 77–92.

2. A detailed account of this period can be found in William J. Lucas and Raymond H. Dawson, *The Organizational Politics of Defense* (Pittsburgh, PA: The International Studies Association, 1974).

3. Hedley Bull, "The Rise of Soviet Naval Power," *Problems of Communism* 30, no. 2 (March/April 1981): 62.

4. Lawrence J. Korb, "The FY 1981–1985 Defense Program: Issues and Trends," *AEI Foreign Policy and Defense Review* 2, no. 2 (1980): 33.

5. Harold Brown, *Department of Defense Annual Report, Fiscal Year 1982*, 19 January 1981, p. 75.

6. John Allen Williams, "U.S. Navy Missions and Force Structure: A Critical Reappraisal," *Armed Forces and Society*, 7, no. 4 (Summer 1981): 499–528, and "Rejoinder" to Rear Admiral John A. Baldwin, *Armed Forces and Society* 8, no. 4 (Summer 1982): 684–85.

7. Catheryn Donohoe, "Lehman Power," *Washington Times*, 20 August 1985, p. 1B.

8. Michael R. Gordon, "Lehman's Navy Riding High, But Critics Question Its Strategy and Rapid Growth," *National Journal*, 21 September 1985, p. 2121.

9. James D. Watkins, "The Maritime Strategy," Supplement to the U.S. Naval Institute *Proceedings*, January 1986, pp. 2–17. For an excellent annotated compendium of relevant writings, see the bibliography by Peter M. Swartz in the same issue.

10. Ibid., p. 5.

11. Captain T.M. Daly, USN, "Maritime Strategy and Long Range Planning," Presentation to the First Annual Long Range Planners' Conference of the Chiefs of Naval Operations (17–18 September 1985), p. 26.

12. John F. Lehman, Jr., "The 600-Ship Navy," Supplement to the U.S. Naval Institute *Proceedings,* January 1986, pp. 30–40.

13. Donald D. Chipman and Major David Lay, USAF, "Sea Power and the B–52 Stratofortress," *Air University Review* 37, no. 2 (January–February 1986): 45–50.

14. See his interchange with Senator Nunn in Senate Armed Services Committee, *Department of Defense Authorization for Appropriations for FY 1985,* Part 8 (Washington, DC: Government Printing Office, 14 March 1984), pp. 3851–3900.

15. John F. Lehman, Jr., "Rebirth of a U.S. Navy Strategy," *Strategic Review* 9, no. 3 (Summer 1981): 13–14.

16. Watkins, "The Maritime Strategy," pp. 8–13. Not surprisingly, Soviet commentators find them "remarkably odious." See Valentin Falin, "Back to the Stone Age," *Izvestia,* 23 January 1986, p. 5.

17. General P. X. Kelley, USMC, *FY87 Marine Corps Posture Statement.*

18. Watkins, "The Maritime Strategy," p. 10.

19. Ibid., p. 11.

20. Barry R. Posen, "Inadvertent Nuclear War? Escalation and NATO's Northern Flank," *International Security* 7, no. 2 (Fall 1982): 28–54.

21. Watkins, "The Maritime Strategy," p. 12.

22. John Allen Williams, "Strategic Alternatives for the 600-Ship Navy," forthcoming.

23. Captain Linton F. Brooks, USN, "Escalation and Naval Strategy," U.S. Naval Institute *Proceedings* 110, no. 8 (August 1984): 33–37.

24. Desmond Ball, "Nuclear War at Sea," *International Security* 10, no. 3 (Winter 1985/1986): 8.

25. John J. Mearsheimer, "Nuclear Weapons and Deterrence in Europe," *International Security* 9, no. 3 (Winter 1984/85): 45.

26. John J. Mearsheimer has argued that Soviets will be deterred only by the knowledge they cannot win a blitzkrieg, to which the contribution of naval forces is minimal. See his *Conventional Deterrence* (Ithaca, NY: Cornell University Press, 1983.)

27. Williams, "Defense Policy," p. 25.

28. Caspar W. Weinberbger, *Annual Report to the Congress, FY 1987,* 5 February 1986, p. 37.

29. See the comments of senior congressional defense analyst John Collins in Benjamin F. Schemmer, "*Defense Guidance* Gives SDI Priority Equal to Strategic Force Modernization" *Armed Forces Journal International* 123, no. 6 (February 1986): 20.

30. Caspar W. Weinberger, *Annual Report to the Congress, FY 1983,* 8 February 1982, pp. III–19.

31. Ibid., p. III–19.

32. Ibid., p. III–21.

33. John F. Lehman, Jr., *Aircraft Carriers: The Real Choices* (Beverly Hills, CA: Sage Publications, 1978).

34. Admiral Thomas B. Hayward, USN, *FY 1982 CNO Report,* pp. 20, 24.

35. Caspar W. Weinberger, "Where We Must Build—And Where We Must Cut," *Defense 81,* December 1981, p. 7.

36. Congressional Budget Office, *Future Budget Requirements for the 600 Ship Navy* (Washington, DC: Government Printing Office, September 1985), pp. 12–14.

37. Ibid., p. 69.

38. Ibid., pp. 72–73.

39. Ibid., p. 47.

40. John F. Lehman, Jr., "The 600-Ship Navy," pp. 38–39. See also his testimony to the House Armed Services Committee, 5 February 1986 (*FY 1987 SECNAV Report*), p. 19.

41. Congressional Budget Office, *An Analysis of the President's Budgetary Proposals for Fiscal Year 1987* (Washington, DC: Government Printing Office), p. 21.

42. Congressional Budget Office, *Reducing the Deficit: Spending and Revenue Options* (Washington, DC: Government Printing Office, March 1986), p. 36.

43. Weinberger, *FY 1987 Report,* pp. 181–82.

44. Tom Burgess, "Lehman to Request Funds for Nuclear Carrier in FY 1988," *Navy Times,* 14 October 1985, p. 4.

45. Watkins, *FY 1987 CNO Report,* pp. 27–28.

46. John F. Lehman, Jr., Testimony to the House Armed Services Committee, 5 February 1986 (*FY 1987 SECNAV Report*), pp. 12–13.

47. Weinberger, *FY 1987 Report,* p. 147.

48. Congressional Budget Office, *Manpower for a 600-Ship Navy: Costs and Policy Alternatives* (Washington, DC: Government Printing Office, August 1983), p. 26.

49. Congressional Budget Office, *Reducing the Deficit*, pp. 62–63.

50. Ibid., pp. 66–67.

51. Lehman, *FY 1987 SECNAV Report*, pp. 23–27.

52. Tim Carrington, ''Panel Releases Details on its Strategy to Streamline Arms-Purchase Process,'' *Wall Street Journal*, 8 April 1986, p. 62.

THE US AIR FORCE: FORCE STRUCTURE, CHANGES, AND IMPLICATIONS

Thomas A. Fabyanic

*B*Y VIRTUALLY EVERY MEASURABLE indicator of merit, the US Air Force after 1986 is a far superior military instrument to the one inherited by the Reagan administration in 1981. The quantity and quality of its manpower, weapon systems, and supporting systems are greatly improved, as are readiness, sustainability, and combat capability.

Collectively, these indices profile a cross-section of what is commonly referred to as the force structure, that is, the basic size and composition of USAF combat capability. That they indicate significant improvement during the past several years is undeniable. Nevertheless, these statistical measures are not real evidence of combat capability. The evidence that determines the capability of the force structure ultimately is provided on the field of battle, for only combat can demonstrate the true military worth of systems and, of infinitely greater importance, the men who employ them. Valid as they are, however, combat judgments are not timely judgments; good or bad, when they are rendered they possess a large measure of finality.

Necessary, therefore, is a combat-oriented conceptual framework for force structure decision-making. Such a framework would include the realities and trends of conflict, followed by technological capabilities and potential, focused threat analysis, and the influence of domestic and international policies. When recent USAF force structure decisions are viewed in the context of their interrelationships, the more optimistic assessments derived from statistical measures give way to a more disquieting picture.

A Conceptual Framework

Although the foundation of US national security policy is deterrence, deterrence may fail, and the nature of war become the arbiter of one's force structure. Evaluations about that force structure, therefore, must be made within the context of war. The purposes for which wars are fought can vary substantially; at one level their intent can be to destroy a nation-state as a political entity, while at another the aim could be the relatively minor one of suppressing insurgency. Clausewitz summed it up quite nicely with his analogy that war has its own grammar (means and methods) but not its own logic (purpose).[1] Because these purposes differ, the methods and means used to achieve the objectives must exhibit an ample degree of flexibility.

War is not deterministic or mechanistic, and thus it cannot be reduced to numbers.[2] Operative in war is Clausewitz's notion of friction. Like its mechanical counterpart, this phenomenon affects all efforts in war, and as a consequence of it even the most simple tasks become difficult; few if any actions occur as expected. Further suggesting that war cannot be reduced to quantitative judgments is the role of chance. Clausewitz understood the role of chance very well when he suggested that

absolute, so-called mathematical, factors never find a firm basis in military calculations. From the very start there is an interplay of possibilities, probabilities, good luck and bad that weaves its way through the length and breadth of the tapestry. In the whole range of human activities, war most closely resembles a game of cards.[3]

An essential element in war's nature is the existence of offense and defense as complementary factors. Neither is perfect, nor dominant; both are operative across the spectrum of war and at all operational levels. Consequently, a force structure that ignores the complementary roles of offense and defense is one that fundamentally is inconsistent with the nature of war.

Aside from the nature of war, any meaningful assessment of a force structure must include an understanding of war as derived from its history. Only history can outline the trends of war and highlight change in its practices. It is history, moreover, that prevents one from viewing war in a vacuum, as something apart from the political, economic, and social conditions that allow war to occur and which tempers its conduct and outcome. History, furthermore, provides a degree of critical judgment and alerts one to the role of subjective elements in war that "cannot be classified or counted" but which must be "seen or felt."[4]

The second variable in the conceptual framework is existing and emerging technology. Technology affects the force structure primarily in qualitative terms, but it also can result in differing quantitive outcomes. What can be referred to as technological *sophistication,* for example, could result in greater numbers of systems, while what one might term technological *complexity* could have just the opposite effect. Technological assessments of force structure decisions can be made by examining the trend of those technologies directly related to military capability and determining the extent to which they are being exploited, individually and collectively, to provide maximum force structure flexibility. But such judgments can be made only if one possesses an understanding of what force structure systems are needed, otherwise the tendency will be to extract maximum benefit from every technology rather than the relevant ones. With regard to its chief adversary, the USSR, the United States holds a commanding lead in basic technologies directly related to military capability. As shown in table 1, the United States is superior in 14, the two countries are equal in 6, and the

Table 1
Relative US/USSR Standing in the Twenty Most Important Basic Technology Areas

Basic Technologies	US Superior	US/USSR Equal	USSR Superior
1. Aerodynamics/Fluid Dynamics		X	
2. Computers and Software	◆X		
3. Conventional Warheads (Including all Chemical Explosives)		X	
4. Directed Energy (Laser)		X	
5. Electro-Optical Sensor (Including Infrared)	X		
6. Guidance and Navigation	X		
7. Life Sciences (Human Factors/ Biotechnology)	X		
8. Materials (Lightweight, High Strength, High Temperature)	X◆		
9. Micro-Electronic Materials and Integrated Circuit Manufacturing	X		
10. Nuclear Warheads		X	
11. Optics		X	
12. Power Sources (Mobile) (Includes Energy Storage)		X	
13. Production/Manufacturing (Includes Automated Control)	X		
14. Propulsion (Aerospace and Ground Vehicles)	X◆		
15. Radar Sensor	X◆		

	US	US/USSR	USSR
Basic Technologies	*Superior*	*Equal*	*Superior*
16. Robotics and Machine Intelligence	X		
17. Signal Processing	X		
18. Signature Reduction	X		
19. Submarine Detection	X⬧		
20. Telecommunications (Includes Fiber Optics)	X		

The list is limited to 20 technologies, which were selected with the objective of providing a valid base for comparing overall U.S. and USSR basic technology. The list is in alphabetical order. These technologies are "on the shelf" and available for application. (The technologies are not intended to compare technology level in currently DEPLOYED military systems.)

The technologies selected have the potential for significantly CHANGING the military capability in the next 10 to 20 years. The technologies are not static; they are improving or have the potential for significant improvements; new technologies may appear on future lists.

The arrows denote that the relative technology level is CHANGING significantly in the direction indicated.

The judgments represent overall consensus for each basic technology area. The USSR may be superior in some of the subtechnologies making up each basic technology. The average assessment can incorporate a significant variance when individual components of a technology are considered.

Source: Caspar W. Weinberger, *Annual Report to the Congress, Fiscal Year 1987* (Washington, DC: Government Printing Office, 1986), p. 255.

USSR leads in none. Since these technologies are available and offer the potential for changing one's military capability in 10 to 20 years, they are essential for arriving at valid judgments about force structure changes.[5]

A closely related third variable is threat analysis and it must address the most serious threat as well as those most likely to result in war. Clearly the USSR falls into the former category and force structure decisions must consider the range of possible conflict that includes a major nuclear exchange, conventional war, and challenges at the periphery. At the same time the United States must consider the threats posed elsewhere, and it is in this respect that the realities and trends of war play such an important role in the analysis. This consideration would make clear the existence of different levels of war and suggest that forces capable of fighting at one level may be totally unsuited for another level. In addition, the analysis would highlight the different ways in which military forces are being used and, by inference, how they might be employed in the future given existing and projected determinants of war.

The final element in the conceptual framework is defense policy, which essentially consists of international and domestic politics. International politics is best viewed as an environment for defense policy in which the key factors are alliance systems, the balance of power among and between states, and the threat or conduct of war. The dominant factor in this environment is existing and potential military power. The environment of domestic politics consists of bureaucracies and interest groups, differing social classes, and political parties. Key factors in this environment are the essential resources of society such as its manpower, money, and material. Any defense policy decision, including force structure decisions, affects to some extent both environments; simultaneously, both environments exert influence on defense policy. The net result is that many policy decisions, and especially those that pertain to the force structure, are not the consequence of logic; rather, they are the result of politics.[6] Indeed, as much as one might wish it to be otherwise, it may well be that the realities and trends of war, technology, and threat analyses are the less influential variables in force structure decisions.

A brief assessment of several ongoing initiatives, when viewed in the context of our conceptual framework, tends not only to suggest the significance of the variables but the extent to which force structure decisions reflect logic or politics.

The Strategic Defense Initiative

Although a Joint Service research program and thus not yet a force structure issue, the potential significance of the Strategic Defense Initiative (SDI) warrants at least a brief examination. Although serious concerns and questions are expressed about SDI, viewing it in the context of war, technology, and threat analysis suggests that it may be one of the wisest decisions of the nuclear era. Above all else, there is a clear conceptual argument for SDI. The majority of those who have expressed their disapproval of SDI belong primarily to a diverse group that includes scientists, physicians, politicians, analysts, and newspaper reporters. The one trait that most appear to have in common in their opposition to strategic defense is a fundamental lack of understanding about the key issue of war. This shortcoming is most regretable, since it is the nature of war and the complementary interrelationship of offense and defense as elements of war that form the essence of the conceptual argument for SDI.

Although it is generally accepted that offense is the dominant form of warfare, much evidence is to the contrary. One merely need compare the objectives of offense and defense to observe, in a metaphysical sense, that defense is the higher form of war. Its purpose is to protect and preserve, but the aim of offense is to destroy and, in some cases, annihilate. One can argue also that defense is the stronger and less demanding type of warfare. Thus, weaker forces can depend on defensive war and survive, but they might be destroyed if they resort to offensive war. Finally, defense permits one to absorb initial attacks and initiate offensive action at a time and place of his own choosing. It is for these reasons that Clausewitz could argue that *"the defense form of war- fare is intrinsically stronger than the offensive,* [and] although it is implicit in the nature of [war], it is at odds with prevalent opinion, which proves how ideas can be confused by superficial writers."[7] (Emphasis in the original.) In other words, the notion of offensive superi- ority apparently has little conceptual basis, but defen- sive warfare has much to justify it. This conceptual validity aside, however, history clearly suggests that warfare is characterized by offense and defense even though one or the other form may take precedence at any given time.

Recent military history clearly shows that the tend- ency to ignore the relationship between offense and defense is not limited to the present generation. For example, strategists in World War I failed, for the most part, to recognize that at some time prior to the war, defense had gained ascendancy over offense. In retro- spect, the US Civil War and the Russo-Japanese War offered ample evidence that the arbitraments of war were defense and attrition, not offense and maneuver. But that lesson did not become clear to most military leaders until the offensives in World War I ground to a halt on the Western Front. By that time, too much had been "invested" to quit.

An additional element in the conceptual argument for defense is the Clausewitzian notion of friction as it applies to war. As a consequence of friction, war does not unfold as planned; troops, weapons systems, and equipment function differently when war imposes its nature upon them. Clausewitz's statement, "everything in war is very simple, but the simplest thing is difficult,'' is a clear recognition of the problem.[8]

By applying the principle of friction to nuclear conflict, one can recognize that ample room exists for it to dominate such conflict. The main cause of friction would be the uncertainty associated with the efficacy of nuclear weapons, none of which have ever been tested in a manner that even remotely approximates war. This potential for friction is enormous and as a consequence of it, no competent military officer could claim a high level of confidence for a nuclear attack. Too many uncertainties exist; US military officers know it and so do their Soviet counterparts. As professional officers, however, they will attempt to reduce the level and effect of friction as it relates to their operations, while realizing that it cannot be eliminated.

Consider, then, how an active US defense would add to the problem of the Soviet attack planner. Of necessity, the entire Soviet attack formulation and the requirements for offensive systems would undergo major modifications. The Soviets would need to contend with a greatly improved US surveillance and reconnaissance system and a layered defense specifically tailored for boost-phase, postboost, midcourse, and terminal defense. Further complicating the attack would be US preferential defense options that would permit defenses of varied intensity. Some targets would be defended heavily and others lightly, but it would be up to the Soviets to figure this out. Above all else, the Soviet attack planner would need to cope with friction and uncertainty. Substantial amounts of both would be generated by US defenses, but much more would occur because of Soviet limitations. Simply put, the Soviets could not test their capability against a US defense system any more than they currently can measure their

effectiveness against the existing US force structure.
Thus, the added friction and resulting uncertainty generated by an active US defense would compound the
Soviet attack calculus in a geometric rather than
arithmetic fashion, and the probability of success would
decrease accordingly. Some Soviet warheads will penetrate and the resulting destructiveness will be of no
small concern, even though the primary targets of the
attack will be US retaliatory systems and not, as some
suggest, US cities. But, arguments that focus on the
imperfectability of an active defense, aside from being
irrational, ignore the larger contribution that defense can
make to deterrence and hence the prevention of conflict.

A chief objection to strategic defense is that it
would lead to instability, either in a crisis situation,
wherein one side might think it possessed an advantage,
or in an intensive development and deployment effort
characterized by some as an arms race in space.[9]
Although the instability argument possesses some validity, it loses much of its relevance when viewed in the
context of military history and our experience with the
deployment of nuclear systems. One probably would
search the annals of military history in vain to find a
war caused by instability resulting from the deployment
of weapon systems. Indeed, all of the evidence appears
to the contrary, even during the nuclear period. As an
example, for almost a quarter of a century following
World War II, US nuclear superiority created force
structure instability *vis-a-vis* the USSR, but it led to no
nuclear conflict.

Additionally, the historical record would suggest
that neither superpower would initiate nuclear war to
prevent the other from deploying a fundamentally new
weapons system. The Soviets, for example, took the
lead in the deployment of land-based missiles and

currently are the only nation to possess an operational antisatellite weapon. The United States, on the other hand, led in sea-launched ICBMs and multiple independently targeted reentry vehicles (MIRVs). In these and other similar deployments, the other side merely developed what amounted to an offsetting capability (which differs substantially from what is referred to as action-reaction).

This trend, moreover, seems to suggest that substantive or dramatic breakthroughs are not a characteristic of Soviet-American arms competition. What one side develops the other soon acquires, although the record does show that, except for a few instances, the United States has maintained a qualitative edge. In this regard, should the United States develop an effective defense system without the USSR's following suit, the United States has pledged publicly to share its technology. Cynics who do not take the United States seriously or critics who argue that providing defensive technology to the Soviets is, to put it mildly, imprudent, perhaps can take some comfort in the realization that the Soviets, through various means, usually have managed to obtain desired military data from the West.

Opponents of SDI also cite its consequences for the 1972 ABM Treaty, the provisions of which would appear to prevent the deployment of an effective strategic defense. This argument, unfortunately, demonstrates a narrow view of the purposes of arms control by suggesting that *its outcomes* are the ultimate measure of merit. That simply is not the case. Arms control is but one (albeit a vital one) of several means used to maintain deterrence. It is not, however, an end in itself, and thus its products should undergo continual assessment.

The concept of defending one's ballistic missile force is militarily sound, a point well understood by military officers, both Soviet and American. Until recently, however, the characteristics of ballistic missiles prevented an effective defense, and because of those circumstances the ABM Treaty made sense in 1972 and for several years to follow. But now we need to question the relevance of the ABM Treaty, since it appears that the concept of defense can become a practical reality by systematic exploitation of emerging technology. The treaty is not sacrosanct and both sides can modify it through negotiations. A refusal to consider that option ignores existing technological realities, the basic elements of deterrence, and the nature of war; moreover, it would confirm the view of arms control critics that the goals of arms control advocates are sadly misplaced.

Those who oppose SDI on technological grounds, like those who raise the instability argument, tend to ignore the historical record. It would suggest the least difficult problem for SDI is technology, comments from scientists opposing strategic defense notwithstanding. (In that regard, one only need recall the distinguished scientist, Vannevar Bush, who ridiculed the idea of ICBMs in the years following World War II.) Although there are serious technological questions pertaining to strategic defense, feasibility is not one of them. The relevant questions are which technologies, of the several that show promise, offer the highest probability of success and how they can be exploited for defensive purposes.[10]

But perhaps the most relevant point about technology is its relationship to the larger scheme of things. During the nuclear era we, as a nation, all too often have allowed technology to dominate or exert undue influence on our decision-making process. Quite often instead of using technology to satisfy conceptual formulations we have permitted the reverse to occur, and as a consequence technology has tended to control our actions. Fortunately, SDI has returned us to a more logical order of things, first by establishing a concept and, as a second step, looking for technology to provide the means or force structure. Should that occur, a measure of intended compatibility would exist between an element of the force structure and the purposes for which it exists. Regrettably, one cannot say that for other Reagan administration structure decisions.

The Midgetman

A classic case of a misguided force structure process and decision can be found in the effort to design, develop, and deploy a mobile small intercontinental ballistic missile (SICBM), referred to as Midgetman. The outgrowth of the President's Commission on Strategic Forces (Scowcroft Commission), Midgetman is quite inconsistent with the realities of war and reasoned threat analysis; as a proposed system, it exists not because of logic but because of domestic politics.

The origins of Midgetman are found in two very debatable and related issues concerning a possible strategic nuclear exchange with ICBMs—land-based missile vulnerability and a concept known as first strike. In brief, the former accepts as valid the assumption that Soviet ICBM reliability and counterforce potential (which derive from warhead yield and accuracy) are sufficient to destroy the majority of US fixed-based systems. First strike simply postulates that the Soviets, by launching a massive nuclear attack first, could destroy enough US systems to render a US response unlikely or impossible. The burden of proof for these positions, of course, rests with the advocates, but despite extensive research, analysis, and argumentation, the evidence remains lacking.

Moreover, it is unlikely that evidence will be forthcoming without extensive operational testing of nuclear-armed ICBMs. Without operational testing the destruct radii of warheads cannot be known accurately; valid calculations for the circular error probable (CEP) cannot be made because they depend on numerous factors, all of which are subject to error under present constraints; bias errors—the distance from the center of the CEP to the target—presently are estimated by unverifiable theoretical calculations based on unproven and unprovable assumptions; nuclear phenomena such as fratricide are not sufficiently understood; and an entire range of issues relating to Soviet alert postures and command, control, and communications procedures and capability are not known with any certainty.[11]

In sum, the realities of war, that is, war as it occurs in practice and not as postulated by unproven theoretical assumptions, would suggest that vulnerability of fixed-based ICBMs is far less than its proponents claim and that a first strike concept will remain exactly that—a concept. Indeed, it is instructive to note that this view is shared by a widely respected Soviet officer, former Chief of the General Staff, Marshall of the Soviet Union, N.V. Ogarkov. In a 1984 *Red Star* article, he observed,

on the one hand, it would seem a process of steadily increasing potential for the nuclear powers to destroy the enemy is occurring, while on the other there is an equally steady and, I would say, even sharper reduction in the potential for an aggressor to inflict a so-called "disarming strike" on his main enemy. The point is that with the quantity and diversity of nuclear missiles that have already been achieved, it becomes impossible to destroy the enemy's systems with a single strike.[12]

Aside from these statements and other arguments found in the nature of war, a host of other reasons make pursuing Midgetman unsound. The first of these is uncertainty about its operational effectiveness resulting from the system's mobility. Errors in location or orientation at launch can lead to significant miss-distances, a condition that is particularly undesirable if one is aiming at hardened targets. An alternate guidance system that relies on stellar-aided inertial or NAVSTAR reception in the missile (as planned for the Navy's Trident II missile)[13] could improve accuracy, but such a system raises reliability and vulnerability questions. Mobility also requires use of a hard mobile launcher (HML) to transport Midgetman. Such a system would require off-road capability and must be able to withstand wind vectors of several hundred kilometers-per-hour and blast pressures up to 40 p.s.i.[14] Finally, from an operational standpoint, the Midgetman's range and penetration capability are doubtful because of congressionally imposed weight restrictions.

Dollar and manpower costs also impugn the wisdom of Midgetman. The General Accounting Office (GAO) estimates that each Midgetman warhead will cost about $100 million as compared to $25 million for an MX warhead. Total cost for the program is estimated at $44 billion. Moreover, GAO concludes that manpower requirements will be on the order of 20,000 to 34,000 additional personnel.[15]

To the foregoing issues one must add the implications for arms control efforts. As is well known, verification is one of the most serious challenges for arms control efforts, and the introduction of mobile systems can only exacerbate that issue. Verification aside, even the monitoring of

total missile limits would apparently require very intrusive cooperative measures that go far beyond relying on national technical means. These intrusive measures would probably include a very detailed listing of all missile production facilities, the establishment of annual production quotas for weapon systems and their major subcomponents and the extensive employment of human inspectors.[16]

Such measures, however, would require a giant step forward for an obsessively secretive society such as the USSR.

The evidence against Midgetman, therefore, appears overwhelming. Nevertheless, the influence of domestic politics, as exerted through congressional pressures, may result in ultimate deployment.

A chief advocate is Representative Les Aspin, Chairman of the House Armed Services Committee, whose primary focus appears not to be the nature of war and its history. Notwithstanding the reasonably obvious irrationality of Midgetman, Aspin not only persists in his support for it but is critical of the USAF and the Pentagon for offering their professional judgments against it. Apparently frustrated because the military does not see it his way, Aspin laments, "now, goddamn it, you got these loons over in the Pentagon trying to cashier the Midgetman."[17] As an eight-term congressman with a Ph.D. in economics and two years of military experience as Pentagon economist, he obviously should have some valued insights on the issue. But he clearly oversteps the bounds of credibility when he argues further, saying,

One of my priorities in this business ... is to solve the vulnerability of land-based missiles.... This government of ours screws around with problems forever. If you've got enough of a consensus to go ahead with it, lets do it.[18]

And therein lies the heart of this force structuring problem. An otherwise intelligent and competent Congressman, whose overall record on defense issues deserves some praise, reveals his utter lack of understanding about war by stating that his priority is to "solve" the vulnerability problem. Such gross misconceptions and efforts at manipulation not only have an adverse affect on the resulting force structure, they have a significant influence on the essential resources, such as manpower, money, and material, that form the essence of domestic policy. But when one recognizes that the decisions made in the environment of domestic politics are ultimately felt in the environment of international politics, then the final consequences of such well intentioned but fundamentally wrong decisions become clear.

The Advanced Tactical Fighter

A major element in the USAF's Tactical Fighter roadmap is a next-generation aircraft referred to as the Advanced Tactical Fighter (AFT). Thomas E. Cooper, Assistant Secretary of the Air Force for Research, Development, and Logistics, sums up its features:

One is ... sustained supersonic flight without using military power. Another key one is affordability, with the great emphasis in the Air Force today on reliability, maintainability, and supportability.

We are also looking for STOL characteristics. The new engine that we are looking at right now will have a two-dimensional nozzle. We are not looking for VSTOL, just STOL, so that we can land and take off on short runways, battle-damaged runways.

A final characteristic we are looking for is a modicum of low observability, and there is a key there, too, as to how much low observability are we talking about, because there are some trade-offs in terms of performance and low observability.[19]

Basically, the ATF is a projected means of defeating an expected Soviet air threat. In the past few years the Soviets have improved their Frontal Aviation fundamentally by moving from short-range day fighters to longer-range aircraft with improved adverse weather capability. Continued improvements can be expected, and it is reasonable to assume that concomitant changes will occur in Soviet operational practices and command and control procedures to exploit the new technology.

However, the projected Soviet air threat, although not to be taken lightly, does not offer ample justification for the ATF. The USAF, therefore, has provided additional rationale that links the emerging Soviet threat to the existence of new and advanced US technologies. In congressional testimony the USAF argues,

we need to take advantage of advanced technologies across the board in terms of low signatures, low observables.

We will look to such advanced technologies for our avionics system for operability and reliability enhancements, in terms of the very high speed integrated circuitry.... We will give it increased range, ... and we will have short take-off and landing capability to let it remove some of the tether to some of the longer bases.

It will have a [deleted] take-off capability, and will also be able to land within [deleted] and we are looking for thrust reversers to help us have that performance regime.[20]

Clearly the USAF is exploiting the opportunities offered by advanced technology and is addressing a key aspect of the Soviet threat expected in a Central European war. What one must question, however, is the extent of the threat analysis. In particular the existing Soviet threat against NATO airfields would seem to question the advisability of continued reliance on fixed bases. Soviet Operational Maneuver Groups and Spetsnaz units (special purpose forces) have the capability and clear potential to penetrate rear areas quickly, while operating independent of main forces. Soviet surface-to-surface missiles, such as the SS–20, but particularly the SS–21, SS–22, and the SS–23

Superscud all pose direct threats against NATO airfields. Finally, emerging Soviet air assets raise fundamental questions about the security of fixed bases.

In a response to these types of threats the USAF's General Charles L. Donnelly, Jr., CINCUSAFE, claimed, ''[The enemy's] taking out a runway slows me down, but it doesn't stop me.'' He further suggested that the combination of an ATF, with a take-off roll of less than 2,000 feet, and some 200 suitable airstrips in West Germany would permit the conduct of operations under a Soviet attack.[21]

Such arguments, although not totally persuasive, do have merit. But what they really suggest is that the USAF must be prepared to fight, under attack, from dispersed locations. How well we should be able to do that appears to be a most relevant question for any fighter force structure decision, but thus far it seems to take a back seat to the potential for advanced technology.[22] The performance characteristics the ATF offers are highly desirable, but they must be put into the context of more probable wartime operations.

By way of analogy, the USAF appears to be following in the footsteps of the US Army Air Corps when it began its search for a long-range escort fighter prior to World War II. The efforts began with assumptions that proved to be wrong: that the aircraft needed sufficient internal fuel to match the bomber's range; that it required two pilots to compensate for fatigue; and that it needed at least two gunners for offensive and defensive action. The resulting designs (such as the Bell XFM–1 Airacuda) proved to be totally unsuitable, of course, simply because their size significantly limited performance characteristics. The answer to the long-range fighter escort came not from a new design but from the application of an existing technology, the external fuel tank. By making it a jettisonable tank, both range and fighter performance were retained.

What this historical example suggests is that the USAF should ask itself a basic question: Are projected fighter designs new *and* innovative, taking advantage of all possible *combinations* of advanced technology, or are they merely straight-line extrapolations from present approaches? The admonishment of a well respected analyst (although offered in a slightly different context) should be heeded.

Those in positions of influence in the ATF program, both now and in the future, must remain keenly mindful of *why* that aircraft is being developed and *what* it is expected to do, lest technological determinism lead us once again to put the cart before the horse.[23] (Emphasis in the original.)

The Special Operations Forces

Perhaps the least glamorous Air Force systems addressed in force structure debates are the special operations forces (SOF). Ostensibly, efforts have been underway since 1981 to revitalize SOF, but the force structure since 1986 clearly demonstrates that little progress has been made. Although several reasons can be advanced to explain this lack of modernization, the key element is a fundamental lack of Air Force understanding about war in general and war at the low end of the conflict spectrum in particular. Nowhere is that intellectual shortcoming more obvious than in Air Force doctrine.

Even a casual reading of the 1984 version of Air Force Manual 1–1, *Basic Aerospace Doctrine of the United States Air Force,* suggests little institutional interest or understanding about the essence of war, that is, its nature. Instead of viewing war in all of its complexity, as a test of independent wills dominated by friction, the Air Force is content to view the phenomenon in terms best described as deterministic and mechanistic.[24] The Air Force's paradigm of war tends to view the phenomenon as an enormous engineering problem to be solved through the application of quantifiable factors, such as men, machines, and technology.

Given this approach, Air Force thinking sees no need to make distinctions about the different levels of war and the challenges they present. As a consequence, the Air Force sees no specific role or function for SOF; indeed, the flexibility postulated for SOF assumes that they are appropriate for use at any number of points on a seamless cloth of conflict intensity.[25] That being the case, specific strategies for employment of SOF at the low end of the conflict spectrum are deemed unnecessary. It follows, therefore, that rationalizations for SOF modernization become equally unnecessary.

Not surprisingly, numerous conceptual challenges have been raised to these Air Force doctrinal judgments concerning SOF.[26] The challenges, however, have been ignored or rejected by the senior Air Force leadership, which continues to argue for SOF applicability across the broader spectrum of conflict. The Air Force Chief of Staff, for example, maintains that although

some perceive Special Operations Forces (SOF) as being primarily employed in very low intensity ... operations ..., *that's the stuff myths are made of.* Our SOF forces are necessarily trained and equipped to fight at all levels of conflict, and the systems we buy have to be robust and affordable and capable across a wide conflict spectrum.[27] (Emphasis added.)

At a minimum, such a view clearly demonstrates a lack of discernment about war, and in particular it ignores the crucial relationship that exists between its ends and means. More important, it explains a clear lack of emphasis on the development of specific SOF weapon systems. The Air Force argument, that SOF are to fight at all levels of conflict, requires SOF to compete with other elements of the force structure, such as F–15s, F–16s, F–111s, and the like. By any measure of performance, however, these latter systems are much more capable than typical SOF aircraft, such as AC–130 gunships and HH–53 Pave Low helicopters. In any performance referenced criteria, therefore, SOF aircraft would appear to possess relatively limited capability and, hence, less potential. If one then imposes fiscal constraints upon the evaluative process, the outcome is foreordained—SOF simply cannot compete. This lack of intellectual discernment about war and the imposition of budget realities have combined to limit SOF enhancement programs severely. Indeed, as noted by two defense-minded senators in a recent letter to the Secretary of Defense,

It is discouraging to note that today we have exactly the same number of MC–130 Combat Talon aircraft (14) and AC–130 A/H gunships (10/10) as we had at the time of Desert One, and two fewer HH–53 Pave Low helicopters than we had in May 1980 (7 today compared with 9 in 1980).[28]

These views, although directed at the Air Force, are representative of a broader concern about SOF found throughout much of the US Congress. Indeed, some members of Congress, who noted that SOF did not benefit appreciably from the Reagan arms buildup, eventually recognized the force structure problem to be a symptom of a deeper, more fundamental issue. In their view, the SOF problem resulted from an organizational arrangement that, in effect, made SOF enhancement an option for the senior Air Force leadership. Consequently, in October 1986, the Congress took SOF prerogatives away from the Air Force (and the other Services as well) by creating a new unified command, the United States Special Operations Forces Command

(USSOFC).[29] The enabling legislation gave the new command responsibility for all affairs relating to special operations activities, including

    a. developing strategy, doctrine, and tactics;

    b. conducting specialized courses of instruction for commissioned and noncommissioned officers;

    c. ensuring combat readiness;

    d. developing and acquiring equipment peculiar to special operations and acquiring special operations-peculiar material, supplies, and services;

    e. ensuring the interoperability of equipment and forces.[30]

Moreover, the legislation directed that the new unified command be headed by an officer of four-star rank; created a new Assistant Secretary of Defense for Special Operations and Low Intensity Conflict; and established, within the National Security Council, a Board for Low Intensity Conflict to coordinate US policy for low-intensity conflict.[31]

This new legislation is important for the United States, in part because of what it portends for future SOF development and employment capabilities. For the Air Force it is important because it virtually assures that capable Air Force SOF will be created not because of institutional leadership but in spite of it.

Judgments and Implications

When viewed in the context of conflict trends, focused threat analysis, technology, and military policy as influenced by domestic and international politics, a number of judgments and implications emerge about USAF force structure changes since 1981. The first judgment is that many of the major force structure initiatives are externally motivated. The Strategic Defense Initiative,

Midgetman, and actual (as compared to intended) SOF
revitalization are the results of pressures exerted from
outside of the military and, for the most part, by civilians. Second, the external judgments appear to be more
accurate when they address broad, conceptual notions,
e.g., SDI and SOF. Conversely, they tend to be at odds
with the purpose of military power when advocating
specific weapon systems such as Midgetman. Third, the
USAF institutionally remains hardware-oriented and as
such found itself responding to Ronald Reagan on SDI.
The hardware focus also has prevented the development
of conceptual arguments against Midgetman, but at the
same time it has surfaced the more serious operational
limitations about the system. The hardware focus is
quite evident in the pursuit of ATF. Regrettably, the
effort appears to be aiming for a straight-line extrapola-
tion of current-generation fighters instead of fundamental departures that might be possible with a combination
of advanced technologies. The final judgment is that the
most influential variables in the conceptual framework
are not the more obvious ones, such as war and threat
analysis; rather, domestic politics are the major determinants. Thus the force structure, although the output of
many things, is not the result primarily of logic.

   The implications of the changes are several. First,
if SDI leads to a credible deployment program, it
clearly will result in the most significant change in the
force structure since the advent of the nuclear age. For
the first time in the history of nuclear deployment a
force structure will be balanced and consistent with the
nature of war and thus will contribute to deterrence.
Second, Midgetman, because it lacks a warfighting
rationale, is unlikely to survive. Perhaps powerful
domestic political pressures can save it, but the long-
term implications of such an outcome would have profound consequences for US military policy. Third, the

externally directed reorganization of SOF creates conditions that might lead to its becoming a meaningful force. The United States needs military power that it can use, and the trends of warfare suggest that SOF capability would be a most appropriate military force for the foreseeable future.

The final implication is the most serious one, because it raises questions about the professional competence of the Air Force to make judgments concerning its force structure. The approach to each of the force structure issues addressed herein—SDI, Midgetman, ATF, and SOF—suggest serious limits to Air Force thinking concerning its fundamental task of understanding and fighting war. The SDI initiative has been long overdue; it comes not from the Air Force, however, but from the President of the United States. And although four years have elapsed since the President's call for SDI, the Air Force has yet to offer a comprehensive rationale for SDI based on the nature of war. Similarly, the Air Force's opposition to Midgetman, although laudable, also exhibits a lack of understanding about war and its nature. The ATF initiative, by contrast, merely demonstrates the Air Force's long-standing emphasis on technology.

To argue, as the Air Force does, that emerging technologies must be incorporated in a new fighter design to replace existing systems, is not without merit. Yet, such rationalizations hardly are sufficient to justify the ATF. The valid and relevant arguments for a new fighter should be found primarily in an understanding of war and strategy and not in technology. But the realm of war and strategy are not part of the Air Force's conceptual landscape; in its scheme of things, technology is the dominant feature. Consequently, it is likely that the Air Force, if left to its own devices, will enter the next conflict unprepared, just as it did in Korea and Vietnam, with a weapons system largely unsuited for the tasks at hand.

Fortunately, the SOF initiatives taken by the US Congress, an institution that clearly exhibits an understanding of the trends of warfare, may result in force structure enhancements that would have been unlikely under Air Force leadership.

In sum, although Air Force readiness trends have shown impressive improvements during the Reagan administration, serious weaknesses for the future are apparent. These weaknesses stem from intellectual deficiencies concerning the nature of war and the mistaken belief that a robust, capable, and flexible force structure is a substitute for conceptual thinking about war.

Notes

1. Karl Von Clausewitz, *On War,* edited and translated by Michael Howard and Peter Paret (Princeton, NJ: Princeton University Press, 1976), p. 605.

2. Lieutenant Colonel Barry D. Watts, USAF, *The Foundations of U.S. Air Doctrine* (Maxwell AFB, AL: Air University Press, 1984), chapter 6, "Friction and 20th Century Warfare," and chapter 7, "Toward A Less Mechanistic Image of War," pp. 105–31.

3. Von Clausewitz, p. 86; cf. p. 134, "Limitation to Material Factors," and p. 149, "Difference."

4. Ibid., p. 184.

5. Caspar W. Weinberger, *Annual Report to the Congress, Fiscal Year 1987* (Washington, DC: Government Printing Office, 1986), p. 255.

6. Samuel P. Huntington, *The Common Defense: Strategic Programs in National Politics* (New York: Columbia University Press, 1961), pp. 1–2.

7. Von Clausewitz, p. 358.

8. Ibid., p. 119

9. Steven J. Cimbala, "The Strategic Defense Initiative: Political Risks," *Air University Review,* 37, no. 3 (November-December 1985): 30–32.

10. Weinberger, pp. 289–291; for contrasting view see Richard L. Garwin, "Countermeasure: Defeating Space-based Defense," *Arms Control Today* 15, no. 4 (May 1988): 2–3.

11. For the vulnerability argument, see General Robert T. Marsh, USAF, "Strategic Missile Debated: Missile Accuracy—We Do Know!" *Strategic Review*, Spring 1982. The opposing view is presented by J. Edward Anderson, "First Strike: Myth or Reality," *Bulletin of the Atomic Scientists*, November 1981, and J. Edward Anderson, "Strategic Missiles Debated: What You Can't Know!" *Strategic Review*, Spring 1982. A trenchant and incisive argument is found in Arthur G. B. Metcalf, "The Minuteman Vulnerability Myth and the MX," *Strategic Review*, Spring 1983. How real war would affect vulnerability is explored in Thomas A. Fabyanic, "Strategic Analysis and MX Deployment," *Strategic Review*, Fall 1982.

12. Leon Goure and Michael Deane, "The Soviet Strategic View," *Strategic Review*, Summer 1984, p. 85.

13. Thomas B. Cochran et al., *Nuclear Weapons Databook,* vol. 1, *U.S. Nuclear Forces and Capabilities* (Cambridge, MA: Ballinger Publishing Company, 1984), p. 145.

14. Matthew Bunn and Kosta Tsipis, "The Uncertainties of a Preemptive Nuclear Attack," *Scientific American* 249, no. 5 (November 1983): 41. For comparison, the Abrams tank can withstand about 10 p.s.i. of overpressure.

15. Scott L. Berg, "Midgetman: The Technical Problems," *Arms Control Today* 15, no. 9 (November-December 1985): 16–18.

16. John C. Baker and Joel S. Wit, "Mobile Missiles and Arms Control," *Arms Control Today* 15, no. 9 (November-December 1985): 13.

17. Michael Canley, "An Exclusive AFJ Interview With: Representative Les Aspin, Chairman of the House Armed Services Committee," *Armed Forces Journal International*, April 1986, p. 38.

18. Ibid., p. 40.

19. US, Congress, Senate, Committee on Armed Services, *Department of Defense Authorization For Appropriations For Fiscal Year 1986, Hearings,* 99th Cong., 1st sess. (Washington, DC: Government Printing Office, 1985), p. 2041.

20. Ibid., p. 2038.

21. John T. Correll, "Tactical Warfare High and Low," *Air Force Magazine* 69, no. 4 (April 1986): 54.

22. This is not an antitechnology argument; rather it is one that suggests careful consideration of where technology would be

applied. For perhaps the best discussion of the technology issue, particularly as viewed by defense planners and reformers, see Walter Kross, *Military Reform* (Washington, DC, NDU Press, 1985).

23. Benjamin S. Lambeth, "Pitfalls in Force Planning: Structuring America's Tactical Air Arm," *International Security* 10, no. 2 (Fall 1985): 118.

24. Watts, *The Foundations of U.S. Air Doctrine*, chapter 7, "Toward a Less Mechanistic Image of War," pp. 105–31.

25. US, Air Force Manual 1–1, *Basic Aerospace Doctrine of the United States Air Force* (Washington, DC: Government Printing Office, 1984), p. 3–4.

26. Noel C. Koch, "Is There a Role for Air Power in Low-Intensity Conflict?" *Armed Forces Journal International,* May 1985, pp. 32–42; "An exclusive AFJ interview with: Noel C. Koch," *Armed Forces Journal International,* March 1985, pp. 36–52; *Joint Low-Intensity Conflict Project Final Report,* vol. 1, *Analytical Review of Low-Intensity Conflict* (Fort Monroe, VA: United States Army Training and Doctrine Command, 1986).

27. *Air Force Policy Letter for Commanders,* 1 December 1986.

28. Deborah Gallagher Meyer and Benjamin F. Schemmer, "Congressional Pressure May Force Far More DoD Dollars for Special Ops," *Armed Forces Journal International,* April 1986, p. 20.

29. US, Congress, House, *Making Continuing Appropriations for Fiscal Year 1987,* Conference Report to Accompany H. J. Res. 738, Report 99–1005, 99th Cong., 2d sess., 15 October 1986, pp. 128–39.

30. Ibid., p. 129.

31. Ibid., pp. 128, 129, 131.

POPULATION DEFENSE THROUGH SDI: AN IMPOSSIBLE DREAM

Jerome Slater
David Goldfischer

PRESIDENT REAGAN'S Strategic Defense Initiative (SDI) has been greeted with widespread skepticism and criticism, especially among scientists and in the arms control community. This reaction is quite understandable, in light of the specific arguments emphasized by the Reagan administration and, equally important, the overall record of the administration in arms control and Soviet-American relations.

To begin, confusion and inconsistency surround the purpose and mission of the proposed ballistic missile defense system. There are four possible missions that ballistic missile defense might perform. First, the President's conception: a full-scale population defense of the United States, to be shared with the Soviet Union at some later date, that will have the effect of ending MAD and rendering nuclear weapons "impotent and obsolete." Second, however, full-scale population defense might be pursued not because it will abolish mutual assured destruction and make all nuclear

An earlier version of this article appeared in *Political Science Quarterly* in 1986, number five, under the title, "Can SDI Provide a Defense?"

weapons obsolete, but in the expectation that it will abolish *Soviet* assured destruction and make *Soviet* nuclear weapons obsolete. This seemed to be the real goal of Secretary of Defense Weinberger and those few other administration officials and defense analysts close to the administration who appeared to believe that full-scale population defense is a realistic goal in the next decade or so. In their view, far from transforming Soviet-American relationships and ending the immoral balance of terror system, SDI will restore US strategic superiority over the Soviet Union, enhance the credibility of the US nuclear commitment to Europe, and give the United States a usable warfighting strategy.[1]

A third mission for ballistic missile defense—BMD—or SDI—would be to protect the US strategic retaliatory force and its command, control, and communications network, rather than populations, with the goal of enhancing deterrence rather than replacing it. Most administration defense officials, including those most closely associated with the SDI program, as well as the nongovernmental defense analysts that the administration heavily relies on, have emphasized that SDI will focus on this mission at least through the end of this century.[2]

To be sure, in theory the two missions of force defense and population protection may be combined to create a new national security strategy of "assured survival" or "defense dominance." After the initial Presidential proclamation of the SDI organization, this emerged as the predominant administration goal, despite occasional reversions by the President and the Secretary of Defense to more radical descriptions. Under the defense-dominance strategy, ballistic missile defenses would begin by protecting the most vulnerable components of the US retaliatory system, particularly

ICBMs in fixed silos, and gradually move toward population defense. Ideally, the transition to population defenses would be negotiated and jointly managed with the Soviet Union, and it would be accompanied by substantial negotiated reductions in offensive weapons. If the Soviet Union refused to negotiate this new joint strategic relationship, however, the United States would proceed unilaterally, relying on the effectiveness of the American system eventually to persuade the Soviets of the futility of seeking to preserve MAD. The eventual outcome would not be the end of nuclear weapons and nuclear deterrence but a new system in which deterrence was a function of the inability of the Soviet Union to achieve a significant military advantage through nuclear attack ("deterrence through denial") rather than fear of unbearable retaliation ("deterrence through punishment"). An official Government statement puts it this way:

Successful SDI ... would not lead to abandonment of deterrence but rather to an enhancement of deterrence and an evolution in the weapons of deterrence through the contribution of defensive systems that threaten no one. We would deter a potential aggressor by making it clear that we could deny him the gains he might otherwise hope to achieve rather than merely threatening him with costs large enough to outweigh those gains.[3]

A final mission of ballistic missile defense might be to provide limited protection of US cities against small-scale nuclear attacks, such as an unauthorized or accidental Soviet launch or a deliberate attack by a small nuclear power. This role has received the least emphasis by the administration and the least attention by defense analysts, whether pro- or anti-SDI. Yet, it is the only mission for ballistic missile defense that makes sense for the foreseeable future.

Population Defense Examined

The arguments against seeking an all-out population defense system as the major goal for SDI in the foreseeable future are by now well known, so I will only summarize them here.[4] Population defenses, it is contended, will be futile, costly, and, most importantly, destabilizing. They will be futile because given the destructiveness of nuclear weapons, a full-scale population defense system would have to work with nearly 100 percent effectiveness to provide any meaningful protection at all. No such system is on the horizon, and it is difficult even to imagine what kind of technology could provide near-perfect protection against a superpower determined to nullify defenses. Even if the various exotic technologies currently being explored by the United States (as well as by the Soviet Union)—supercomputers, software programs of unprecedented complexity, orbiting space stations, lasers or particle-beam weapons, for example—prove to be feasible in principle, which is by no means assured, there would still be perhaps insoluble operational problems of joining the various technologies together into a complex weapons system that would have to work in near-perfect fashion the first time it was actually used in battle.

Thus, even without assuming an adversary determined to nullify defensive systems, the problem of creating a near-perfect population defense system against a nuclear superpower would be formidable indeed. In any case, it is certain that under the present international circumstances and in reaction to the President's specific SDI program, the Soviet Union *would* seek to counter any American defensive system, just as the United States has made it clear it will seek to counter any Soviet defensive program.[5] Given the context of ongoing and indeed intensified Soviet-American conflict, this kind of superpower behavior is inevitable, for worst-case analyses will continue to drive the military strategies and weapons systems deployment of both sides. Each fears a situation in which its adversary simultaneously deploys both an effective defense system and highly accurate counterforce offensive missile forces. Such a system might be designed only for defensive damage-limitation purposes in the event deterrence fails: counterforce weapons to destroy the other side's nuclear weapons, defensive systems to shoot down those that are missed. However, such a force posture would be indistinguishable, certainly in capability and possibly in motivation as well, from an offensive first-strike force. As is well known, when faced with potential enemies, nations assume the worst about intentions and base their military planning on their opponent's capabilities; as a result neither side will allow the other to achieve an even theoretically effective defense.

Thus, the consensus among scientists and other experts on BMD is that any system deployed by either side designed to protect its population against a full-scale retaliatory attack by the other can be destroyed, overwhelmed, or circumvented by the other side. Among the steps that could be taken are a preemptive attack on the space-based defense systems, various countermeasures to protect retaliatory forces against laser or particle beam weapons, the overwhelming of defenses by much larger offensive missile deployments or the retargeting of existing missiles to aim at cities instead of military forces, and the circumvention of BMD systems through low-flying cruise missiles or depressed-trajectory ballistic missiles, launched from submarines close to American shores. And if all else fails, high-technology systems could be dispensed with, and nuclear weapons "delivered" clandestinely in the holds of commercial ships or airlines, or even by a man with a suitcase.

Secondly, a full-scale population defense is bound to be extremely costly. Although the Pentagon's SDI organization has so far been unable or unwilling to provide even rough cost estimates to Congress,[6] a number of authoritative critics have estimated the costs as ranging from a minimum of $100 billion for an ICBM protection system to over a trillion dollars for an all-out population defense.[7]

Perhaps even more significantly, few analysts believe that a defensive system could be made "cost-effective" against a determined superpower adversary—that is, in the inevitable contest between offense and defense, it will always be cheaper for the offense to add new capabilities to overcome the defense than the reverse.[8] The administration began the SDI program with the forthright acknowledgment that it would not make sense to deploy a defensive system unless it met the criterion of being cost-effective, but recently—obviously in response to a variety of studies (including its own internal ones) that predicted the unlikelihood of meeting this standard—it has begun to suggest that a vague "affordability" standard may suffice.[9] But unless the cost-effective criterion is met, the United States could spend hundreds of billions of dollars without any net gain in defensive capabilities—indeed, it might be even worse off if the Soviet Union should choose to counter by emphasizing countercity rather than counterforce targeting.[10]

Third, it is argued that in the current international context, SDI will surely end serious efforts at arms control and will provoke an intensified arms race. The deployment or even anticipated deployment of defensive weapons will stimulate the deployment of new offensive weapons to overcome the defense.[11]

Fourth, some critics have argued that even if perfect defenses should eventually be deployed, they might have the paradoxical effect of increasing the probability of superpower conventional wars, on the assessment that fear of escalation terminating in nuclear destruction is one of the major constraints on conventional wars today. In light of the massive destructiveness of modern conventional weaponry, and the likelihood that even a purely conventional war in Europe would be far more destructive than World War II, it might be concluded that the trade-off between reduced risks of nuclear war and increased risks of conventional war is an undesirable one, even if that choice should become a technologically feasible one.[12]

Perhaps the most serious criticism of SDI is that it will be destabilizing, particularly in a serious superpower crisis. In such a crisis, it is argued, defensive systems would give both sides a high incentive to initiate a nuclear attack, either in a deliberate aggressive attempt to disarm the other side, or as a desperate, essentially defensive, measure to "preempt"—that is, strike first when war seems inevitable, in order to minimize the destruction to one's homeland.

Some opponents of SDI have argued that the dangers of either surprise or preemptive attack are greatest when one side has a unilateral edge, regardless of which side has it. For example, Drell and his associates have argued as follows:

An effective but imperfect ABM on one side would exacerbate the risk [of war] because the side that did have an ABM might calculate that it would be better off if it struck first and used the ABM defense to deal with the weakened response.... Similarly, the side that did not have ABM might calculate that its situation would be better (however bad) if it struck first and avoided being caught trying to retaliate with a weakened force against the ABM defense.[13]

However, the dangers of either surprise attack or preemptive war are probably exaggerated, even in the case of serious defensive asymmetries. No rational government would initiate nuclear war in the expectation that it would be "better off" merely in the sense that it would gain a *relative* advantage in the postwar balance of power; surprise attack could be considered only if one could be confident that the other side would be disarmed with little risk of one's own cities being destroyed in retaliation. In practice, though, no rational government could have such confidence, for it would surely make conservative estimates: that its offensive weapons might function below their theoretically expected effectiveness, that its opponent's defenses might perform at a better-than-expected level, and that its own defenses might be less effective than predicted.[14] Thus, the range of operational uncertainties would weigh very heavily against a deliberate attack. It follows, of course, that the logic of a deliberate attack is even less persuasive for the side with no or lesser defenses.

The dangers of preemptive war also appear to be exaggerated. In theory, it is true that the desire to exploit any plausible first-strike advantage would be increased to the extent that the outbreak of war is deemed inevitable. In practice, however, there is little reason to fear preemption because of asymmetries in defensive capabilities. First, as long as there is mutual awareness that neither side can confidently preclude massive retaliation by striking first, it is hard to see how either side could decisively conclude that nuclear war was "inevitable."

Further, the most likely effect of concern over imminent war would be the adoption of a "launch on warning" posture, thereby undercutting or negating any remaining first-strike incentive. Indeed, the side with no ABM would be particularly inclined to launch on warning, so that the side with a defensive advantage could never count on facing only a weakened retaliatory strike. Thus, no matter how severe the crisis, states should always prefer not to strike first, for war may not, after all, occur. On the other hand, the state choosing to preempt thereby *guarantees* that there will be war, and must assume that its cities will be vulnerable to a retaliation it cannot prevent.[15]

In short, a first strike against a superpower can *never* make sense: even if the motive is defensive rather than aggressive, even if the attacker has a less than perfect population defense system and his opponent doesn't, and even in a high crisis. In each case a first strike converts an uncertain probability of war in which one's weapons are the target into the certainty of war in which one's cities face catastrophic damage.

Even if the destabilizing dangers of SDI are exaggerated, though, the other arguments against it are decisive: the extreme unlikelihood that effective population defenses could work against a determined adversary, the huge costs of making the attempt, the destruction of existing as well as potentially more effective arms control agreements and the likelihood of an all-out arms race.

The arguments against seeking a full population defense in the hopes of abolishing MAD are equally or more applicable to the argument that SDI will enhance US nuclear superiority, strengthen the credibility of extended deterrence, and allow the United States actually to employ nuclear weapons in war ("take a controlled and limited strategic nuclear initiative on behalf of beleaguered overseas allies.")[16] The American commitment to use nuclear weapons if necessary to repel a

Soviet conventional invasion of Europe, it is argued, has lost its credibility, for the United States itself could be completely destroyed in a Soviet retaliatory strike. Since no country will commit suicide on behalf of its allies, the reasoning continues, the Soviets will doubt the credibility of the US commitment, and hence will no longer be deterred from a conventional invasion of Europe. Thus, an effective population defense of the United States would restore the credibility of the US nuclear commitment to Europe, for nuclear war would no longer be suicidal for the United States (whatever the effects on Europe). Similar logic would also apply elsewhere where US interests might be sufficiently vital to justify a strategy of the first use of nuclear weapons to offset Soviet conventional advantages, for example, to repel a Soviet invasion of the Persian Gulf.

However, neither the portrayal of the alleged problem nor its suggested remedy are convincing. There is no evidence that the Soviet Union regards the American commitment to use nuclear weapons in defense of Europe as noncredible. The credibility problem is at least 30 years old, for the Soviet Union has had the capability of striking the United States with nuclear weapons for this long—yet the Soviets have not taken advantage of their conventional superiority to invade Europe. Moreover, if today there is a serious credibility problem with extended deterrence, a population defense of American cities would not remedy it. For all the reasons already discussed, no rational American President could order the use of nuclear weapons in Western Europe on the assumption that even if the Soviets chose to escalate they lacked the capability of hitting the United States.

Perhaps in response to these criticisms of the population defense mission (whether linked to the end of nuclear deterrence or, more characteristically, to the restoration of US nuclear superiority), most Reagan administration officials have emphasized that at least initially the goal of SDI will be to protect military targets (ICBM silos and command and control systems) rather than cities, with the aim of enhancing deterrence rather than eliminating it. The chief virtue of this mission is that it appears to be technologically feasible in the near future, especially within a system employing preferential defense and/or deceptive basing of ICBMs. Unlike population defenses, hard-point defenses of military targets would not have to be nearly leakproof to be effective, for even 50 percent effectiveness would make a disarming Soviet first-strike far more uncertain and difficult. Moreover, ICBM defenses are not subject even in principle to the criticism that they will increase crisis instability, for they would not diminish either side's second-strike, countercity retaliatory capability and so, in the logic of the nuclear age, they would not add to the theoretical dangers of surprise or preemptive attacks.

On the other hand, even ICBM defenses would be expensive—the usual estimate is at least $100 billion.[17] More important, they might also stimulate a further arms race, for both the Soviet Union and the United States would probably seek to counter ICBM defenses, in pursuit of their current counterforce strategies. Still, these might be costs worth bearing if it were indeed the case that the theoretical vulnerabilities of US strategic forces created a real-world risk of a Soviet deliberate or preemptive attack. In fact, though, it is extremely unlikely that there is such a risk. Such an attack would not, of course, disarm the United States. A Soviet attack on ICBM silos might precipitate an American decision to launch on warning or under attack, leaving only empty holes for the attacking missiles to strike. Even if the Soviets irrationally choose to ignore the possibility of that kind of US response, their attack would be unlikely to achieve the 95 percent kill rate that some theoretical contributions attribute to it.[18] Finally, no matter how successful an attack on ICBM silos might be, such an attack would still leave untouched thousands of American strategic weapons, including cruise missiles and other nuclear weapons carried by SAC bombers and SLBMs aboard the largely invulnerable US submarine force. With these forces the United States could either attack the remaining Soviet strategic forces, or completely destroy Soviet society, or both.

The typical response of those who believe the problem of ICBM vulnerability is real is to acknowledge the potency of US retaliatory power under any conceivable circumstances, but to contend that the Soviets might attack vulnerable components of the retaliatory force anyway, counting on their ability to "deter our deterrent." The reasoning is that our surviving forces would lack a meaningful counterforce capability, and could only destroy Soviet society—ensuring our complete destruction in retaliation. Thus, a well-executed first strike would confront the United States with a choice of "suicide or surrender," and Soviet leaders might reason that the United States would prefer surrender.

Such a scenario, however, is bizarre, for it assumes a propensity to take literally insane risks that no Soviet leaders have ever demonstrated. A Soviet attack on US silo forces would nonetheless kill 20 to 40 million Americans, almost guaranteeing an American response, which even if confined to military targets would be at least as devastating to the Soviet Union as World War II.[19]

In any case, even if it is desirable to guard against remote contingencies, there are a number of other less costly and probably more effective ways to do so, including relying more extensively on the air and under-sea components of the US retaliatory forces, phasing out vulnerable ICBMs that could serve as a lightning-rod for a Soviet attack, developing mobile land-based systems such as the proposed "Midgetman" system, relying more extensively on cruise missiles (though both of these latter measures might seriously complicate the possibilities of arms control), or—best of all—placing greater reliance on arms control measures, such as banning or reducing the number of multiple-warhead missiles.

In summary, no rational government could risk launching an attack when its cities are hostage, despite bizarre scenarios to the contrary. Thus, even though ICBM defenses are much more feasible and less provocative than full-scale population defenses, they are still a costly and unnecessary response to a largely non-existent problem that, if it were real, could be far better remedied by a variety of other measures.

If there are good arguments for BMD—as the analysis that follows will contend—they have been all but buried by the bad arguments made by the Reagan administration. More generally, because of the administration's continued buildup of offensive nuclear weapons, its rejection of a variety of serious arms control agreements, and its overall confrontational posture toward the Soviet Union, even the good arguments receive little attention from either the Soviet Union or by Americans concerned with arms control and détente.

Unfortunately, we have seen something like this before. The current situation bears an uncanny resemblance to the 1965–1972 period, when the earlier

ABM debate took place. By the mid-1960s earlier model ABMs had become operational, but there was considerable uncertainty about how and for what purpose they should be deployed. Then as now, the rationale was that ABMs could provide a meaningful defense against a full-scale Soviet attack on cities. Then as now, an intense national debate generated mounting skepticism toward the claim that we could find real safety against the Soviet nuclear arsenal by deploying ABMs. Then as now, commentators worried that an American effort to protect its cities would be seen by the Soviets as a provocative step requiring Soviet counteractions that would escalate the arms race and might prove destabilizing in crises. Then as now, as these apparent defects of heavy population defense systems gained wider recognition, new rationales for ABM were devised. The Johnson administration briefly argued for deploying an ABM system against the hypothetical kind of ICBM attack that China might be capable of mounting in the mid-1970s, but this rationale was dropped as the Vietnam war wound down and rapprochement with China was undertaken. Then, the Nixon administration once again changed the rationale of the ABM system; the new "Safeguard" ABM system was designed to protect land-based ICBMs, even then said to be vulnerable to a surprise Soviet attack. Once again, though, the rationale proved unpersuasive as critics demonstrated that the overall US deterrent remained unchallengable. More and more the ABM appeared to be a Pyrrhic technological triumph, a weapon in search of a rationale. Faced with strong public and congressional opposition to ABMs of any kind, the Nixon administration was compelled to seek the strict limitations on ABM development and deployment that were embodied in the 1972 SALT treaties.[20]

Thus, in both the earlier period and today, defense has been championed primarily by strategists and political figures committed to hard-line Cold War policies; moreover, even on the merits the criticisms of defensive systems have been much more persuasive than the ever-changing rationales for them. Unfortunately, however, once again Gresham's Law has prevailed: all but lost in the chaff of bad ideas has been the germ of a good one.

What is worth saving in SDI? To begin with, the underlying critique of MAD is sound; indeed, there is a growing consensus cutting across the ideological spectrum of American politics that in the long run MAD must be replaced. A conservative administration, conservative military strategists (like Donald Brennan and Herman Kahn earlier and Colin Gray, Keith Payne, Albert Wohlstetter, and many others today), and long-term liberal critics of current strategies (for example, Freeman Dyson, Jonathan Schell, the American Catholic Bishops Conference) agree that MAD has three fatal defects. First, MAD is radically immoral: it directly violates the most fundamental moral and legal norms limiting war, for it explicitly threatens to annihilate millions of innocent people in retaliation or revenge for actions of their governments over which they have little or no control. Second, MAD is ultimately unstable: even though it has prevented nuclear war so far, it cannot be relied upon to do so indefinitely. Sooner or later a system so complex, so dependent on the sanity and rational self-restraint of all future decisionmakers of all nuclear powers, so increasingly decentralized, and so dependent on advanced technology is bound to fail for one reason or another. Finally, the consequences of failure will be catastrophic. Even relatively minor failures that do not result in full-scale war are likely to produce disasters unprecedented in human history, and a general breakdown of MAD might well imperil human life on earth.

It is not enough, then, to seek to deter war through a balance of terror. We must also seek to defend our civilization, society, economy, and lives in case deterrence fails. And in the long run, we must seek to abolish the balance of terror itself.

But where to begin? The gravest defect of MAD is not that it is unreliable as a means of deterring the superpowers from deliberately initiating nuclear war against each other. On the contrary, MAD has worked very well for that purpose, and there is no reason to think that will change in the future. The destructiveness of nuclear weapons is so great and so evident that no minimally rational government can deliberately initiate war against a nuclear-armed adversary.

Put differently, the balance of terror—*defined as the state of mutual deterrence between the governments of the major powers*—has not been "delicate" since at least the mid-1950s; it is not delicate now, and it will not be delicate in the foreseeable future, regardless of any currently imaginable technological change. However, nuclear holocaust could occur in a variety of ways that are simply undeterrable, such as an accidental launch of nuclear weapons as a result of a communications or technological failure, an unauthorized launching by an insane or fanatical lower level commander, or a clandestine attack on one of the superpowers by a third party, such as a terrorist group or renegade government. Yesterday's science-fiction nightmares could easily become today's realities: despite technological and other efforts to prevent such events, the odds of a catastrophe mount as the number of nuclear weapons increase, as weapons-grade nuclear materials proliferate around the world, and as the knowledge of how to build nuclear weapons becomes increasingly diffused.

Thus, MAD cannot deter human error, technological breakdown, or ideological or criminal fanaticism. Indeed, against such increasingly likely incidents, MAD is *worse* than useless, for a limited launch of nuclear weapons could trigger a spasm exchange between the superpowers, turning a horrible but limited catastrophe into apocalypse. And even if total war were averted, the prospects are not very comforting. Consider this: a single American Trident submarine can today target 240 separate Soviet cities, and Soviet submarines will soon have comparable capabilities. Thus, an unauthorized mistaken attack by a single submarine would produce a holocaust far more destructive than a deliberate, all-out total war would have been some 25 years ago.

Against such prospects we need defense, not (or not merely) deterrence. Put differently, MAD overdeters but underdefends. That is, it provides a redundance of deterrence but no defense against the least likely contingency—a deliberately initiated nuclear war by a superpower—but neither deterrence nor defense against the much more likely contingencies of accidents, unauthorized launches, or third-party attacks. Even worse, by proliferating the sheer numbers and types of nuclear weapons and delivery systems, MAD makes such events both more likely to occur and more likely to escalate into full-scale nuclear war.

The central argument here is that it is both desirable and possible to defend against limited nuclear attacks without reducing deterrence against a full-scale superpower nuclear attack. Superpower defenses against light attacks have long been recognized as a potentially feasible mission for BMD systems, but both proponents and critics of BMD generally have paid scant attention to the matter.[21] Proponents of BMD tend to treat defense against various light attacks as a desirable but relatively marginal bonus of heavy defenses against the Soviet Union. As a result, critics of BMD—even when they recognize the desirability of light defense in principle—tend to reject it because of fears that light defenses will be only the opening wedge for heavy defenses.

The legitimate concerns of critics of SDI and other proposed missile defense systems could be met by the careful negotiation of a new superpower nuclear regime. This new regime would allow for limited population defense systems, and it would have two purposes. First, it would provide at least some defense against various forms of light attack, particularly unauthorized or accidental superpower ballistic missile launchings and deliberate third-country or terrorist group attacks. To be sure, determined terrorists might circumvent defenses by a variety of means, but, nonetheless, defensive systems against the ballistic missile systems that are spreading around the world would at least modestly augment the security of both superpowers.[22] Second, and perhaps more important, a joint regime for initially modest purposes could provide a model and basis for a far more comprehensive regime that would substitute defense dominance for MAD at some future date.

The new strategic regime will be based on the assumption that as long as the Cold War persists each superpower will seek to maintain its deterrence capabilities, each will define deterrence as requiring the capacity to destroy the other side completely, and that neither side can be denied that capacity. In other words, MAD is a function of both the existence of nuclear weapons and high political conflict, and in that situation a population defense system can succeed only if the superpowers choose not to exercise their capacity to overwhelm it. However, mutually negotiated limited population defense systems, large enough to provide significant protection of cities against accidents, unauthorized launchings, and third-party attacks, but not large enough to undermine deterrence of a deliberate superpower retaliatory strike, would serve the common interests of each side, regardless of the level of political conflict or arms competition. Thus, at least in principle it ought to be possible to build on these minimal superpower common interests not to destroy or be destroyed by accident, lunacy, or third parties, and design population defenses that neither side will have any rational incentive to overcome.

What might such a system look like? As soon as nonnuclear city defense systems are technologically feasible in both the Soviet Union and the United States, the two superpowers should agree on a joint negotiated deployment of limited defense systems to defend their cities, industries, and command and control centers against all kinds of nuclear missile attacks *except* for very large, deliberate superpower attacks. To be sure, there might be formidable technical problems to be resolved, particularly if missile defense systems were to be based on exotic, space-based laser or particle-beam weapons. The task would be to devise systems that would have defensive capabilities only and that would provide each side with a specified and equal degree of limited defense. Assuming these problems can be solved, the design of the system would provide significant defense against accidents, unauthorized launches, and third-party attacks but would do nothing to destabilize the underlying superpower balance of terror.

At the same time, other stabilizing measures could be undertaken, and should be feasible even in the absence of more fundamental political settlements. For example, if both sides were to move toward more invulnerable second-strike retaliatory forces, whether unilaterally or by joint agreement, a limited population system would be even more attractive, though it would not *require* such steps. In particular, if both sides were to reorient their strategic nuclear forces away from theoretically vulnerable fixed land-based ICBMs and toward submarine forces, mobile missiles, cruise missiles, and the like, the incentives to overcome limited population defense systems would be diminished further (although this would have to be weighed against the possible complications for arms control). There would then be no possibility that a counterforce surprise attack could reduce the other side's retaliatory forces to a level that could be reliably neutralized by the aggressor's city-defense systems.

Moreover, even more far-reaching arms control measures might be feasible, still within the context of a continued US-Soviet adversary relationship. The elimination of multiple warheads and major reductions in overall numbers of strategic nuclear weapons would further diminish the possibility of a disarming first strike, lessen the chance of accidents and unauthorized launchings, lessen the task of limited population defense systems, and lessen the destructiveness of accidents or unauthorized attacks that occur regardless of precautions and defense. Doing so would stabilize MAD and increase the security of both the United States and the Soviet Union—all without assuming an overall Cold-War settlement or utopian agreements on true disarmament.

Let us now consider the principal objections to a limited ballistic missile system. First, it has been argued that BMD cannot work. However, nearly all such arguments are based on the key premise that each superpower will seek to overwhelm defensive systems; in the context of a limited-defense arms control regime this should not occur. The reorientation of SDI to such a finite and far more realistic objective, together with recent advances in laser technology as well as precision-guided conventional weapons, could make operational systems feasible within the next decade.

Conversely, there is concern that any BMD system might prove to be destabilizing. As I have argued, though, this argument is based on the assumption of a competitive, unconstrained offense-defense arms race, and even in that context fears of destabilization seem exaggerated. In any case, a joint Soviet-American deployment within negotiated limitations that were carefully designed to hold the BMD system below the threshold at which it would theoretically threaten the MAD regime would meet most of those concerns.

Another concern is that one or the other of the superpowers will suddenly seek to "break out" of negotiated limitations and attempt to upgrade limited defensive systems into full-scale population defenses.[23] Of course, such concerns are a potential problem with any negotiated arms control treaty, not just a BMD treaty. Any such behavior would be irrational, for the other side would quickly detect major breakout moves and would undertake a variety of countermeasures in order to nullify the effort; meanwhile the side that cheated would have irrationally destroyed the regime that it had agreed to create because it served its own high self-interests to do so. Put differently, all arms control treaties assume rationality, but at the same time hedge against irrationality. It would not be difficult to deter as well as simultaneously hedge against efforts at unilateral breakouts from an arms control regime that incorporated limited population defenses.

Would the Soviets agree to negotiate a bilateral deployment of limited defensive systems? Surely the present Soviet rejection of the Reagan administration's SDI program does not make it inevitable that they would reject a very different system. The earlier history of the ABM treaty is instructive in this regard. In the early 1960s the Soviets strongly favored building defensive systems and curtailing offensive systems, presumably in accordance with their long military tradition placing the highest emphasis on defense of their homeland. When the Johnson administration, especially Secretary McNamara, tried to convince the Soviets to eschew defenses in favor of institutionalizing MAD, the Soviets initially resisted. Premier Kosygin indignantly replied, "Defensive systems which prevent attacks are not the cause of the arms race, but constitute a factor preventing the death of people."

True, the Soviets were eventually persuaded to abandon these views, and they joined in signing the ABM Treaty in 1972. This shift, however, may have been less a result of a new "sophistication" in their strategic thinking than of a resigned realization that they were on the wrong end of a self-fulfilling prophecy. McNamara had repeatedly argued that "neither side" would allow the other to create a theoretically effective defensive system, and that defensive systems always could and inevitably would be overwhelmed by additions to the opposing offensive systems. These arguments were hardly hypothetical; rather, they were a concrete warning of what the United States would in fact do if the Soviets sought to build a heavy ABM system.

Thus, McNamara had the unquestioned capability to ensure he was right in "predicting" that the deployment of ABM systems would only stimulate an offensive arms race, create dangerous new tensions and interacting fears, and end by being futile as well as dangerous.

Today, in the context of intensified Cold War and the Reagan administration's SDI program, the positions have been reversed, and Gorbachev is just as correct as McNamara was earlier in predicting the consequences of a *unilateral* defensive deployment. However, in light of Soviet unhappiness with the doctrine of assured destruction, the traditional Russian emphasis on defense, their present efforts to limit homeland destruction of nuclear war by antiaircraft defenses and counterforce targeting, and the specific arguments that can be made for the deployment of limited defensive systems, it is reasonable to hope that the Soviets could be persuaded to reassess the situation. This would be particularly the case if negotiations should occur in a less confrontational context and were accompanied by serious arms control limitations on offensive weapons.

Still another concern is that limited missile defenses would require the abrogation or renegotiation of the SALT I ABM Treaty, the most successful arms limitation treaty of the nuclear age. This would not be a high cost, however, as long as the deployment of BMD was not unilateral but followed from bilateral negotiations. The ABM Treaty was not supposed to be an end in itself. It was not based on the rationale that defense *per se* was bad but, rather, that drastic limitations of defenses were a necessary means to an undeniably desirable end: meaningful cutbacks of offensive systems. The underlying assumption was that limitations of ABMs would leave both superpowers unambiguously hostage to each other, would institutionalize MAD, and would thus eliminate the forces driving the offensive arms race.

In retrospect, however, we can now see that in this crucial respect the ABM Treaty has been a dismal failure. The rationale—such as it was—for a continuing offensive arms race may have been eliminated, but the race has nonetheless been substantially escalated since the treaty was signed in 1972. What went wrong? It is now clear that the notion that the arms race was primarily a function of an action-reaction cycle between offense and defense underestimated other potent forces driving that race: the underlying Soviet-American ideological and political conflicts; the implementation of particular military strategies, like counterforce or damage-limitation; worst-case reasoning in both superpower defense establishments; the inexorable march of technology; the impact of domestic politics, interservice rivalries, and bureaucratic competition; and the desire for negotiating advantages in arms control talks themselves, that is, "bargaining chips."

Thus, 15 years after the ABM Treaty ended the prospects of protection against any kind of nuclear attack, little or nothing has been done to inhibit the arms race seriously or stabilize mutual deterrence. Put differently, the single weapons system meaningfully constrained after 25 years of more or less serious superpower arms control negotiations has been the single weapons system that was defensive, that actually had some promise of saving lives rather than destroying them. Surely we can do better than that. A joint renegotiation of the ABM Treaty is hardly too high a price to pay for a limited defensive system that will not destabilize the underlying mutual deterrence relationship.

Another potential argument against limited population defenses is that a Soviet BMD system large enough to deal with accidental and third-party attacks might nullify the British and French independent nuclear deterrent forces, and require those states radically to increase the numbers of their offensive weapons. The argument seems implausible. Not only would rational Soviet leaders lack confidence that their defenses would be impenetrable to the already-substantial British and French forces, they would further have to assume that an attack on Europe would lead to American as well as British and French retaliation.

Moreover, if the British and French deterrent were undermined by superpower deployment of limited defensive systems, the same logic would apply with considerably greater force to other potential nuclear powers. Thus, limited defense systems could provide an additional disincentive for further nuclear proliferation (although, admittedly, nth-country nuclear powers might continue to have incentives other than their capacity to attack a superpower). On balance it seems more likely that superpower defensive systems would inhibit rather than stimulate the deployment of nuclear weapons by all other states. And if this predication should prove wrong, the price of some increase in British and French forces would be worth the benefits.[24]

Finally, one has to consider the economic costs of deploying defensive systems. A limited defense that did not have to guard against superpower countermeasures would of course be much less expensive than Reagan's SDI, although undoubtedly it would cost many billions of dollars.[25] However, this expense would be spread out over a number of years, and furthermore it could be offset by negotiated reductions in offensive systems. In any case, it would be worth billions to protect our society against the most likely threats of nuclear catastrophe.

* * *

The replacement of the present MAD regime with one of ''defense dominance'' is a good idea whose time has not yet come. The political obstacles are even greater than the technological ones, for no matter what technological advances may be made in the foreseeable future, it will still remain the case that no defense can succeed against a powerful adversary determined to nullify it. If anything, in recent years the political conditions for defense dominance have become even more unfavorable, even as the technology begins to show promise, because the predominant intellectual and political champions of defense dominance today are also militantly anti-Communist, confrontationist, and committed to the restoration of US nuclear superiority and perhaps even warfighting capabilities, rather than arms control.

Over the longer run, though, it seems unexceptionable that the end we should aim at is not (or not merely) the stabilization of MAD but its elimination, through the progressive dismantling of the doomsday machine that we have created. The ultimate goal should be the complete elimination of nuclear weapons, though the feasibility of this is indeed questionable. However, it is much less utopian to think in terms not of nuclear disarmament but rather of a shift in strategies and weapons systems toward defense dominance, in which the superpowers agree to agree mutually to deploy heavy population defense systems to defend against full-scale nuclear war.

There would be two fundamental preconditions that would have to be met for such a regime to be implemented. The first would be that each superpower would have to refrain from nullifying the other side's defensive systems. Since effective full-scale population defense systems would mean the end of the balance of terror system, this could happen only in conjunction with an end to the Cold War and an overall political settlement between the United States and the Soviet Union. Put differently, however paradoxical it might superficially appear, no nuclear defense against a major power can succeed unless it is grounded in a cooperative rather than adversarial relationship.

The second precondition is that major reductions in offensive weapons would have to accompany the deployment of heavy population defensive systems, for it could never be assumed that *any* defensive system could provide meaningful and reliable protection against thousands of nuclear warheads.

If these preconditions were met, the superpowers could gradually move from thin population defenses, not dependent on a transformation of political relations but only on recognition of the most minimal common interests in survival, to thick defenses, which are indeed dependent on radical psychological and political changes in the international political environment, or at least in the bilateral US-Soviet relationship.

Why, it might be objected, would defenses be necessary at all after an end to the Cold War? Why not just proceed directly to the elimination of nuclear weapons instead of defending against them? For a number of reasons, complete nuclear disarmament would require more than a Soviet-American political settlement. Such a settlement would still leave many nations with nuclear weapons and a number of unresolved serious international conflicts. Even more important, it is difficult even to imagine how a reliable international regime for the complete elimination of nuclear weapons could be established, in light of the well-understood difficulty of disinventing an established technology. And even if one day serious efforts are made in this direction, population defensive systems would undoubtedly play an important role, as a means of providing a safeguard against clandestinely retained nuclear weapons.[26] Thus, strategic defense, if regarded as an instrument of arms control rather than of military strategy, may offer the most viable basis for a safe and durable arms control regime.

For the present, however, we need not be concerned with how to convert utopias into realities, for there are two important and quite realistic functions that defenses against nuclear weapons could play in the near future: to provide at least modestly effective defense against a variety of possible limited attacks, and to serve as a base and model for a future defense-dominant world.

Notes

1. Weinberger's remark that with the success of SDI, "We could be back in a situation we were in ... when we were the only nation with a nuclear weapon." Quoted by George Ball, "The War for Star Wars," *New York Review,* 11 April 1985. See also the various writings of Colin S. Gray, a close adviser of the administration, especially "A New Debate on Ballistic Missile Defense," *Survival,* March–April 1981.

2. For example, James Abrahamson, the SDI Program Director, told Congress in 1984 that, "First and foremost, an effective defense against ballistic missiles would improve stability and reduce the likelihood of war by removing the military utility of a preemptive nuclear strike." Quoted in Peter A. Clausen, "SDI in Search of a Mission," *World Policy Journal* 2, no. 2 (Spring 1985). For an extended, quasi-official development of the administration's ideas, see Keith B. Payne and Colin S. Gray, "Nuclear Policy and the Defensive Transition," *Foreign Affairs* 62, no. 4 (Spring 1984).

3. US Department of State, "The Strategic Defense Initiative," June 1985. For similar statements by high administration officials, see Paul Nitze, "SDI: Its Nature and Rationale," Bureau of Public Affairs, Department of State (Washington, DC: October 1985), and Fred C. Ikle, "Nuclear Strategy: Can There Be a Happy Ending?," *Foreign Affairs* 63, no. 4 (Spring 1985).

4. The most important criticisms include Union of Concerned Scientists, *The Fallacy of Star Wars* (New York: Vintage Books,

1984); Sidney D. Drell, Philip J. Farley, and David Holloway, *The Reagan Strategic Defense Initiative* (Cambridge, MA: Ballinger Publishing Co., 1985); Harold Brown, "Is SDI Technically Feasible?" *Foreign Affairs* 64, no. 3; Brown, "The Strategic Defense Initiative," *Survival* 27, no. 2 (March/April 1985); McGeorge Bundy et al., "The President's Choice: Star Wars or Arms Control," *Foreign Affairs* 63, no. 2 (Winter, 1984–85); Ashton Carter, *Directed Energy Missile Defense*, Office of Technology Assessment (Washington, DC: Government Printing Office, 1984); Office of Defense Technology, *Ballistic Missile Defense Technologies* (Princeton: Princeton University Press, 1986).

5. In the last few years Soviet political and military leaders have repeatedly warned that the deployment of American defensive systems would be countered by a variety of Soviet measures. Similarly, the Reagan administration, even while proclaiming that SDI is in the joint interest of both sides and will lead to the abolition of nuclear weapons, is already at work on offensive systems to counter any Soviet defensive systems. *New York Times,* 15 December 1985.

6. Union of Concerned Scientists, *Nucleus* 8 no. 2 (Summer 1986).

7. Brown, 1985; James R. Schlesinger, "Rhetoric and Realities in the Star Wars Debate," *International Security* 10, no. 1 (Summer 1985).

8. Wolfgang Panofsky, "The Strategic Defense Initiative," *Physics Today,* June 1985. As Panofsky points out, the scientific consensus on this point is overwhelming. It may also be noted that while there may be no way to demonstrate conclusively in advance the feasibility of new technology, the historical record is quite discouraging. In the 1950s the Soviets poured vast resources into bomber defenses that were easily overwhelmed by US bomber capabilities, and a similarly intense Soviet commitment to ABM in the early 1960s foundered on the US proliferation of missiles and warheads.

9. For a review of the administration's progressive abandonment of the cost-effective criterion, see *New York Times,* 1 May 1986.

10. Union of Concerned Scientists, 1984, p. 166: "To the extent that defenses pose a serious threat to the 'assured destruction' capability of either side, they invite retargeting to retain such destructive capacity."

11. Clausen, p. 269; Clausen's argument that the arms race effects of SDI will be felt in the very near future, "long before

actual deployment and quite possibly even if deployment is ultimately rejected.''

12. Charles L. Glaser, ''Why Even Good Defenses May Be Bad,'' *International Security* 9, no. 2 (Fall, 1984).

13. Sidney D. Drell, Philip J. Farley, and David Holloway, ''Preserving the ABM Treaty,'' *International Security* 9, no. 2 (Fall 1984), p. 21. For other arguments stressing the destabilizing potential of SDI, see Jonathan B. Stein, *From H-Bomb to Star Wars* (Lexington Books, 1984) and Union of Concerned Scientists, 1984.

14. Stephen Weiner, ''Systems and Technology,'' in Ashton B. Carter and David N. Schwartz (eds.), *Ballistic Missile Defense* (Washington, DC: The Brookings Institution, 1984).

15. The would-be preemptor cannot rationally assume a better outcome if he ''decapitates'' his enemy with a surprise attack against its command, control, communications, and intelligence systems (C^3I), for it must be assumed (as, indeed, both the United States and the Soviet Union have already strongly implied) that both sides have predelegated the authority to respond to a successful decapitation attack to lower-level military commanders. Indeed, under such an assumption it would be much worse for the attacker to destroy the enemy's C^3I systems that to preserve them, for in the latter circumstance there is at least a chance that the attacker may avoid a devastating ''spasm'' retaliatory attack.

For other arguments questioning the destabilizing dangers of defensive systems, see Charles W. Glaser, ''Do We Want the Missile Defense We Can Build?'', *International Security* 10, no. 1 (Summer 1985). Glaser notes that even if the superpowers do eventually deploy defenses that significantly reduce the vulnerability of their homelands, these defenses would also make their retaliatory forces highly survivable, thereby greatly reducing any preemptive incentives.

16. Colin Gray, in Carter and Schwartz, p. 405.

17. *New York Times* summary of a study by Barry Blechman and Victor Utgoff, 23 July 1986.

18. For an authoritative analysis of the purely technical problems of a coordinated attack on ICBM silos, see Matthew Bunn and Kosta Tsipis, ''The Uncertainties of a Preemptive Nuclear Attack,'' *Scientific American* 249, no. 5 (November 1983).

19. Bunn & Tsipis; Albert Carnesale, and Charles L. Glaser, ''ICBM Vulnerability: The Cures Are Worse than the Disease,'' *International Security* 7, no. 1.

20. The preceding paragraphs are drawn from Jerome Slater, "Population Defense Reconsidered: Is the ABM Really Inconsistent with Stability?" *Policy Sciences Journal* 8, no. 1 (Autumn 1979).

21. For brief discussions of light defense, see Freeman Dyson, *Weapons and Hope* (New York: Harper & Row, 1984); Office of Defense Technology, *Ballistic Missile Defense Technologies;* Ashton Carter, "BMD Applications: Performance and Limitations," in Carter and Schwartz; Drell, Farley & Holloway, 1985; William Schneider & Donald Brennan, *U.S. Strategic-Nuclear Policy and Ballistic Missile Defense* (Cambridge, MA: Institute for Foreign Policy Analysis, 1980).

22. On the spread of ballistic missiles, see Aaron Karp, "Ballistic Missiles in the Third World," *International Security* 9, no. 3 (Winter 1984–85).

23. Brown, *Survival;* Glaser, 1985.

24. It is possible, however, that the Soviet Union would refuse to accept *major* increases in British and French forces in the interest of a limited defense agreement, and for that reason negotiations for such an agreement will probably have to take into account European security concerns.

25. There have been no careful studies of the costs of a limited defense system. However, the recent Blechman/Utgoff study estimated the cost of a system that provided both terminal defenses for ICBM silos and limited defenses of the 47 largest US cities as about $160 billion. Clearly a limited population defense system alone would be substantially less, although the costs cannot be meaningfully estimated at this time. *New York Times,* 23 July 1986.

26. For arguments on the role defense systems might play in conjunction with far-reaching nuclear disarmament, see Dyson, Payne, and Gray.

Part IV

☆☆☆

ACQUISITION
AND READINESS

BUILDING REFORM IN
WEAPONS ACQUISITION

Jacques S. Gansler

*T*HE REAGAN ADMINISTRATION entered office with a strong mandate to increase defense expenditures and reverse a perceived decline in the relative position of America's military posture around the world. The two main thrusts of the administration's initiatives were a trillion-dollar defense buildup—the largest in peacetime history—and a commitment to building some high-visibility systems, for example, the MX missile, the B–1B bomber, and an increased number of large warships.

As a result of the deterioration of America's military posture in the post-Vietnam era and the continued buildup of Soviet forces, the increase in US defense expenditures was clearly warranted, and it had the desired impact, both in military and economic terms. However, towards the end of the first term of the Reagan administration questions began to be raised about whether taxpayers were getting their money's worth. Issues varied from whether we were buying the right systems (highlighted by the controversy surrounding radios that did not allow the Army to talk to the Navy during the Grenada conflict), to the glaring newspaper "horror stories" about weapons that didn't work, and grossly overpriced toilet seats and hammers. With the deficit rising dramatically and the perception of "chaos and corruption" in defense procurements increasing, defense expenditures began leveling off and there was a rising intensity in congressional and executive branch attacks on the defense industry—again, fueled by the press. Efforts were made by the Pentagon to shift public attention from "management issues" to "criminal actions," giving many the impression that acquisition management was becoming primarily an issue for auditors and lawyers.

Congress picked up on this attack and began issuing hundreds of new "procurement reforms" aimed at correcting the apparent abuses. For example, Senate Bill 1958 was introduced on 17 December 1985, stating, "wherein, no funds appropriated to or for the use of the Department of Defense may be obligated or expended for the procurement of any plastic toilet cover shrouds, identified as toilet assembly #941673–101, at a unit cost in excess of $125.00." Congress got more into the detailed management of each and every procurement line item—changing more than half of them in one way or another, and requiring detailed studies to be done by the Department of Defense and submitted to the Congress in many others. Thus, instead of industry getting Government "off its back," the trend has been toward increased auditing (by the General Accounting Office, the Inspectors General, and so forth) and greater regulation of defense contractors.

Fortunately, in parallel with this mainstream focus on "fraud and abuse," there has been a broader, and far more important, rising concern about "waste"—a new look at the effectiveness and efficiency we realize from our defense dollars and the broad structural changes that are needed to increase the cost-effectiveness of our expenditures. Again, at the beginning of the Reagan administration the Defense Department took the lead in initiating these reforms. The so-called "Carlucci

Initiatives'' were a set of acquisition reforms (proposed by then Deputy Secretary Frank Carlucci) aimed at correcting many of the historical abuses in the system. They focused on such goals as increasing program stability, improving production efficiency, and establishing greater realism in program costs. While highly desirable, such thrusts ran up against the "traditional way of doing defense business" and were hard to implement— especially in an environment where everyone was in a hurry to make short-term "fixes."

However, by the end of the first term of the Reagan administration, the movement towards broad structural reform had gained momentum. The call for reform permeated all levels of DOD: the Office of the Secretary of Defense, the Joint Chiefs of Staff, the military services, and the defense industry, as well as all of the major DOD processes: the "requirements process" (for weapons selection and specification), the planning, programming, and budget process (for resource allocation), and the procurement process itself.

In early 1985 a bipartisan report on the findings of an independent 18-month study on defense organization was released,[1] reiterating the need for such broad changes. The study panel included members from Capitol Hill, many former Defense Department officials, and military leaders such as General David Jones, former Chairman of the Joint Chiefs of Staff, General Edward Meyer, former Chief of Staff of the Army, and Admiral Harry Train, former Commander-in-Chief of the Atlantic Command. Additionally, the recommendations of this study were endorsed by six former Secretaries of Defense who in their introduction stated, "There are serious deficiencies in the organization and managerial procedures of the U.S. defense establishment."

This study was followed by the release of a similarly detailed investigation by the Senate Armed Services Committee.[2] This also recommended broad institutional changes and was supported by a bipartisan coalition led by Senators Goldwater and Nunn. On the House side, Congressman Les Aspin (the new Chairman of the Armed Services Committee) initiated a far-reaching set of hearings on broad defense procurement and management issues. Finally, in February 1986, the President's Blue Ribbon Commission on Defense Management (the so-called Packard Commission, named after the Chairman of the Commission, industrialist and former Deputy Secretary of Defense David Packard) released its set of recommendations on defense reorganization and procedural changes.[3]

Again, the focus was on broad, structural changes in the acquisition process itself rather than on the narrower issue of "fraud and abuse," with the recommendations centering on the need for a new planning and budgeting system, significant reorganization of both the Office of the Secretary of Defense and the Joint Chiefs of Staff, and significant changes in the acquisition process as well as the management and buying practices of the Congress and the DOD.

Thus, the Congress and the executive branch are faced with a choice. They can either continue their detailed attack on "fraud and abuse"—through greater regulation and stepped-up auditing—or they can shift the debate to the higher plateau of broad structural reform in the way the Department of Defense will do its business over the coming years. Obviously, this examination argues that latter approach. However, the argument comes with a warning: it is possible to go too far and seek change for its own sake, thus "throwing away the good with the bad." One after another, independent studies comparing defense management with that of other Government agencies (at Federal, State, and local levels) have found that the Department of Defense is one of the best managed—if not *the* best managed of all Government agencies.[4] This is easy to see when defense overruns are compared with those occurring in other agencies' major projects. For example, Defense horror stories pale in comparison to cost, schedule, and management problems encountered in the building of mass transit systems, and congressional office buildings. Thus, while making necessary and dramatic changes in the way the Department of Defense does its business, it is important not to ignore the many important lessons we've learned in buying DOD weapon systems over the past 40 years. Nonetheless, there is much room for improvement, as the following discussion of current problems makes quite clear.

The Acquisition Process

There are essentially four sets of adverse trends which must be reversed if the DOD is to get its money's worth and public confidence is to be restored. The first of these is *increasing concern about the choice of weapon systems themselves.* Essentially, there is a perception that "the existing institutional structure" does not provide for the selection and development of the most cost-effective weapons. This concern is typified by the extensive debates over the past several years regarding the $20 billion requested for 100 MX missiles, a second $20 billion for 100 B–1 bombers, and third $20 billion for two additional aircraft carrier task forces. The issue is not whether these weapon systems are desired but whether they represent the best way (among many other possible alternatives) to spend $60 billion to enhance the nation's security. Similarly, there has been much debate—but, again, no clear consensus—over the allocation of incremental defense funds: whether a 600-ship Navy, more Army units, or more Air Force fighter wings should have the highest priority. These questions of strategy and the resultant weapon selections are compounded by inter-Service rivalry for resources. They are still further complicated by the opportunities for revolutionary change in force structure that are offered by future technological changes capable of multiplying relevant military capabilities if the new technology can be "absorbed" by the military institutions.

However, proposals for such dramatic change often fall into an ambiguous region between traditional Service equipment and missions, which makes it difficult for the armed services to accept such concepts "culturally." For example, perhaps the Navy could carry out its mission of denying use of the surface of the seas to an enemy with reconnaissance satellites and land-based missiles. But such concepts are so foreign to traditional notions of naval operations that they receive little attention.[5] Instead, we continue to concentrate on building improved versions of traditional platforms—ships, planes, and tanks.

Moreover, the armed services insist that each item of equipment be the "best possible." This leads to the second of the adverse trends, namely *rapid growth in the cost of defense equipment*. The United States has clearly kept its military equipment at the forefront of the technological state-of-the-art, but the cost of this improved performance—from generation to generation of weapon systems—has been increases of around 6 percent per year in the unit price of each new generation of equipment (even after adjusting for inflation, as well as the higher unit price associated with the reduced quantities typically purchased today.)[6] Since the cost of a single ship currently is measured in hundreds of millions and even billions of dollars, and an individual plane in the tens or even hundreds of millions, and each new tank in the millions, it is clear that under any realistic projection of resources likely to be made available for defense, if unit costs continue to increase the nation will be able to buy fewer and fewer weapon systems each year.

Recognizing the difficulty of buying enough weapons within the dollars available, the armed forces historically have been optimistic in estimating the "likely" cost of these weapon systems, especially when first requesting funds for their development. Their hope has been either that costs will, in fact, be unexpectedly low, or that more money will become available in the future. More cynically, some suggest that unrealistically low cost estimates reflect a bureaucratic tactic whose purpose is to get the development program started and to leave the problem of how to pay for it to those in office in later years. Indeed, as weapons are actually developed and procured, far too often their realized costs have been significantly higher than the initial estimates. This program cost growth historically has averaged between 50 and 100 percent of the original cost estimate of each weapon system.[7]

Naturally, if there are only a certain number of dollars available for buying a given system, and its costs double, we can only afford to buy half as many. Thus, while the United States has been buying extremely capable weapon systems, the total result of both types of cost growth—from generation to generation, and between initial estimates and final price tags—has been fewer and fewer systems bought each year. For example, in the 1950s the United States bought around 3,000 fighter planes each year; in the 1960s, the number purchased declined to 1,000 per year; and in the 1970s, the figure was only 300 fighter planes per year. (Norm Augustine has pointed out that a continuation of this trend would result in our building one fighter plane per year in the year 2054.)[8]

There is, however, a minimum quantity of weapon systems which is absolutely critical for the successful completion of any military mission, especially as the Soviet Union has been steadily improving the quality of its weapons, while still maintaining equipment stocks and production rates that are very high compared to American defense numbers. Thus, these cost-induced reductions in the quantity of US weapon purchases could be devastating.

The increasing cost of US weapon systems also adds to the third of the undesirable acquisition trends, namely, a *lengthening of the acquisition cycle*—the time required to move from the initiation of development through the completion of production. Part of this lengthening is due to the increasing complexity of modern weapon systems, but two more important causes are (a) stretchouts resulting from an increasingly burdensome and indecisive managerial and budgeting process (in both the executive and legislative branches) and (b) stretchouts resulting from program cost growths and budget reductions. It used to take 5 to 7 years to acquire a weapon system, but new systems now often take 12 or even 15 years to move from exploratory development to initial deployments in the field. Even after development is complete, the high costs of each weapon mean that only a few production units can be purchased each year, so the deployment of any significant number is still further delayed. It becomes a vicious circle, since an added effect of lengthened acquisition cycles is reduced efficiency in the acquisition process, and therefore still greater unit costs and still lower quantities. Thus, the lengthening acquisition cycle has a compound military effect. First, it results in a decline in America's technological advantage over the Soviets, since most of the systems deployed in the field are older designs, and, second, the longer cycle itself causes higher costs and therefore reduced quantities.

Adding to these undesirable weapon system acquisition trends—and to a considerable extent being caused by them—is the fourth of the adverse trends, *worsening problems in the US defense industrial base.* With the long-term decline in rates of production, one would expect to see the industrial base "drying up." In fact, during the shrinkage in defense procurements in the early 1970s (the annual procurement account dropped from $44 billion to $17 billion, excluding inflation effects, from 1969 to 1975), the large prime contractors remained in business by building equipment at very low rates, for example, one aircraft per month in an extreme case, while suppliers of parts and subcontractors were allowed simply to disappear. A series of reports in late 1980 all indicated significant problems in the US defense industrial base.[9] These studies identified areas of substantial inefficiency for normal operations in peacetime, as well as critical bottlenecks (for example, in selected critical parts and production equipment), such that there was almost a total lack of capability to respond rapidly to any emergency condition with a surge in production. For example, it was reported that it would take over three years for an existing aircraft production line to increase its output significantly.

Oddly, America's national security strategy was itself partially the cause of this declining industrial responsiveness. After World War II, the United States shifted to a strategy and military force posture that relied very heavily on US nuclear superiority to deter war in any form. Under this posture, the US ability to mass-produce huge quantities of weapons rapidly—as demonstrated during World War II—was no longer considered a part of America's security strength. Beginning in the 1960s, however, as the USSR began to acquire strategic nuclear parity, the threat of a US nuclear response to a conventional attack became less credible as a deterrent to war. Thus, the United States shifted to a strategy of "flexible response": attempting to respond to conventional aggression with conventional weapons, while maintaining nuclear weapons as a deterrent to nuclear attacks and for "first use" if conventional defenses fail. To prevent the United States from being forced to employ the "nuclear option," however, the conventional warfare portion of this strategy has to count more heavily on US industrial responsiveness—to be prepared to beef up the relatively small peacetime standing forces in the event of crisis.[10] But improving industrial responsiveness also requires money, which compounds the squeeze on available acquisition funds, so successive US administrations have been reluctant to take significant steps in this area.

Reversing these four undesirable acquisition trends can be accomplished neither quickly nor easily. The complexity and magnitude of the defense acquisition system does not lend itself to simple solutions. However, partly out of frustration and partly to react to the public and press clamor for corrective actions (brought on more by the revelations of $400 hammers, $900 stool caps, and $600 toilet seats than by the above-noted broad trends in defense procurement), "quick fixes" have been the attempts pursued by both the Congress and the DOD. For example, recently the Congress had over 150 different defense procurement reform bills being processed—many of which would, in fact, be counterproductive and even self-contradictory, while the DOD, to correct the "spare parts problem," added literally thousands of people (the Air Force added over 3,000 people for spare parts alone), and the net result was to double the processing time for ordering spare parts with actually negative impact on force readiness as a result of this "fix." Clearly, primary attention needs to be addressed to the large-dollar items if significant impacts on defense procurement are actually to be realized—rather than to the small items. The latter, unfortunately, are the ones that have been grabbing the headlines, and thus receiving a disproportionate amount of the attention. An example of the mismatch in resources would be the fact that the DOD now has 30 to 40 percent of the government's plant representatives, auditors, etc. looking at spare parts, which actually represent only 3 to 4 percent of the total DOD dollars.

Needed Changes

If these significant and undesirable trends in the Department of Defense's acquisition practices are to be reversed, there are four broad sets of changes required. In priority order, these are (1) improved long-term resource allocations and weapon system selections (there's no value in properly buying the wrong systems); (2) improving the stability in programs and budgets (how can you possibly manage efficiently if the programs, and the dollars for them, are continuously changing?); (3) shifting from a current system that *regulates* quality and costs to one that creates natural *incentives* for higher quality and lower costs (it's harder to get people to do things right by directive rather than by choice); and (4) there is a need for greater emphasis on the importance of the health and responsiveness of the defense industrial base (its role as a vital part of our national security posture must be recognized and steps taken to revitalize the "arsenal of democracy").

Clearly, these four actions are inter-related, yet all four are required if there is to be a broad "cultural change" in the way DOD does its business. A more detailed discussion of the four actions follows.

1. Improved methods to allocate defense resources and establish weapon system requirements. At present, weapons and other equipment are selected almost solely by each military service acting independently. The Army, Navy, Air Force, and Marines each choose the systems that appear best suited for their unique, historical missions, according to their own perceptions of requirements. Thus, the armed services design the structures of their forces as if they intended to fight *independent* land, sea, air, and amphibious wars. (This explains why—as noted before—in the Grenada operation of 1983, the radios of the Army and Navy operated differently, prohibiting the needed direct communications between them during the conflict.) All military experts agree that future battles will be fought with integrated forces, so clearly weapons and equipment should be selected to complement one another, and thus maximize the combined capabilities of the armed forces.

Unfortunately, those who have the responsibility for planning how wars will be fought—the Chairman of the Joint Chiefs of Staff and the Commanders of the Unified and Specified Commands (CINCs)—do not develop weapon requirements, nor approve the selection of weapon systems, nor establish the priorities for resource expenditures among the various competing demands. Thus, the sole responsibility for imposing some coherence upon the uncoordinated procurement programs of individual Services has been assumed by the Office of the Secretary of Defense, with frequent advice from the Congress.

To get resource and equipment planning done by the *military* on a unified basis would require a strengthened Chairman of the Joint Chiefs and an organization and staff more independent of the Services, as was suggested by President Eisenhower (but not implemented) in 1958. Thus, long-range, mission-area resource plans would be generated based on guidance from the Office of the Secretary of Defense with total dollar levels established by the President that would make more effective use of the overall resources and the changes in technology now available. It is the latter which has resulted in the present considerable overlap in individual Service traditional roles and missions.

Such long-range plans—tied to military mission future needs—would place an "affordability constraint" on deciding which future weapon systems would be developed and procured, and in what numbers. The Chairman would also recommend a strategy that would be tied to these resource plans, a link which, many have noted, is currently missing. Such a plan would not only have the military making explicit trade-offs between quantity and quality (the result of a resource-constrained plan), it would also require explicit trade-offs between dollars for force modernization and dollars for force readiness (the input from the CINCs is particularly important in the latter regard).

Much of what fits into this recommendation is contained within the movement for "JCS Reform."[11] However, many of these reform proposals tend to emphasize exclusively the military "chain of command" issue. They need to be expanded to include the resource planning issue also. If properly implemented, these reforms would significantly strengthen the role of the Secretary of Defense. He would then have far greater assistance in achieving integrated planning—from the Chairman of the Joint Chiefs of Staff, the CINCs, and the more independent staff of the Chairman of the JCS. Similarly, they would make clear the specific role of the Services, which is—by law—that of organizing, equipping, training, and supporting their respective forces.

Overall, the effect of this broad reform would be to shift more towards *centralized decisionmaking* and *decentralized implementation,* with the Services having full authority and responsibility for the execution of the weapon systems developments and procurements—as well as their subsequent support.

The long-range, integrated, resource plan generated by the Office of the Secretary of Defense and the Chairman of the Joint Chiefs of Staff would then form the basis for the second of the needed defense acquisition reforms.

2. Greater program and budget stability. The United States is one of the few nations in the world, if not the only one, to run its defense establishment on an annual budget cycle. Single-year defense budgets encourage the Services, the administration, and the Congress to meet annual total budget limits by stretching out the purchases of most weapons over several additional years—a far less difficult action than actually canceling an entire weapon program. Such "stretchouts" are short-sighted, as they force contractors to produce equipment at inefficient rates of production, causing higher unit costs and the overall procurement of fewer systems. For example, the three-year production "stretchout" of the F–15 aircraft in the mid-1970s resulted in a two-billion-dollar increase in program costs (excluding the effects of inflation). Eighty-three fewer fighter aircraft were purchased than would have been possible—for the same dollars—had the original plan been adhered to.[12]

Congress could make a very significant contribution to controlling procurement costs by adopting a multiyear defense budget.[13] Two- or three-year budget cycles would introduce the greater stability necessary for contractors to plan more efficient production rates and lower the unit costs of new systems. Furthermore, the stability of multiyear budgeting would encourage the application of multiyear procurement contracts—a far more efficient technique. Finally, and most important, multiyear budgets would encourage the Defense Department and the Congress to consider more carefully the long-term fiscal and strategic implications of procurement decisions. Naturally, multiyear budgets could be reviewed at any time in light of changes in world conditions.

Encouragingly, during the past year both the Senate and the House have introduced bills for a biennial budget process, wherein a two-year defense budget would be established during the first year of the new Congress. The Department of Defense has strongly supported this initiative. It might be noted that the Congress's annual budget resolutions actually have three-year budgets contained within them, but only the first year is *binding* on the executive branch, while the second two are considered "targets." Making these out-year targets binding as "nominal budgets," with the President permitted to submit amendments as the economic picture changed, would introduce a major element of the needed stability without requiring radical changes in procedures.

A second beneficial congressional reform would be to reduce the number of committees involved in the Defense budget process. In 1983, Defense Department witnesses testified on the 1984 budget before 96 committees and subcommittees; 1,306 witnesses provided 2,160 hours of testimony. The redundant hearings are time-consuming (for both Defense management and for the Congress) and focus extensive attention on the details of the budget, rather than on broader policy issues. Additionally, the many small changes that result from this process (last year over 1,000 line items were changed) introduce great instabilities into defense programs and uncertainties about future funding levels and schedules. An Air Force study estimated that savings of 20 percent could be achieved—after a few years' time— by stabilizing the Department of Defense budget;[14] congressional reforms would help to make these savings possible.

The Defense Department also could help achieve greater budget stability. The Department might begin by recognizing how much it hurts itself by not making realistic total program cost estimates. Historically, the cost associated with the *uncertainty* of developing new advanced-technology weapons has not been included in most program initial estimates, since potential price tags look more attractive without these "contingency dollars." Optimistic initial estimating is a problem throughout the various levels of the Defense Department, as well as in the Congress. There is no question, however, that there are major uncertainties in the development of weapon systems, and that factors to cover these risks must be included if costs are to be estimated realistically—this is basically a management issue, not a cost-estimating issue. Clearly, realistic program cost estimates are critical to the achievement of stability—and, therefore, efficiency—in the defense acquisition process. Low estimates always result in "cost growth" and stretchouts later on. Naturally, if realistic program cost estimates were used, it would result in fewer programs in the total budget than currently exist. However, each of the programs which survived could be managed more efficiently and, in the end, a great deal more equipment could be procured for the same amount of money.

One technique that the Services have recently begun implementing to achieve greater stability is called "baselining." Here, an internal "contract" is written on each program—between the program manager and his Service. For example, the Air Force is now trying to discipline itself to operate within the $20 billion estimate for 100 B–1B aircraft. A baseline has been signed (and if revisions are required, re-signed) which commits—at the very top levels of the Service—to all of the key parameters of the program, for example, performance, annual budgets, quantities, schedules, support plans, operational plans, etc. Traditionally, such commitments have not existed. So the Services have felt free to change their minds frequently on both program requirements and budgets, thus creating turmoil and instability in the program and allowing the industrial suppliers to operate "flexibly" on contract costs—even if the original contract had been a fixed-price contract. Underlining this concept of baselining is the assumption that the Service program manager is given sufficient authority to reject changes that come in from other staff areas. Of great help to the effective management of these programs would be greater DOD reprogramming authority for the Congress to permit the necessary managerial flexibility.

Inherent in this concept of program stability are two basic assumptions: (1) *never start the program until you're ready;* that is, don't initiate full-scale development unless the technology has already been demonstrated, firm requirements have been established, and relevant operational concepts have been settled; and (2) *recognize that, historically, a commitment to full-scale development is a commitment to production.* There have been no programs cancelled by the Services after full-scale development has begun, and very few have been cancelled by any other authority—either in the executive or legislative branches. Under this concept, the dollars must be available for production and the planning done to have a smooth transition from development into production, with proper production planning done early enough to achieve the desired efficiency of production operations. Such planning and commitments would encourage both efficient production rates and efficient multiyear contracting.

The first two reforms in defense procurement—improved planning and selection of weapon systems, and stability in programs and budgets—are the highest priority. With these two reforms in place, it would then be possible to manage each weapon procurement program far more efficiently and effectively. However, to do so the two reforms discussed below are also necessary. The combined effect of all four will achieve the needed overall "cultural change" in the way defense does its business.

3. Shifting from regulations to incentives to achieve higher quality and lower cost equipment. Here we come to the area of specific "procurement reforms"—the types of measures that most discussions of "getting more bang for the buck" normally start with. In this case there are two choices. Either a large number of new laws and/or regulations are issued, covering every detail of defense costs and "how to" rules; *or* one creates a new environment, one in which the government and its contractors have natural incentives, such as promotion, profit, increased sales, professional pride, etc., which lead the government and industry managers to want to figure out ways to improve the quality of their products and lower the costs. As will be seen below, such "market incentives" rarely exist today in defense procurement. They need to be created in order to achieve the necessary changes.

The following 10 specific techniques might achieve the "natural incentives" needed for improved efficiency and effectiveness of defense resource management.

ENHANCED PROFESSIONALISM. Because experienced Government managers are essential for the successful acquisition of new multibillion dollar high-technology, high-risk weapon systems, incentives must be created for the retention, and especially the promotion, of effective military and civilian personnel in the agencies that manage the acquisition process. Historically, such stability and rewards have not existed. For the military, promotion potential lies elsewhere in operational positions. Rotation rates are high in management billets, and inexperience—or even no experience—is common. However, in recent years the Air Force has made some significant strides in the right direction, and in 1985 Navy Secretary Lehman directed that 40 percent of all future admirals must come from the acquisition community. Similar upgrading of status and promotion potential is also required on the civilian side.

The first and most obvious step is a reclassification of procurement from "administrative" to "professional" categories, including all of the corresponding changes in training and experience. Until the personnel system is fully reformed—on both the civilian and military sides—it will be difficult to recruit and retain the most capable and experienced people in the acquisition process.

INCREASED PROGRAM MANAGEMENT AUTHORITY. In recent years, "priesthoods" of individuals with extensive authority have built up on the Service and Secretary's staffs. These people have the right to tell a program manager exactly what he must have in his program—from the point of view of the "competition advocate," the "streamlining advocate," the "reliability expert," the "logistics expert," the "military component specification expert," and so forth. Since all of these individuals have veto power over a program, the program manager must agree to meet their diverse requirements if he wants his program approved, regardless of the costs. In addition, in order to "sell" a program on up the line, the program manager must go through innumerable sets of "reviews"—often over 40 individual sets of briefings for one decision on how the program will be run. A look at either commercial programs or well-run defense programs shows that what successful programs have in common is a strong program manager with full authority to do the job, and the full support of those senior to him who can force the system to allow it to happen. Defense "layering" has built up to such a point that, in some cases, it is nearly impossible for this to occur. In 1985 Navy Secretary Lehman took a dramatic step to eliminate a whole layer, or organization, by removing the Chief of Navy Materiel and all of his supporting staff. This also had the desirable effect of eliminating much of the staff from the next layer down, whose principal job was supplying data to the upper layer. He also streamlined the reporting chain from the program manager directly upward. Thus, the program manager was given both the authority and the responsibility associated with his job, and was free to manage in the most effective and efficient fashion practical within the limits set by program dollars.

This is an essential step in more effective acquisition management.

CONTINUOUS ALTERNATIVE. In the nondefense world the maintenance of some form of continuous alternative (for example, competition between two or more suppliers for the same product, or between at least two different products for the same mission) is the normal way of doing business. Since such a competition assures the continual creation of incentives for lowering costs and improving performance, it has proven to be an effective technique. By contrast, the normal approach for the Department of Defense is to have an initial competition for the development of a weapon system, followed by sole-source contracts to the winner. The thousands of subsequent program changes are bid in a monopoly environment, thus invalidating the initial contract bid. Similarly, all follow-on contracts—especially for the large production dollars—are bid on a sole-source basis over the next 10 to 20 years.

The DOD must figure out ways to shift from this sole-source environment to some form or forms of continuous alternative. In the commercial world, if one supplier raises his prices significantly, you'll switch to another. In the DOD world—with only one supplier of a badly needed weapon system—the option is simply to buy fewer systems this year and the rest a few years later, at still higher prices. While continuous competition may not always be practical, most of the time it is. Certainly, it should always be considered, and efforts made for its achievements. Where it is not possible or practical at the weapon system level, continuous alternatives can be used for critical subsystems. The emphasis here—as with all the required acquisition initiatives—must be on incentives for the achievement of both higher quality and lower costs. Studies have shown that when the Defense Department has used such continuous competition in the past, program cost savings on an average of 25 to 30 percent have been realized, along with significant performance improvements.[15]

Recognizing these potential benefits, on 1 April 1985 the Congress mandated that the "Competition in Contracting Act" be fully implemented. This law not only requires the consideration of competition on all major weapon systems but it also establishes the requirement to report on this to the Congress. While the Competition in Contracting Act is clearly a move in the right direction, that is, toward more use of competitive incentives, there is a danger that the intent of the increased competition—improved performance at lower costs—will be subverted through its improper implementation. We have already begun to see this happen. What has captured the attention of both Congress and DOD is the short-term benefits of holding "auctions" for low-bidder awards, without adequate attention given to the attendant risk (given the highly complex, high-technology makeup of most advanced weapon systems) of achieving very low reliability and very inferior performance from the "budget-priced" goods.

It is necessary for the DOD to learn how to do "value competition"—as is done in the nondefense/commercial world—where the competition is held for the best goods at a reasonable price. Most often, the buyer will see that it's to his advantage to spend a little more money to get a lot more quality.

INCREASED USE OF COMMERCIAL SYSTEMS, PARTS, AND SPECIFICATIONS. Until recent years, defense technology was far ahead of its commercial counterpart. However, in many areas this is no longer the case—better and cheaper equipment is available in the highly competitive and fast-growing commercial marketplace. Nonetheless, Defense has held on to its traditions, and has insisted upon extensive use of special-purpose equipment and parts built to special military specifications. The overall result is that the DOD often pays dearly for the specialized nature of its parts and equipment, and yet gets inferior results. For example, in microelectronics, today's commercial equipment is built to withstand environments (such as being mounted on automobile engines) that are as difficult as those stipulated by DOD. But the commercial equipment is far more reliable, is lower in cost, and embodies much more advanced technology than that of comparable military equipment. It is time for Defense to shift to the selection and use of existing commercial systems, parts, and specifications as its first priority. These parts have all met the "market test" for both quality and price.

Thus, the DOD will have all the advantages of the "continuous competition" of the commercial marketplace, without having had to create the market itself. This approach has the added benefit of increasing the integration of the military and commercial industrial worlds, introducing not only far more cost sensitivity to military procurements but also providing the potential for a rapid surge in production. Our surge capabilities would be greatly enhanced if existing commercial production lines could be rapidly converted to defense production in periods of crisis.

REWARD GOOD PERFORMANCE WITH FUTURE BUSINESS. Defense contractors are primarily sales-oriented, that is, they are continuously striving to achieve increased levels of business on the assumption that profits will follow sales. This sales emphasis will grow even stronger if the recommendation for more competition is implemented. However, current source selections are based almost completely on promises in the proposals that are submitted for a particular award. There is very little institutional consideration of the performance (in terms of quality, delivery, or cost) that was achieved by that supplier on prior programs. Thus, awards are based more on promises than on past performance. The opposite approach is taken in the commercial world, where firms are rewarded with increased business if their past performance has been good, and are closed out of future business if their performance has been poor. Secretary McNamara tried to implement a performance-based source-selection system when he first came to the Defense Department, but his efforts were unsuccessful and were subsequently dropped.

Nevertheless, the need to reward success has not diminished and new efforts should be made in this direction.

PROFIT. Clearly, industry is motivated to enhance its profit margins. However, the Defense Department follows the perverse practice of negotiating a contractor's profit margin each year without regard to how the product's costs in prior years have compared to expected costs. For example, the cost basis used for profit negotiations in production programs is that of the previous year's costs. The higher the costs, the more profit dollars next year, since the profit margin (percent) tends to remain about the same from year to year.

A far better approach would be for the government to allow a higher profit margin in subsequent years if the costs fell below that which was expected for the prior years. If costs rose one year, the contractor would receive a smaller profit the next year, but if costs actually fell in one year, the contractor could be assured that his profit margin would rise in negotiations for next year's contract. Similarly, profit margin could be tied to a system's demonstrated reliability, in order to create an incentive in this area. These proposed changes would essentially constitute a move toward the commercial practice of rewarding good performance with higher profits in the future.

PRICE ELASTICITY. The military services' incentives to achieve lower costs could be greatly enhanced by a policy which permits the Services to buy larger quantities, or improve the performance, of those particular systems for which unit costs fell below expectations. Thus, part of the cost savings would be returned to the Services for the acquisition of greater military capabilities. As is now the case, the relevant program office loses the money if costs are reduced.

Instead, savings could be used to improve the performance of systems (for example, through increased reliability testing), to buy more of them, or to pay for needed product modifications. A version of this "price elasticity" incentive was tried successfully by former Secretary of Defense James Schlesinger when he offered the Air Force a choice between a larger number of fighter wings if lower cost F–16 aircraft were purchased, or a smaller number of aircraft if they chose to buy the more expensive F–15s. The Air Force decided to buy the lower-performance, lower-cost, *greater-quantity* option—so today we have F–16s in the Air Force inventory.

TECHNOLOGY DEMONSTRATIONS. Faster, more efficient major weapons acquisition programs require that high-risk, high-cost subsystems that incorporate next-generation technologies—such as radars, engines, and computers—should, whenever possible, be developed independent of the complete weapon system. They should then be fully tested before a commitment is made to include them in the overall weapon system. This demonstration of new technology, prior to application in a weapon system, is the proper use of the "fly-before-buy" concept. It would reduce the cost risk of major weapon system development programs and reduce the time necessary to complete them. When new subsystem technology has been demonstrated, it can be quickly inserted into the overall program and brought into the field. This "modification" approach has already proven to be an extremely efficient way of developing new weapon systems both in the United States and other countries, but the DOD acquisition and budget processes are structured primarily around the development of complete new weapon systems.

"DESIGN-TO-COST." In the commercial world advanced technology is used simultaneously to lower equipment costs and to improve the performance of new systems. In the defense world technology is used almost exclusively to maximize performance. It has been estimated that achievement of the last few degrees of performance tends to raise defense system costs by 30 to 50 percent—correspondingly reducing the number of weapons which can be acquired.

If unit cost were made an important *design* criterion—along with performance—then the DOD could take advantage of new technologies both to improve the quality of its equipment and to increase the quantities it is able to purchase, thereby trading a very small reduction in an individual system's performance for a larger increase in the number of systems acquired. Similarly, an important early design consideration must be the development of innovative techniques to reduce subsequent logistics costs. Today, support costs are prohibitively expensive; their reduction must be recognized as an early engineering design task, not something to be fixed later.

FUND NONTRADITIONAL CONCEPTS. In order to encourage the development of new technology that can be used to improve overall military effectiveness in nontraditional ways, especially when it would cut across historical Service roles and missions, it is necessary for the Services and the Defense Advanced Research Projects Agency (DARPA) to "hedge" funds for such nontraditional systems and technology. These nontraditional technologies otherwise remain underfunded, as the institutions that control the research process consider them to be a "lower priority."

For example, both the Army and Air Force have had trouble funding and utilizing remotely piloted-vehicles, even though Israel has clearly shown their military value in conflict. If a special allowance was made for the prototype development and demonstration of prototypes of nontraditional systems, and the money not counted against a Service's budget (that is, charged to the Office of the Secretary of Defense), a form of internal competition could be set up between improvements in traditional systems and innovative ways of accomplishing the same task. The innovative alternatives could then be tested against the traditional approaches. To create the proper incentives, it is desirable that these nontraditional approaches be pursued by separate organizations within each Service, and/or that increased funding be given to DARPA.

To summarize this third broad acquisition initiative, i.e., the substitution of regulations with natural incentives, it is important to emphasize that these 10 "incentives" will not be easy to implement, yet the government has already begun moving on some of them, and many of the others are very similar to practices that are widely utilized in the commercial world. Thus, there is a large body of "lessons learned" that could be applied. The combination of these changes clearly would result in a very significant "cultural change" within the Department of Defense, shifting from a heavy dependence on regulation for improved performance and lower cost to the use of natural incentives to attain these same objectives. Many believe that the use of such incentives will, in fact, be far more effective than the historic regulatory approach.

All three of the broad recommendations for change that are described above have in common a "demand side" perspective through revisions to the budgeting and program management process, and to incentives to create higher performance and lower cost in weapon system procurements. However, stopping with only these changes would leave out a major potential area of improved effectiveness and efficiency, namely the "supply side," that is, the defense industrial base. This brings us to the fourth and last of the broad reforms required.

4. Industrial base visibility. Historically, the assumption has been that a free market has been operating in the defense arena, one which adjusts to changing conditions and achieves economic efficiency and strategic responsiveness to the nation's security needs. Unfortunately, this has not actually been the case, the principal reason being that the overall defense market is unique, consisting of one buyer and in many instances, only one supplier. Under these conditions, the Defense Department, as the only buyer, has an obligation to concern itself with the health and responsiveness of the defense industry. In order to do this, it needs to have some organization responsible for the industry's health and in a position to take action to assure it. At times, such an office would encourage the establishment of a second or even third producer. At other times, it might encourage the awarding of a contract so as to achieve greater labor stability. At still other times, it might investigate the critical lower tiers of the defense industry to assure that similar efficiency and responsiveness is attained in the supply of critical parts.

The United States is the only nation in the world which does not treat its defense industry as a vital national resource. Today, the Defense Department does not have the means to achieve these ends, at either the prime contractor level or at the critical lower-tier levels. Specifically, what it is missing is governmental insight into the conditions of efficiency and effectiveness in critical sectors of the industrial base. This insight can be provided by gathering data in such areas as the amount of competition in given sectors, labor force stability, bottlenecks, capital investments, foreign dependency, long-term R&D, capacity utilization, surge capability, and integration of civil and military production.

When provided with insight into the health and responsiveness of the industrial base, the DOD can then include such considerations in its major acquisition and budget decisions. For example, DOD could make informed decisions, not possible now, on the best time and location to start up a new production line, whether to obtain a second supplier to do research in a critical component area, or where to target investments to allow the rapid surge of a production line in the event of a crisis.

Today these supply-oriented decisions are not part of the DOD's acquisition process, nor is the necessary data base—insight—available. With the addition of such considerations, far greater efficiency and effectiveness could be achieved in this unique marketplace. Additionally, industrial responsiveness could be made a more significant part of overall US national security.[16]

* * *

The last few years have clearly been dramatic ones for "defense reform." Much new legislation was implemented with a clear trend towards increased—and more detailed—regulation of all aspects of the defense industry. This trend was further heightened by actions within the Department of Defense itself, which moved towards the turnover of greater acquisition management responsibility and authority to the "lawyers and auditors" as the short-term solution to perceived increases in "waste, fraud, and abuse." In parallel with these negative trends, however, both the executive and congressional branches initiated far broader and perhaps more long-reaching efforts at the needed basic structural reforms. Activities are underway that promise still greater results in these more significant directions. The big unknown is whether these activities can realize a payoff, in terms of improvements in the effectiveness and efficiency with which Defense spends its annual budget. This examination argues for significant structural changes within the current overall institutional pattern. The other options are either "minor adjustments" to the current system ("if you believe it's working well, why fix it—just correct the abuses") or, at the other extreme, radical changes to Service roles and missions as well as the use of a single civilian buying agency ("the current system will never work, so let's scrap it and start over"). Nonetheless, even the middle-of-the-road set of four recommendations contained herein still will result in rather dramatic changes in organizations and procedures—and ultimately, in a significant "cultural change" in the way the DOD conducts its business.

The implementation of the above four changes will be difficult and will take significant time. So to avoid totally disrupting the system, these changes must be implemented on a relatively gradual basis. Mostly what will be required is a desire for change—on the part of the legislative and executive branches, particularly the latter.

Today, many on Capitol Hill and in the Pentagon are attempting to achieve procurement reform in a very piecemeal fashion—from a new "spare parts czar" to a corps of new auditors, and from hundreds of pieces of new procurement-reform regulations and legislation to even greater congressional micromanagement of every defense budget line item. However, the coming years will represent an even more significant challenge for the defense procurement world. No longer can one expect the large increases in defense budgets that were seen in the first Reagan administration. Thus, in the presence of significant budget constraints there will be even greater political infighting—again, both on Capitol Hill and within the Services. In this environment there are likely to be increasing cries for "immediate reform," with its associated flood of new legislation and newspaper head-lines. The challenge will be to achieve the required broad changes in this environment—without damaging what is worth saving in the existing system.

If these necessary changes can be made, then the public's confidence in DOD management can be restored, the taxpayers can get their money's worth, and our national security can be strengthened. Clearly, these results are worth the extra effort.

Notes

1. "Toward a More Effective Defense," the final report of the CSIS Defense Organization Project, Georgetown University, Washington, D.C., February 1985.

Also, it should be noted that many of the ideas contained in the present paper resulted from the deliberations of this activity's Working Group on Weapons Acquisition. The members were: Chair: Dr. J.S. Gansler; members: Dr. R. Art, Lieutenant General E.J. D'Ambrosio, Mr. D. Church, Mr. J. Ford, Professor R. Fox, Rear Admiral R. Freeman, Representative D. McCurdy, Dr. J. Shea, Dr. M. Stern, Lieutenant General G. Sylvester, Major General R.F. Trimble, and Rear Admiral R. Wertheim.

2. "Defense Organization: The Need for Change," Committee on Armed Services, US Senate, 16 October 1985.

3. President's Blue Ribbon Commission on Defense Management ("Packard Commission"), Initial Report, 28 February 1986.

4. For example: Rand Reports R–3373–AF/RC, January 1986, p.10; R–2481–DOE, July 1979; R–3387–GRI. Also see, "System Acquisition Performance of U.S. Government Agencies," Department of Defense memorandum, Pyatt, OSD, 14 April 1976, (comparing federal agency program acquisition cost reports to Congress). Numerous GAO reports have had similar results.

5. For a more extensive discussion of the emphasis on and resistance to technology in traditional and nontraditional weapon systems refer to J.S. Gansler, "The U.S. Technology Base: Problems and Prospects," which is chapter 4 of *Technology, Strategy and National Security* Margiotta and Sanders, (Washington, DC:

National Defense University Press 1985); and for an excellent historical perspective see: Morrison, Elting, *Men, Machines, and Modern Times,* (Cambridge, MA: MIT Press, 1966).

6. Defense Systems Acquisition Review Council Working Group "Final Report, Weapon Systems Costs," 19 December 1972. Also see J.S. Gansler, *The Defense Industry* (Cambridge, MA: MIT Press, 1980), p. 16 for a more recent update.

7. The higher range comes from both a GAO study of 1972 (Comptroller General of the United States, "Acquisition of Major Weapon Systems," DOD report B–163058, July 1972) and a 1979 report ("Inaccuracy of DOD Weapons Acquisition Cost Estimates," House Committee on Government Operations, 16 November 1979, Washington, DC); it was again reconfirmed as slightly over 2 to 1 in 1981 by the "Affordable Acquisition Approach," Air Force Systems Command, 9 February 1983. The lower range comes from attributing more of the cost growth to inflation effects.

8. Norman Augustine, "Augustine's Laws," American Institute of Aeronautics and Astronautics, Inc., 1982.

9. House Armed Services Committee, Industrial Base Panel report, "The Ailing Defense Industrial Base: Unready for Crisis," (Chairman, Richard Ichord), 31 December 1980; Defense Science Board Task Force report on industrial responsiveness, (Chairman, Robert Fuhrman), 21 November 1980; the Air Force Systems Command statement on defense industrial base issues, (General Alton Slay), 13 November 1980; Jacques S. Gansler, *The Defense Industry* (Cambridge, MA: MIT Press, October 1980).

10. For a fuller discussion of this strategy shift see J.S. Gansler, "Industrial Preparedness: National Security in the Nuclear Age," *Military Engineer,* November–December 1983, pp. 483–490.

11. Reorganization of the Joint Chiefs of Staff was discussed at length in the 1984 *Annual* by Phil Odeen. Also, refer to Archie Barrett, "Reappraising Defense Organization," (Washington, DC: National Defense University Press, 1983). Also see "Understanding U.S. Strategy: A Reader" ed. T.L. Heyns, (Washington, DC: 1983); National Defense University Press, especially the two articles on reform of the Joint Chiefs of Staff by General David C. Jones, USAF (Ret.) p. 307, and by General Edward C. Meyer, USA (Ret.) p. 327.

12. For a detailed discussion of schedule stretchout, its effects, and possible corrective actions—as well as the specific F–15 example—see "Affordable Acquisition Approach," Air Force Systems Command, 9 February 1983.

13. For more discussion of multiyear budgeting refer to J.S. Gansler, "Reforming the Defense Budget Process," *Public Interest Magazine,* Spring 1984.

14. For a discussion of the effects of instability see "Affordable Acquisition Approach."

15. For a brief summary of some examples see J.S. Gansler, *L.A. Times,* op-ed article, "There's Precedent for Pentagon Thrift," p. 5, part IV, 2 October 1983. For more details see: L.W. Cox, and J.S. Gansler, "Evaluating the Impact of Quantity, Rate and Competition," *Concepts,* The Journal of Defense Systems Acquisition Management, Autumn 1981.

16. For a more detailed discussion of the needed industrial base actions see J.S. Gansler, "Can the Defense Industry Respond to the Reagan Initiatives?" *International Security,* Spring 1982, pp. 102–21.

DID READINESS GET ITS FAIR SHARE OF THE DEFENSE BUILDUP IN THE FIRST REAGAN ADMINISTRATION?

Lawrence J. Korb

*B*ETWEEN fiscal year 1980 and fiscal year 1985 the defense budget doubled, growing from $144 billion in fiscal year 1980 to $292 billion in fiscal year 1985. If one discounts for inflation, the real growth over this period was $104 billion or *52* percent. Total defense spending for the first part of this decade was $1.7 trillion, and, for the first time in our nation's history, the budget increased in real terms more than three successive years. In fact, it went up for six consecutive years.

Despite this outpouring of money, many people have argued that the Department of Defense did not receive commensurate improvements in its military capabilities. These arguments usually are based on one or all of the following assumptions: that the DOD had no coherent strategy, it simply threw money at the military departments to spend as they saw fit; the military balance actually deteriorated during this period; and too much money was spent on hardware or modernization and not enough on readiness and sustainability.

Although the first two assumptions are certainly worthy of analysis, they are quite properly the subject of separate and detailed discussions. This examination will focus on the third assumption—that sufficient monies were not spent on readiness or sustainability.

The Meaning of Readiness

Before beginning an analysis of this issue, it is important to be precise about how we define and apply the term readiness.

One of the long-standing problems in discussing defense readiness has been that "readiness" means many things to many people. Too often both unsophisticated private citizens, members of the Congress, and even some senior DOD officials—both military and civilian—have used the term "readiness" to refer to our overall defense capabilities. In 1981, in an attempt to define the terms precisely enough so that they could be measured, and for an understanding of how changes in resource levels influence different aspects of overall defense capabilities, DOD devised and officially issued some standard basic definitions. Overall military capability is a function of four attributes:

Force structure: The numbers, size, and composition of the units that comprise our defense forces, for example, divisions, ships, and air wings.

Force modernization: The technical sophistication of all the elements of the force.

Force readiness: The collective ability of the elements of the force to deliver the outputs for which they were designed.

Force sustainability: The "staying power" of the force during combat operations, often measured in numbers of days.

Thus, "readiness" as it is defined, measured, and reported is a much narrower concept than the size of the force or the rate at which it is modernized. Those who make such pronouncements as "you've got to modernize to be ready" merely confuse an already complicated issue. The term "force readiness" or "readiness" means a measure of the pre-D-day status of the force as it pertains to its wartime requirements for operationally available materiel, and appropriately trained manpower; "sustainability" measures post-D-day staying power.

Thus, "force readiness" is only one of the key components of the broader concept of "military capability." It should be noted that it is possible for a force to be 100-percent ready—all equipment operational, all personnel trained—and still not provide adequate military capability because of a deficiency in one of the other components that determine that capability, for example, force structure. On the other hand, it is possible for a force to perform adequately in combat even though it is less than 100-percent ready. Unless this distinction is kept in mind, force modernization, a component of military capability, can very easily be confused with force readiness.

As shown in figure 1, force readiness has both materiel and personnel dimensions. Each of these is

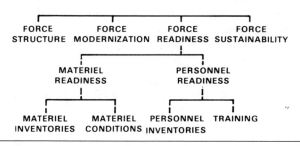

Figure 1
Military Capability

driven by the resources available to the commander for the performance of his wartime mission.

Materiel readiness for a unit consists of two elements: the inventories of equipment and supplies on hand relative to the wartime requirement; and the ability of this hardware to perform the functions needed.

The two corresponding considerations in personnel readiness are the inventories of personnel on hand relative to the wartime requirement, and the status of training of these personnel for the functions they must perform in wartime.

Thus, the factors at the bottom of figure 1 yield the basic measures of readiness. In order to measure materiel and personnel inventories, the percentage of people and critical equipment items on hand, as contrasted to what is necessary in wartime, are used as the basic measures. Likewise, for training, the percentage of training accomplished as opposed to what is required is used as a basic readiness measure. Materiel condition is slightly more involved: the readiness measure used most often here is the mission capable (MC) rate. This is essentially the average percentage of time a weapon system or equipment (or a collection of them) is able to perform the functions for which it is needed.

The principal measures of unit readiness are the C-ratings (that is, combat readiness ratings) from the Joint Chiefs of Staff unit status and reporting system, (UNITREP). The UNITREP is designed, managed, and controlled by the Office of the Joint Chiefs of Staff (OJCS). The Services collect and report their readiness statistics (up through the several levels) to the OJCS in accordance with specific Service-developed reporting rules within broad OJCS guidelines.

It is important to understand that the UNITREP system was designed primarily, if not exclusively, to measure the day-to-day readiness of the operating forces. It was never intended as a tool for developing budgets and outyear financial programs nor, because of changing criteria, does it always give a completely accurate view of readiness trends over time. Its primary purpose is to tell the Secretary of Defense, the Chairman of the Joint Chiefs of Staff, the Commanders in Chief, and the service Chiefs what units are ready *today* to go to war on short notice, which are not, and for those that are not, what lacks of resources constrain them.

The UNITREP assigns one of these overall C-ratings to each combat unit: C–1 (fully ready), C–2 (substantially ready), C–3 (marginally ready), C–4 (not ready), and C–5 (not ready, but for reasons previously planned). Examples of C–5 units are ships undergoing scheduled overhaul, or units in the process of being activated or deactivated.

For each combat-oriented unit, a C-rating is computed for each of the four resource measures, equipment fill readiness, equipment status, personnel fill readiness, and personnel training. The basic readiness percentages in each of the four resource categories are translated into C-ratings in accordance with criteria that are standard across Services and equipment types. For example, if a unit has between 70 percent and 90 percent of its wartime requirement for selected critical items, it is given a C–2 rating for equipment readiness (inventory). The *overall* C-rating for the unit is the lowest C-rating in any of the four readiness categories.

In addition to the basic measures of readiness (shown on the left-hand side of table 1), the ancillary indicators, shown on the right, provide some insight into what is contributing to increases or decreases in the basic measures of readiness. For example, mission-capable rates should improve as maintenance backlogs

Table 1
Measures of Readiness

Basic Measures	Ancillary Measures
Percent equipment versus requirements	Maintenance backlogs
Percent personnel inventories versus requirements	Supply fill rates
Percent training versus requirements	Supply backorders
Mission-capable rates	Cannibalization rates
	War reserve withdrawals
	Flying hours/steaming days/ battalion training days
	Exercises
	Reenlistment rates
	Mental categories of enlistees
	Match of skills and grades versus jobs
	Personnel turbulence/stability

are reduced, supply backorders are cut, and supply fill rates are increased. Also, a healthy supply system, with adequate spares, is reflected in reduced cannibalizations and fewer withdrawals from war reserves. Similarly, training improvements should come with increased training exercises and increases in flying hours, steaming days, and battalion training days. Also, the percentage of personnel inventories as contrasted to requirements improves with positive enlistment trends and reenlistment rates, and the extent to which positions are filled with personnel in the required skill/grade category.

Just as some people confuse the meaning of readiness, others confuse the budget accounts that actually contribute thereto. For example, many people believe that *all* operation and maintenance (O&M) funding and *only* operation and maintenance funding has a direct impact on readiness. This is a serious misconception. As detailed in table 2, several budget accounts affect readiness. The budget accounts that have a major impact on readiness are (1) operations and maintenance, (2) procurement, (3) military personnel, and (4) stock fund. In addition, some projects in the military construction account can have a significant direct or indirect effect on readiness or on other attributes of defense combat capabilities.

Purchases made through the procurement accounts enhance readiness by acquiring some of the spare parts needed to replace those parts that fail in our weapon systems and equipment; also modification kits are acquired to improve the reliability and maintainability (R&M) of our hardware (some R&M modifications buy "readiness"; other modifications buy "modernization"; some modifications buy both); and equipment items (for example, tanks, howitzers, and trucks) bought to fill shortages in existing force structure.

Table 2
Key Budget Accounts Affecting Readiness

Procurement	Military personnel
Spare parts	Pay
Support equipment	Bonuses
Modification kits	Incentives
Major equipment items	
Operations and maintenance	Stock fund
Depot repairs	Peacetime augmentation
Installation or modifications/	War reserve materiel
alterations	
All force operations	
Flying hours	
Steaming days	
Battalion training days	

These procurement accounts are very important to readiness, but there is a significant lag time between appropriation of procurement funds and the effect they have on readiness. Typically, it takes two years or more between the appropriation of dollars to buy spare parts, repairs, and equipment and the delivery of these to the field. In early 1986, DOD was just beginning to accept delivery of those parts procured with fiscal year 1984 funds. The full effect of the procurements on readiness was not fully felt until late 1986.

It is true, however, that the O&M appropriation generally influences readiness more quickly and efficiently than does the procurement account. They produce quicker results because O&M funds finance depot repairs, installation of modifications, force operations, and training, beginning six months from the time they were appropriated. It is more efficient because repairing an item usually costs approximately 15 to 20 percent of the cost to buy a new item. This difference in lag times and efficiency is the basis of DOD's general policy that repairing an item takes priority over procuring an item of the same type.

Military pay, bonuses, and other incentives help recruit and retain the numbers and types of people needed in our armed services. As shown below, because of additions to this account personnel readiness has increased dramatically since 1981.

Let me conclude this review of basic concepts and definitions with a brief description of the critical components of sustainability, i.e., the staying power of the force in combat. To sustain our forces, planning must be undertaken in peacetime to replace those resources that will be consumed or suffer attrition during combat. These post-D-Day supplies come from either war reserve stockpiles or the mobilization production base.

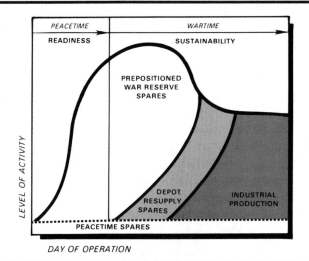

Figure 2
Materiel Sustainability

As shown in figure 2, ideally, sufficient stocks should be available and properly positioned at D-Day to meet combat consumption demands until the production base (and transportation pipeline) can be expanded to meet the demand.

The primary components of manpower sustainability, analogous to war reserve materiel and the production base, are a pool of trained individuals to serve as replacements, and unit fillers. Furthermore it is necessary to have training bases to process volunteers or conscripts in time of war. Those components must be balanced in a manner comparable to the materiel components.

The Real Issue

With this as a background, let us now focus on the argument that readiness has not received its fair share of the budget. The dispute is based on two propositions. First, as indicated in table 3, between fiscal year 1981 and 1985 the defense budget increased by 60.7 percent. However, over that same period, operation and maintenance grew by only 40.1 percent while procurement grew by slightly over 100 percent. In real terms, or constant fiscal year 1987 dollars, the O&M increase was 25 percent while procurement rose by almost 70 percent. Thus, whereas in fiscal year 1981 procurement accounted for $7 billion less than O&M, by fiscal year 1985 it received almost $20 billion more.

Second, by DOD's own measurements between 1980 and 1984, the percentage of Army units rated C–1 or C–2 actually dropped by 25 percent while the percentage of Air Force units rated C–1 or C–2 showed a drop of 15 percent. Only the Navy showed improvements in this period, and this change was primarily in the manpower area.

Both of these propositions are misleading. Not all the readiness funds are in the operation and maintenance account, and the entire procurement account is not dedicated just to modernization. A more accurate way to analyze the mix of modernization readiness is presented in table 4. Rather than using the five budget titles as in the DOD budget, this table breaks the budget down into eight categories, thereby enabling us to see which portions of the procurement account go for modernization and which actually are allotted to readiness.

As the table suggests, the largest area of real growth in the DOD budget since fiscal year 1980 is in materiel sustainability, which has grown in real terms by almost 21 percent a year. While growth in modernization and force structure equipping has been substantial, nearly 16 percent per year, so also has been the growth in materiel readiness, almost 15 percent per year. The

Table 3
Department of Defense—by Appropriation[a]
(dollars in millions)

| | Fiscal Year | | | | | 1981–85 | |
	1981	1982	1983	1984	1985	Increase Amount	Increase Percent
Current dollars							
Military personnel	36,909	42,875	45,688	64,866*	67,773*	17,024	33.6
Retired pay	13,840	14,986	16,155				
Operation and maintenance	55,548	62,466	66,540	70,950	77,803	22,255	40.1
Procurement	48,025	64,462	80,355	86,161	96,842	48,817	101.6
Research, development, test, and evaluation	16,609	20,060	22,798	26,867	31,327	14,718	88.6
Military construction	3,398	4,916	4,512	4,510	5,517	2,119	62.3
Family housing and homeowners assistance program	2,004	2,203	2,712	2,669	2,890	886	44.2
Revolving and management funds	2,677	2,494	1,075	2,774	5,088	2,411	90.1
Total—Direct program	178,365	213,751	239,474	258,150	286,802	108,437	60.7
Constant fiscal year 1987 dollars							
Military personnel	49,844	51,496	52,752	72,762*	73,182*	5,312	7.9
Retired pay	18,026	18,315	18,663				
Operation and maintenance	64,908	69,315	72,657	76,552	81,231	16,323	25.1
Procurement	62,029	78,115	92,689	95,757	103,876	41,847	67.5
Research, development, test, and evaluation	20,974	23,973	26,272	29,887	33,662	12,688	60.5
Military construction	4,240	5,886	5,182	5,004	5,904	1,664	39.2
Family housing and homeowners assistance program	2,491	2,583	3,093	2,951	3,092	601	24.1
Revolving and management funds	3,461	2,997	1,242	3,087	5,466	2,005	57.9
Total—Direct program	225,138	251,807	272,133	285,279	305,941	80,803	35.9

[a] Numbers may not add to totals due to rounding.
*Includes retired pay accrual.

Table 4
DOD Funding Trends by Function
(TOA in constant FY 1985 dollars in billions)

	Fiscal Year						Compounded Annual Real Growth Rate FY 1980–85
	1980	1981	1982	1983	1984	1985	
Force structure equipping and modernization	50.0	57.6	70.4	85.7	89.1	104.4	15.9
(annual percent growth)		(15.2)	(22.2)	(21.7)	(4.0)	(17.2)	
Military personnel readiness[1]	51.2	52.3	54.7	56.2	58.3	60.5	3.4
(annual percent growth)		(2.2)	(4.6)	(2.7)	(3.7)	(3.8)	
Peacetime force operations[2]	14.4	15.8	17.6	18.3	19.0	20.6	7.4
(annual percent growth)		(9.7)	(11.4)	(–4.8)	(3.8)	(8.4)	
Centrally managed materiel readiness[3]	14.6	18.3	20.6	22.9	26.2	28.8	14.6
(annual percent growth)		(25.3)	(12.6)	(11.2)	(14.4)	(9.9)	
Other central logistics[4]	15.2	17.3	19.3	18.8	18.8	23.7	9.3
(annual percent growth)		(13.8)	(11.6)	(–2.6)	(0)	(26.1)	
Materiel sustainability	5.3	8.3	11.3	10.4	10.8	13.5	20.6
(annual percent growth)		(56.6)	(36.1)	(–8.0)	(3.8)	(25.0)	
Military construction, facilities, and other support	25.2	27.7	29.9	30.7	31.7	36.6	7.8
(annual percent growth)		(9.9)	(7.9)	(2.7)	(3.3)	(15.5)	
Retired pay[5]	15.4	16.0	16.3	16.5	16.8	17.6	2.7
Total DOD	191.3	213.2	240.1	259.6	270.8	305.7	9.8
(annual percent growth)		(11.5)	(12.6)	(8.1)	(4.3)	(12.9)	

[1] Military personnel appropriation, individual training, medical, and other personnel support.
[2] Includes below-depot maintenance, supply, fuel, and other force operating costs.
[3] Depot maintenance, spares procurement, and stock fund augmentation.
[4] Equipment modifications and alterations, supply operations, transportation, procurement of logistics support equipments, and other logistics support.
[5] Fiscal year 85 on actual basis; other years on cash payment basis.

only account not to show improvement is military personnel. The compounded real growth in this area is only 3.4 percent. Yet personnel is the area of greatest improvements. In the fiscal year 1981–85 period, the quality of recruits is at an all-time high and retention is at record levels.

The second proposition is equally misleading. It is true that from 1981–84 the number of units rated C–1, fully ready, and C–2, substantially ready, did decline for the Army and Air Force units. However, during that same time the criteria to achieve these higher levels of readiness were made more stringent. For example, in 1981, tactical air squadrons in the United States were rated fully combat-ready in equipment if they had enough materiel to fight for 15 days. However, in 1982 the criteria for C–1 in this area was changed to 30 days. As a result a unit could have increased its resources from 16 to 25 days in the 1981-to-1985 period but dropped its readiness rating from C–1 to C–2.

Similarly, during this same period, the Army began introducing M–1 tanks into its combat forces and revised its full-readiness criteria for tank battalions so that only those possessing M–1 tanks could be rated C–1 in equipment. Thus units still possessing M–60A3 tanks suffered a decline in readiness "on paper" solely because they had not yet received the M–1 Abrams tank.

The only meaningful way to answer the second proposition is to take a broad look at the warfighting capabilities of armed forces, noting whether they have improved significantly over the past five years. Since exact readiness figures are classified, we need to be content with some broad indicators.

The most important single indicator of the strength of any organization is its people. What happened to the

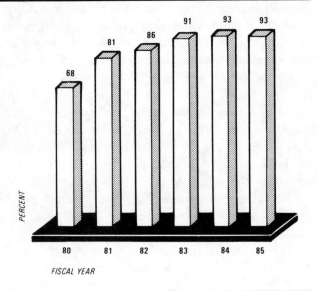

Figure 3
Recruits with High School Diplomas (all Services)

quantity and quality of the people in the armed forces between 1981 and 1985?

The size of the total force, active duty and Selected Reserves, grew significantly in the first part of this decade. In 1980, there were 2.95 million people in the total force, 2.05 million individuals on active duty and 0.9 million active (drilling) reservists. By 1985, the total force had increased in size to 3.3 million, an increase of 350,000 or 12 percent. By 1985, the active force stood at 2.15 million and the Selected Reserves had reached an all-time high of 1.1 million.

Not only has the quantity of military personnel increased, so also has the quality. In 1980, for example, only 54 percent of the Army's new recruits were high school graduates. By 1985 that number had risen to 91 percent. For all the services, the number of high school graduates entering the military grew from 68 percent in fiscal year 1980 to 93 percent in fiscal year 1985. Figure 3 displays this large jump in the number of high school graduates over the 1980–85 period.

As suggested in figure 4, the aptitude level of the new recruits also has increased markedly since the Reagan administration took office. In fiscal year 1980 about 66 percent of those entering the services scored average or above average on the Armed Forces Qualification Test. This was slightly below the average for the nation's youth population. In fiscal 1985 over 93 percent were in that category. The change was even more dramatic for the Army. In fiscal year 1980, 55 percent of those entering the Army were in the below-average category. Last year less than 10 percent of the new recruits scored below average.

Retention also improved substantially in the first

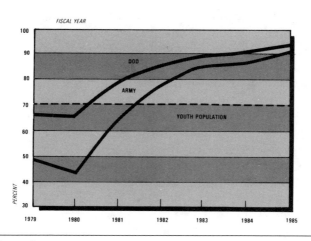

Figure 4
Aptitude Level of Recruits (Percent Scoring Average and Above)

Reagan administration. The first-term reenlistment rate rose from 38 percent in 1980 to 48 percent in 1985. The career retention rate jumped from 71 percent to 84 percent in that same period. This has resulted in a more experienced force better able to handle the more complex weapon systems and has substantially eliminated the much-discussed NCO and petty officer shortages of the past decade. From 1980 to 1985, the average years of service of those on active duty increased from 5.5 to 6.0 years.

In addition to the dramatic improvements in the personnel area, the operating forces have all received large amounts of modern sophisticated equipment. Moreover, as indicated in figure 3, increased funds have been provided to maintain the equipment, train the people to operate and maintain it properly, to buy sufficient spares and repair parts, and to purchase adequate ammunition to ensure the staying power of this equipment.

As a consequence, the warfighting capability of our land, sea, and air forces has improved dramatically in the first Reagan administration. Compared to 1980, the warfighting capability of the Army's infantry active divisions has gone up by about 60 percent, while that of its National Guard counterpart has improved by almost 40 percent. Similarly, over the past five years, the ability of the tactical air forces to generate sorties has risen by almost 80 percent. Finally, the overall readiness of Navy's deployable battle force is up by 32 percent over the same period.

In addition, our ability to deploy our forces has also improved greatly. In 1980, DOD could airlift only 28 million ton-miles per day. By 1985 that figure had increased to 40 million ton-miles. Similarly, in 1980, DOD possessed only 80 short tons of sealift capability. But, by 1985, it had grown to almost 400 short tons.

* * *

During the first Reagan administration, there was an appropriate balance between the funds spent for readiness and hardware. This is apparent if one understands the definition of the terms used in the debate, and the budget accounts that contribute to readiness and sustainability, and if one uses common-sense indicators to measure the improved warfighting capabilities of our land, sea, and air forces.

However, the second Reagan administration is not like the first. The fiscal year 1986 Defense Department budget declined by 6 percent in real terms, the largest decline in 15 years. Moreover, the fiscal year 1986–90 defense program was reduced by $400 billion or 20 percent between January 1985 and January 1986. Given the passage of Gramm-Rudman-Hollings, the short-term outlook does not appear to be hopeful. The challenge will be to maintain that balance between modernization and readiness in a period of fiscal austerity. If this is not done, the gains of the first Reagan administration will be eradicated.

THE EDITORS
AND CONTRIBUTORS

William P. Snyder is professor of strategic studies at the Air War College. Following his retirement from the Army in 1975, he joined the political science faculty at Texas A&M University. He is the author of *The Politics of British Defense Policy, 1945–1962,* articles on defense and foreign policy issues, and co-editor (with James Brown) of *The Regionalization of Warfare: The Falkland/Malvinas Islands, Lebanon, and the Iran-Iraq Conflicts.* Professor Snyder organized the Southwestern Regional Program in National Security Affairs in 1980 and directed the program's activities until he joined the Air War College faculty in 1985. He is a member of the Inter-University Seminar on Armed Forces and Society and of the American Military Institute.

James Brown is professor of political science, Southern Methodist University. His doctoral degree in political science is from the State University of New York at Buffalo. He has written extensively on national security policy and civilian-military relations in Greece and Turkey, and his work has appeared in *Armed Forces and Society, Air University Review, Defense Analysis,* and *Polity.* Professor Brown is an associate chairman of the Inter-University Seminar on Armed Forces and Society and a fellow of the International Institute for Strategic Studies.

* * *

Thomas A. Fabyanic earned his doctoral degree from St. Louis University. He is a retired Air Force officer and a veteran of some 200 combat missions in Vietnam. His publications have appeared in *Air University Review, Armed Forces and Society,* and *Strategic Review.* He is currently an analyst with a Washington-based research organization.

Schuyler Foerster, Major, US Air Force, is assigned to the Office of the Defense Adviser, US Mission to NATO. A graduate and former faculty member at the US Air Force Academy, he holds a doctoral degree in politics and strategic studies from Oxford University. Major Foerster served as a combat intelligence officer in Southeast Asia and as an intelligence analyst on Soviet political-military affairs in Washington, DC. He is co-editor (with Major Edward N. Wright) of *American Defense Policy* and the author of numerous articles on arms control.

Jacques S. Gansler is Vice President and Director of Analytic Science Corporation. He received his doctoral degree from American University. Gansler holds visiting professorships at the University of Virginia and at the Industrial College of the Armed Forces. He served as an adviser to the Packard Commission; his most recent book is *The Defense Industry.*

Paul H. B. Godwin is professor of national security policy at the National War College. Godwin holds a doctoral degree from the University of Minnesota. He has published articles in *Studies in Comparative Communism, Comparative Politics,* and *Air University Review;* his most recent book is *The Making of a Model Citizen in Communist China* (co-author).

David Goldfischer is a graduate student completing degree requirements toward a Ph.D. in political science at SUNY-Buffalo.

John F. Guilmartin, Jr., is a visiting professor at the Naval War College. Editor of the *Air University Review* from 1979 until his retirement from the US Air Force, Guilmartin also served as director of the Space Shuttle History Project at the Lyndon B. Johnson Space Center in Houston. He holds a doctoral degree in history from Princeton University, and has written extensively on the technological and operational aspects of maritime and military history. He is the author of *Gunpowder and Galleys: Changing Technology and Mediterranean Warfare at Sea in the Sixteenth Century.*

Nathan L. Hibler is a graduate student completing degree requirements toward a Ph.D. in sociology from the University of Maryland.

Dennis S. Ippolito is the Eugene McElvaney Professor of Government and chairman of the Political Science Department at Southern Methodist University. His doctoral degree in political science is from the University of Virginia. A national authority on the budget process, Ippolito has published extensively; his most recent volume is *Hidden Spending: The Politics of Federal Credit Programs.*

Lawrence J. Korb is dean of the Graduate School of Public and International Affairs at the University of Pittsburgh. A noted expert on the national security issues, Korb has published over 100 books, monographs, and articles on these topics. His doctoral degree is from SUNY-Albany. Prior to joining the University of Pittsburgh, Korb served as Assistant Secretary of Defense responsible for manpower, logistic, and reserve component matters.

David R. Segal is professor of sociology and of government and politics at the University of Maryland, and a Guest Scientist in the Department of Military Psychiatry, Walter Reed Army Institute of Research. He is an associate chairman of the Inter-University Seminar on Armed Forces and Society, and is the editor of *Armed Forces and Society*. He is co-author of *The All-Volunteer Force,* and co-editor of *The Social Psychology of Military Service.*

Jerome Slater is professor of political science at SUNY-Buffalo. His doctoral degree is from Princeton University. Slater has written extensively on security issues and is a leading authority on US policy toward the Caribbean nations. His numerous articles that have appeared in *International Organization, Yale Review, Armed Forces and Society,* and *World Politics.*

William O. Staudenmaier is a colonel in the US Army and is the director of strategy at the Center for Land Warfare, US Army War College. He is a graduate of the University of Chattanooga and of Pennsylvania State University. His military service includes combat tours in Vietnam and staff assignments at Department of the Army. His articles have appeared in *Foreign Policy, ORBIS, Naval War College Review, Military Review, Army,* and *Parameters.* He is co-author of *Strategic Implications of the Continental-Maritime Debate* and co-editor of *Military Strategy in Transition: Defense and Deterrence.*

Roy A. Werner has a graduate degree in political economy and strategic studies from Oxford University and an MBA from Claremont Graduate School. Werner served as a professional staff member on the Senate Committee on Foreign Relations and as Principal Deputy Assistant Secretary of the Army. Presently, he is associated with a major defense contractor.

John Allen Williams is an associate professor of political science at Loyola University of Chicago, and also executive director of the Inter-University Seminar on Armed Forces and Society. His publications are in the areas of US and Soviet naval forces, strategic nuclear policy, and defense organization. Professor Williams is also a commander in the US Naval Reserve.

Edward N. Wright, Major, US Air Force, is associate professor of political science and director of American and Policy Studies at the US Air Force Academy. Wright has a doctoral degree in government from Georgetown University. He is the co-editor (with Major Schuyler Foerster) of *American Defense Policy.*

Dov S. Zakheim is Executive Vice President of Systems Planning Corporation and a former Deputy Under Secretary of Defense for Planning and Resources. A Phi Beta Kappa, his doctoral degree is from Oxford's St. Antony's College. Zakheim has written and lectured widely on issues relating to the US Navy and the Rapid Deployment Force. He serves on the Maritime Policy Study Group of the Center for Strategic and International Studies, Georgetown University, and is a member of the Royal Institute of International Affairs, the International Institute for Strategic Studies, and the Council on Foreign Affairs.

Peter R. Zwick is chairman of the Political Science Department at Louisiana State University. His doctoral degree is from Duke University. Zwick is a noted authority on Soviet politics and his latest volume is *Soviet Foreign Relations: Process and Policy.*